INTENSIFYIN CLASSROOM ROUTINES

in Reading and Writing Programs

Michael P. Ford

MAUPIN HOUSE BY
CAPSTONE PROFESSIONAL
a capstone imprint

Intensifying Classroom Routines in Reading and Writing Programs
By Michael P. Ford

Cover Design: Charmaine Whitman and Lisa King
Book Design: Charmaine Whitman and Lisa King

Library of Congress Cataloging-in-Publication Data
Cataloging-in-publication information is on file with the Library of Congress.
978-1-4966-0835-2 (pbk.)
978-1-4966-0837-6 (eBook PDF)
978-1-4966-0839-0 (eBook)

Image Credits:
Capstone: 125; Shutterstock: Monkey Business Images, cover, Naddya, 26

Maupin House Publishing, Inc. by Capstone Professional
1710 Roe Crest Drive
North Mankato, MN 56003
www.capstonepd.com
888-262-6135
info@capstonepd.com

DEDICATION

To Pat

For her unending support

ACKNOWLEDGMENTS

After nearly 40 years in education, it's hard to tell where your ideas begin and the influences of others end. I have been fortunate to have been surrounded by great colleagues and collaborators throughout my teaching career. Many of those may see their insights and ideas incorporated into what I have written. None have been more influential than my longtime collaborator and friend, Michael Opitz. I also want to thank Mary Jo Fresch, who was my go-to person for questions about word study and Louis Chicquette, who always reminded me of the power of the morning message. I want to acknowledge my friend and colleague, Debra Zarling, who is the Oshkosh Area School District PreK–6 Reading Coordinator. She invited me to work with the staff and students of Jefferson Elementary School while I was writing this book, which helped ground my insights and ideas in real classrooms. I want to thank Principal Rhonda Buchanan; Instructional Support Teachers Carrie Boettcher and Julie Ruck; and staff members Craig Clark, Rebecca Gerl, Katie Herrick, Stephanie Hibbs, Nick Kelley, Wanda Kerns, Brenda Orde, Alyssa Rumlow, and Heather Swenson. I want to especially acknowledge kindergarten teacher Monica Huebner, who allowed me to work with students in her classroom as we rolled out a five-day cycle for routines included in this book. Finally, this book would not have been possible without the staff at Capstone, including Karen Soll for embracing this project; Emily Raij for her close attention to the manuscript; and Mary McCarthy, David Willette, and Kim Smith for their continual support and promotion of my work.

Table of Contents

Introduction 7

CHAPTER ONE:
Laying the Foundation 11

CHAPTER TWO:
Intensifying Your Shared Writing 31

CHAPTER THREE:
Intensifying Your Shared Reading 79

CHAPTER FOUR:
Intensifying Your Word Wall 135

CHAPTER FIVE:
Putting It All Together 163

Appendices 169

References 201

Introduction

> **How can our works and thoughts, if they are always to be the fittest, continue always the same? Change, indeed, is painful, yet ever needful.**
>
> *Thomas Carlyle, philosopher*

I am a former first-grade teacher, Title I K–3 reading teacher, teacher educator, researcher, and consultant, who has observed and participated in many elementary classroom literacy and language arts programs. In repeated visits to these classrooms for more than 30 years, I have seen three common elements in almost every primary literacy and language arts program: the use of shared writing (usually in the form of a classroom morning message), shared readings, and a word wall. While these were not the exclusive features of the primary programs I have visited, these three common large group routines were more often seen than not. Sometimes they were used as separate instructional activities in addition to the typical language arts instruction. Other times, they were integrated with the total language arts program. (For the record, I will argue the latter is the best way to use the routines, and in this book, I will explain how to do that.)

In observing all three of these routines through the years, I began to wonder if teachers were getting the most bang for their buck from these activities. Were teachers maximizing the power of these three popular routines? Based on my observations across multiple classrooms, I started having concerns about the implementation of these popular activities. I often saw classroom morning messages (shared writing) become routinized very quickly and repeat the same experiences over and over again. They seemed to be conducted with only some regard for what the curriculum expected or what the students needed. Similarly, large group shared readings were conducted with a typical lesson plan that offered little variation over time in spite of changing demands from the texts being used and changing needs of the learners. I would see word walls that were put up with careful attention early in the year but that remained unchanged as the year moved forward. The word walls blended in with other things posted on the classroom walls, rarely used by teachers or students as a resource to support instruction and learning.

I began to ask this question: How could teachers intensify these routines, or maximize their power, to help provide more intentional instruction that would target and impact learners in a more productive way? These routines seemed to be consuming valuable instructional time, so could they produce more value for learners during that time? I started experimenting with a systematic approach to help teachers become more intentional in their use of these routines. I modeled and demonstrated how this might work with undergraduate students in an interim course focused on early literacy. I began to share it with teachers in professional development forums and model potential rollouts and sequences in receptive classrooms. I thought the ideas might be helpful for an increasing audience of educators, which is why I proposed this book.

The purpose of the book is to provide a how-to resource focused on getting more instructional mileage out of three common classroom routines frequently used in primary literacy and language arts programs: shared writing (also referred to as interactive writing and commonly seen through the use of the classroom morning message), shared reading (also referred to as interactive reading), and the word wall. The book lays out step-by-step, day-by-day plans to put those three key routines on a systematic, coordinated, weekly five-day cycle that would change as students move through increasingly sophisticated developmental phases as readers and writers. The desired outcomes from the use of this book is to maximize the power of these routines to offer more intentional and focused teaching in classroom literacy and language arts programs and to achieve the student outcomes toward which educators are striving.

The structure of the book is as follows. Chapter One examines the importance of routines in elementary literacy and language arts programs. It looks at the research base for including instructional routines in classroom programs. It argues for the need for intensification of these routines, including the need for systematic instruction, explicit instruction, common language across reading and writing, and the use of the gradual release of responsibility model. The chapter reviews two key phases of readers and writers (emergent and early learners) and makes a case for what skills and strategies are critical for each of those phases. With emergent readers and writers, the focus is on needs for both reading and writing related to concepts of print, alphabetic knowledge, and phonological—including phonemic—awareness. With early readers and writers, the focus is primarily on word strategies, including sound analysis, sight vocabulary, structural analysis, and context clues to assist reading and writing.

The subsequent chapters look separately at each of these routines. Chapter Two is focused on shared writing (interactive writing and morning messages). It examines the purpose of shared writing routines discussed in light of current theory, expert opinion, and research. Then a five-day sequence is provided for conducting the routine of shared writing with early readers. The chapter shows how to modify the routine for emergent literacy (focusing on concepts of print, alphabetic knowledge, and phonological—including phonemic—awareness) and early literacy (focusing on word identification using sound, sight, structure, and context analysis). For each sequence, practical ideas and illustrated examples are included that can be used to focus shared writing instruction on different skills and strategies. A sample five-day sequence of lessons is provided for the early phase of reading development.

Shared reading is discussed in Chapter Three. The purpose of the shared reading routines (interactive read-alouds) is also discussed in light of current theory, expert opinion, and research. The five-day sequence for shared reading is aligned with the sequence for shared writing. The chapter shows how to modify shared reading for the same two phases of reading development: emergent literacy and early literacy. For each sequence, practical ideas and illustrated examples are included that can be used to focus shared reading instruction on different skills and strategies. Another sample five-day cycle sequenced plan is provided for this routine for the early reading phase.

Chapter Four is focused on word wall routines. As with the other routines, the purpose of word walls are discussed in light of current theory, expert opinion, and research. The daily sequences for activities involving word walls are aligned with the sequences for shared writing and shared reading. The chapter shows how to modify word wall activities for the two phases of reading development: emergent literacy and early literacy. Again, for each sequence, practical ideas and illustrated examples are presented that can be used to focus word wall instruction on different skills and strategies. Another sample of sequenced plans for early readers is provided for this routine as well.

In Chapter Five, I show how to bring these three routines together to systematically and intentionally address and teach needed skills and strategies for learners in specific phases of literacy development over time. I look at how to get started, allocate time, and align the routines.

The book concludes with references to allow readers opportunities to explore more deeply any additional issues, ideas, or insights related to these routines. Reproducible materials are provided so that teachers can more easily implement these ideas.

This book will allow you to examine your practices related to these three common routines, determine how to intensify those practices, and then see how intensification can lead to greater results for the readers and writers in your classroom.

CHAPTER ONE:
Laying the Foundation

> A natural outgrowth of the biological rhythm is a regular sequence of daily events that helps children and adults know what to expect and contributes to everyone's sense of security.
>
> *Hearron and Hildebrand, 2013*

The Importance of Routines in Elementary Literacy Programs

The importance of routines in elementary literacy programs can probably be summarized in a single word—predictability (Hearron and Hildebrand, 2013). For students, many who are coming from chaotic worlds outside the school walls for a variety of social, cultural, and economic reasons, predictability may offer a needed contrast to other events in their day. Epstein (2007) concluded that routines "provide children with emotional stability and security (13)." Knowing what will happen when and what will happen next allows many students to prepare, regulate, and evaluate their own behaviors in school settings (Hill and Ekey, 2010). It lessens the confusion encountered in moving from one new activity to the next new activity if the students can instead move from a known activity to the next known activity. The more predictable the flow of activities, the less students will need new directions or reviews of previous directions. Routines allow for more inherent connections in terms of behavioral and cognitive expectations between days. They allow students to actually build on what was learned and practice from one day to the next. With routines, students can be more independent and more time can be spent learning (Ganske, 2013; Rose-Duckworth and Ramer, 2009).

The benefits, however, are not just for students; routines can help teachers as well. Most teachers hear this common mantra: "Don't work harder; work smarter!" Routines are actually one way to achieve that. Instead of planning something new at the end of the day, routines provide a framework that makes planning more efficient. Minor adjustments in focus and techniques can replace starting over with new plans every day. Routines will also guarantee that what you need to focus on gets regular systematic attention instead of being visited occasionally when time allows. The day-to-day nature of these routines allows for tighter connections from one lesson to the next—building continuity. Review is also built into the framework of the routines. While specific outcomes related to knowledge, skills, or dispositions may need to be reviewed, the need to reteach them every time you start a lesson is reduced. The day-to-day nature of these routines also allows for a more gradual ramping up of expectations, building on instruction from the previous day. As Hill and Ekey (2010) conclude: "You can focus on teaching (77)." In the end, it saves instructional time. This is a major advantage. Routman (2008) reminds us that we should always teach with a sense of urgency. There is not a minute to lose. It may not seem like a lot of time for any one lesson, but if you can gain five minutes of instructional time each day, that adds up to more than 900 minutes of instructional time over a 180-day school year.

The Need for Intensification

There are many metaphors that can be used to discuss intensification. Bomer (1998) talked about the need to turn up the heat and focus more light on practices in literacy and language arts instruction. I (1996) have written about tightening up practices to get more mileage out of them. Intensification invites teachers to look at practices currently being used in new ways. In this book I invite teachers to look specifically at their use of shared writing, shared reading, and word walls. Intensification encourages teachers to consider how to increase intentionality in using these routines to maximize their power in reaching more learners with what they need to become proficient readers and writers. Intensification focuses on four critical aspects: making instruction more systematic, making instruction more explicit, using common language to connect reading and writing instruction, and structuring instruction through a gradual release of responsibility model.

Systematic instruction is planned instruction. It is intentional, purposeful teaching (Epstein, 2007; Rose-Duckworth and Ramer, 2009). It considers the needs of the learners and the expectations of the curriculum in short-term planning for an individual lesson and for long-term planning across lessons (Zarrillo, 2007). In this resource, each routine will be placed on a five-day cycle (one school week), which clearly describes what will happen on each day and coordinates the instruction across the days. Systematic instruction often values the frequency of lessons focused on skills and strategies instead of just the duration or length of an individual lesson. In other words, systematic instruction recommends a little bit of attention every day versus a lot of attention every once in a while. Systematic instruction intentionally structures short daily lessons and avoids single-shot, lengthy, isolated lessons, often with little thought about setup or follow up. Others have developed and advocated for similar structures to create systematic instruction for small groups and independent centers (Bear, et al., 2015; Fox, 2003).

In some ways, systematic instruction is a bit like an exercise routine. Most experts on exercise recommend a moderate amount on a daily basis. Many of us try to make up for an absence of exercise over many days by overdoing it on a single day. Instead of that becoming the start of a more regular program, it often becomes the only exercise we do until we feel the need to make up for lost time again. Systematic instruction tries to avoid the notion of teaching by overdoing on a single day to make up for not doing something over several days. At the same time, consecutive instruction in and of itself may not be the solution. Like exercise, while doing the same thing over and over again may help you maintain a certain outcome level, it is usually more effective to change your routine over time to move toward new outcome levels. Systematic instruction is both consecutive and increasingly more sophisticated over time.

When I have significant periods of unscheduled time, like on summer break, I use a technique I learned to actually make productive use of that time to accomplish things I have had to postpone because of the busyness of my regular school schedule. I developed a schedule where I give 30 minutes of daily attention to tasks that need to get done (updating financial records, organizing files, working on writing projects, reading recent journals, completing personal correspondence, etc.). By systematically giving these tasks a little bit of time on a daily basis, I've noticed tasks get done over time. Otherwise, it is too easy to ignore overlooked tasks because they will require too much time or to tire quickly from working on them for big chunks of time on one day. In many ways, making instruction more systematic leads to the same advantages. Tasks get done without being overlooked or taught to death in a single block of time.

Explicit instruction is more direct instruction in which skills and strategies are taught through clearly articulating what the strategy is, when and why the strategy is used, and how the strategy is done. This explanation is followed by modeling and demonstrating for the learners by the expert (usually the teacher, though it could be a peer) (Routman, 2000). One of the most critical features of explicit instruction is the think-aloud (Rose-Duckworth and Ramer, 2009; Oczkus, 2010). Teachers need to make their thinking public as they complete reading or writing tasks in front of their students. They need to verbally model the thought processes of skilled readers and writers as they interact with or compose text (Wilhelm, 2001). Think-alouds ask teachers to take what they do automatically internally and externally share that with the students. Akhavan (2008) says this is a chance to "become a reader and writer in front of your students each day (70)." This might be especially important for those readers and writers who need our help the most. Cambourne (2001) reminds us that two of the most common reasons students struggle with reading and writing is that they received faulty demonstrations of how to read and write and/or quality demonstrations that did not engage them.

Explicit instruction is often contrasted with instruction in which the skills and strategies are more embedded, taught indirectly, and learned more implicitly (Zarrillo, 2007). For most of the critical concepts, skills, and strategies needed by emergent, early, and transitional readers, research suggests explicit instruction will be beneficial (Cunningham and Allington, 2016). Explicit instruction does not have to be used exclusively, but for many learners, access to explicit instruction will help them with phonemic awareness, phonics (Stahl, 1992; Ganske, 2013), vocabulary (Bromley, 2007), comprehension (Pardo, 2004; McLaughlin, 2012), and word analysis—including spelling (Gunning, 2001). Others have acknowledged the importance of explicit instruction in writing instruction as well (Calkins and Ehrenworth, 2016). Remember, however, that explicit instruction without many opportunities to read and write will probably fall far short of its potential impact. Explicit instruction and process-oriented instruction can and should complement each other.

Common language is used to show the connections between two processes, such as reading and writing. Research acknowledges that, while the reading and writing process are not exactly the same, they share a number of common elements (Shanahan, 1988). Reading and writing are parallel processes that complement each other (Pinnell and Fountas, 1998). This is especially seen in the orthographic knowledge shared between reading words and writing words. In one case, students are mapping letters to sounds when they spell, and in the other case, they are mapping sounds to letters when they decode (Ganske, 2013). It makes sense to show students the commonalities between these two processes. Instruction in reading should intentionally show how the strategies can also be used by learners during writing, and instruction during writing should intentionally show how those strategies can be used during reading. The line between when students are learning about writing and when they are learning about reading should begin to blur. One way to do this is to use language that is common with both processes. While we might think the connections should be obvious to students, for many students, they aren't. Students may assume what they learn during reading is used primarily during reading and what is learned during writing is only used during writing. One school I recently worked with attributed their disappointing performances on writing benchmark assessments to the disconnect between their reading and writing instruction. They weren't seeing the transfer of what was learned about print in reading instruction being applied in writing contexts. Common language is also critical in seizing the opportunities to connect reading and writing to content areas so that what is learned in one context is seen as applicable across the curriculum (Cunningham and Allington, 2016).

The gradual release of responsibility acknowledges the importance of always teaching for transfer with an intentional effort to lead students toward independent use of the skill and strategy (Pearson and Gallagher, 1983). Instructional models based on the gradual release of responsibility acknowledge three critical phases of the lesson: *I do, we do,* and *you do* (Ellery, 2014). In the *I do* phase, explicit instruction through explanation, modeling, and demonstrating from the teacher usually begins the lesson. This is the important role explicit instruction plays as previously described.

We do first uses guided practice to invite the learner in through prompting, strategic questioning, and probing as the teacher takes the lead while the students practice with the teacher. Then, guided practice asks the students to take the lead and practice while the teacher monitors that effort. This usually happens in small groups or with partners (Fisher and Frey, 2013). The key to effective guided practice is knowing your students and knowing your curriculum well enough that you can provide the optimum amount of guidance as they practice. Dorn and Jones (2012) remind us that the optimum amount of guidance is the least amount of help students need to complete the task. Wood, et al. (1995), offered this instructional contingency rule: Offer more help when the learner runs into trouble and less or the same amount of help when the learner experiences success. In other words, try to avoid doing most of the work for the students, so they can do the work they need to do to increase their competence and confidence (Burkins and Yaris, 2016). To help make decisions about what level of support to give students, Rodgers, et al. (2016), have identified five levels of support to consider in prompting and questioning students. (See Figure 1.)

Figure 1: Hierarchy of Support, Rodgers et al.

Level of Support	Teacher's Role	Sample Language
Level One: Prompting	Teacher provides no information	"Try that word again."
Level Two: Prompting with Information	Teacher provides some general information	"We practiced that word before we started reading the story."
Level Three: Directing	Teacher provides specific information	"Think about what word would make sense."
Level Four: Demonstrating	Teacher provides information though modeling	"Watch as I reread the sentence, and think about what would make sense."
Level Five: Telling	Teacher provides all the information, including the answer	"That is the word ________."

Finally, the responsibility is transferred to the learner in the *you do* phase. The learner independently practices the skills or strategies in authentic situations with the teacher monitoring or assessing the use of the strategy. Monitoring the learner means there is also intentionality in collecting information (data) while the learner is performing during the routine. These data should inform our thinking as we plan what the learner needs to do next. (See Figure 2.)

Figure 2: Gradual Release of Responsibility

I DO	• Teacher reads aloud, thinks aloud, writes aloud • Explain, demonstrate, and model
WE DO (Part One)	• Teacher and students read, think, and write together • Guided practice with teacher leading
WE DO (Part Two)	• Students read, think, and write together • Guided practice in small groups/partners with teacher monitoring
YOU DO	• Students read, think, and write independently • Independent practice with teacher monitoring

Remember one caution in using the gradual release of responsibility. This instructional framework is often discussed in a fairly linear hierarchy. (e.g., *First you do this, and then you do this.*) In some ways, it might be better to present the gradual release of responsibility in more of a circular sequence, which can be entered at any point and then continued to move forward. One veteran reading specialist expressed a preference to start her instruction with the *you do* phase. By watching the independent level of performance of her learners as they read or write and prompting them with the question, "What was the difficult part for you?," she is better able to determine a focus for the *I do* stage. It also gives her a better sense of how much support to give during the *we do* stage. Similarly, Calkins and Ehrenworth (2016) remind us in writing instruction, methods should include elements from the gradual release model (demonstration, guided practice) but also inquiry, responsive observation, and coaching. In more inquiry-based approaches, the learner takes the lead and the teacher follows that lead. The students provide the cue for the level of support and practice instruction that will be needed.

Description of Key Phases of Readers and Writers

Recently, in looking at *Guided Reading: What's New, and What's Next?* (Ford, 2016), I discussed what others typically define as the four phases of learners in literacy and language arts classrooms (Ellery, 2014; Rog, 2012; Richardson, 2009): emergent readers, early readers, transitional readers, and fluent readers. Others present continuums of learner development that include additional stages (Saunders-Smith, 2009) or with significantly more complexity (Fountas and Pinnell, 2016). In order to make the routines in this book more doable and less daunting, I'm going to focus on distinctions between two types of learners: emergent and early.

Emergent readers and writers are trying to answer the question of how print works. They are searching for ways to make connections across various sign systems, including oral and written language. They are trying to figure out what reading and writing are as they become immersed in worlds filled with language, including oral conversations, storybook readings, environmental print, and visual graphics, and are making meaning through marking on paper (among other things!). The emergent reader and writer has to come to understand concepts in how print works, alphabetic knowledge in exploring why letters are important and how they work, and phonological (including phonemic) awareness in discovering and manipulating sounds within language.

Emergent readers and writers are expanding vocabulary and world knowledge needed to eventually bring meaning to the pages they will read and write. The emergent reader and writer needs to find the joy that leads to a positive identity as a reader and writer. Richardson (2009) suggested that some English language learners (ELLs) may actually be pre-emergent. Saunders-Smith (2009) echoed a similar concern for some kindergartners with less experience and stamina. Both suggested that these students may still benefit from what Saunders-Smith (2009) called "bridging experiences." These often include whole class routines like shared reading and writing experiences. In this book, learners who some may label pre-emergent will be addressed within discussions of emergent readers.

Early readers and writers have figured out how print works. They have developed most concepts of print and a foundation in phonemic awareness and alphabetic knowledge. They have the oral language and world knowledge they need to begin bringing meaning to the page and making meaning on a page. They have experienced enough joy to want to embrace their identities as readers and writers. While they may continue to firm up their foundations in those areas, they begin to shift attention to the question of how to figure out print. Their focus becomes acquiring the tools needed to become readers and writers. They move from learning about what reading and writing are to learning about how to read and write. In this phase, much attention is given to the micro aspects of the texts, or what Fitzgerald (1999) called "local knowledge." They use different strategies to figure out words. For example, they'll draw upon sound, visual, structural, grammatical, and semantic clues. Early readers and writers are figuring out multiple strategies to use when searching, monitoring, and cross-checking the words they encounter or record in print (Schwartz, 2005). They get better at using what they know about sounds and letters to decode and encode words. They begin to recognize and produce more words automatically on sight, especially those high-frequency words they see and use over and over again. They are spotting patterns in words that they can use to assist in morphemic analysis as they read and spell longer words. They grow in their ability to use context clues to figure out the meanings of unknown words, which helps them monitor the words they use as they write. By seizing control of their reading and writing, their self-efficacy grows. They see themselves as readers and writers. They begin to experience success, want to experience more success, and develop their knowledge base of how to continue their success (Opitz and Ford, 2014).

Looking at these two phases of readers helps teachers define predictable common patterns across their learners. This narrows the focus of instructional needs as teachers plan to support learners during the common routines of shared writing, shared reading, and word walls. Let's look at those instructional needs in the next section of this chapter.

What Skills and Strategies Are Critical for Emergent Readers and Writers?

Let's look at planning for and supporting the emergent reader and writer. Instruction related to routines needs to be planned to help the learner move forward to these key outcomes:

- **Understanding concepts of print:** The foundational standards for reading, recently published within the College and Career Readiness Standards (CCR) (NGA, 2010), focused on four key areas. One of those areas was print concepts. Emergent learners (primarily in kindergarten and first grade) need to "demonstrate understanding of the organization and basic features of print." Clearly, it is important to determine what the reader knows about how reading, books, and print work. Understandings about directionality (moving left to right on a page and left to right in a sentence, using a return sweep at the end of a line, moving top to bottom, starting at the beginning, finishing at the end, moving page by page, etc.) need to be developed. Understandings about reading (e.g., knowing print differs from pictures, has meaning, and has practical uses) are also critical. The learner must also know the distinguishing features of a sentence (e.g., first word, capitalization, ending punctuation). One indicator includes the ability of the student to show a "voice-print match" between the words on the page and the words said initially by pointing to each word and eventually relying less on pointing with a finger. The reader must have an understanding of instructional terms (academic language) related to reading: *letter, word, page, capital/uppercase, small/lowercase, start, end, beginning, front, back, first, last, print, picture, line,* and *sentence*. Appendix 1 (pp. 170–171) provides a record-keeping sheet for keeping track of the status of instruction on concepts of print. Add extra rows as needed for other expectations or outcomes defined in your local program, framework, or standards.

- **Securing alphabetic knowledge:** An emergent reader needs to learn what a letter is, that each letter has a name, and that a letter or group of letters represents certain sounds. This is called alphabetic knowledge. Alphabetic knowledge is critical for building a foundation for phonics and spelling instruction that will follow later (Piasta, 2014). For emergent readers and writers, I suggest focusing on helping them first learn what letters are and then the names of each letter. Connecting the letters to their sounds will be a focus of later instruction.

- Learning about the alphabet for some emergent readers and writers starts with the ability to visually discriminate. For emergent students with limited alphabetic knowledge, this begins by noticing features as they match and sort letters, often before they even know letter names. Can they find letters that match? Can they sort letters by features (circle parts, straight lines, tails, or diagonal lines)? Can the child find features of letters within words (words that start with the same letter,

EVALUATION IDEA:
Formal assessment of concepts of print can be done using a subtest from tools like Clay's (2013) *An Observation Survey of Early Literacy Achievement* (OSELA), but any teacher can create a simple survey to observe behaviors when the child attempts to read or write, like those identified in Appendix 1 (pp. 170–171).

end with the same letter, etc.)? Be careful to avoid visual discrimination that strays too far from letters and words. Gross visual discrimination activities (i.e., finding the two animals that match) have little bearing on the child's ability to discriminate between two similar letters (*t* from *f*) or two similar words (*was* and *saw*).

- Once students can see visual differences among letters, it might be good to introduce letter names. So what does the research reveal about how emergent readers and writers learn letters and their names? Piasta (2014) identified a number of factors that may make a letter easier or harder to learn. Letters in the names of students—especially initial uppercase letters—may be the first with which children become familiar. They also learn the lowercase letters in their names fairly quickly. Student names are often a good starting point. Look at the names of your children and think about starting to teach those letters that occur with greater frequency.
- Another influence is the alphabetical order of letters. Children learn letters earlier in the sequence like A, B, and C more frequently than those later in the sequence like X, Y, and Z. The theory is those early in the sequence are often seen, said, and repeated more often than others. Though this may suggest teaching the letters in sequential order, other factors also contribute to whether a letter is easier to learn. The shape of the letter may make it easier to learn. A letter with a more distinctive shape (such as the letter X) may be easier to learn than letters with harder-to-distinguish shapes (like C versus G). So while X is at the end of the alphabet, which might make it harder to learn, its shape might make it easier to learn. Likewise, while C is at the beginning of the alphabet, it might be confused with other curved letters more frequently. Additionally, the frequency of letters seen in print and the environment may also influence how quickly they are learned. T is seen a lot more than Q or Z, which may make it easier to learn (though research is mixed on the influence of frequency).
- Considering all these confounding influences, how should decisions be made about what letters to teach? While sequences of letters to teach are available, reflecting some of this research (Piasta, 2014), teachers may want to determine their sequence of letters to teach in light of the students sitting in front of them. Quick assessments of letter knowledge of students can be aggregated to inform instructional decisions about what to teach across students. Keep in mind that in any classroom, there will be a range of alphabetic knowledge in your students. Also, your students may acquire their alphabetic knowledge on slightly different pathways. Since no one plan will probably capture every need, start with a plan that will help you address the common patterns across your students. As you prepare subsequent lessons, consider how to address individual variations as well. Appendix 2 (pp. 172–173) provides a record-keeping sheet for keeping track of the status of instruction on alphabetic knowledge. Include additional rows as needed for other alphabetic knowledge expectations or outcomes defined in your local program, framework, or standards.

EVALUATION IDEA:
Piasta (2014) identified a number of formal tools to assess alphabetic knowledge, but any teacher can create a simple tool using letter flashcards to get a sense of a child's knowledge about letters using the guide in Appendix 2 (pp. 172–173) as a survey.

ENGAGEMENT IDEA: Many classrooms have purchased commercial displays of the alphabet that are often put up on the wall long before students arrive and receive very little attention once students show up. Hayes and Creange (2001) suggest that if you are going to use an alphabet display, raise the value of the display by engaging students in creating it. Student ownership can be fostered by having the students create posters using their drawings to illustrate words that go along with each letter. This calls more attention to the alphabet display and increases the chances that students might actually use it as a resource. Creating new pictures as the year goes along will bring renewed attention to this resource.

- **Developing phonological awareness (including phonemic awareness):** An emergent reader needs to figure out that oral language is made up of groups of sounds and individual sounds. He or she needs to be able to identify, match, blend, segment, and manipulate the sounds in words, syllables, and clusters, as well as individually. The student needs to be able to hear separate words in sentences, syllables within words, clusters of sounds within words, and eventually individual sounds in words. This is called phonological awareness. Phonemic awareness is specifically focused on working with individual sounds within words primarily through the use of auditory tasks.
- While identifying a hierarchy of phonological awareness outcomes may suggest a linear progression of skills, keep in mind that acquisition of outcomes in this area may be anything but linear. There will be individual differences in the rate and order of acquisition in this skill area (Yopp, 1992). Caution should be exercised in labeling, classifying, and sorting young children based on assessment of these outcomes. A suggested hierarchy starts with the broadest forms of phonological awareness. Student *I can* statements might be as follows:
    - ❑ I can hear and identify individual words in sentences. (word awareness)
    - ❑ I can hear and identify parts or chunks in words. (syllable awareness)
    - ❑ I can hear and identify ending clusters of sounds in words. (awareness of rimes)
    - ❑ I can hear and identify the same ending cluster of sounds in different words. (rhyming)

Then hierarchies often move to more narrow forms of phonological awareness, including phonemic awareness, which is the knowledge that a spoken word is made up of individual sounds or phonemes. These outcomes often move from what are easier tasks for most emergent learners to those that are more sophisticated.

The student *I can* statements might be as follows:

- ❏ I can hear and match individual sounds in words.

  EXAMPLE: Which of these words start the same: *bat, ball, hit*?

- ❏ I can hear and isolate individual sounds in words.

  EXAMPLE: What is the first sound you hear in *bat*?

- ❏ I can add individual sounds to words.

  EXAMPLE: What word do you get if you add /s/ to the end of *bat*?

- ❏ I can blend individual sounds into words.

  EXAMPLE: What word is made of these sounds: /b/ /a/ /t/?

- ❏ I can segment all the individual sounds in a word.

  EXAMPLE: What are all the sounds you hear in *bat*?

- ❏ I can substitute one individual sound for another in a word.

  EXAMPLE: What word do you get if you switched the /b/ in *bat* to /h/?

Remember, the focus is on identifying and manipulating sounds within words. The examples above would all be done through auditory activities. The students are not seeing the words or letters in these activities. For most emergent learners, phonemic awareness activities are typically easier if the focus is on initial sounds first, then ending sounds, and finally, medial sounds. Blending and segmenting sounds in words may be the most helpful to support emergent learners with decoding and spelling words (Fox, 2003). Appendix 3 (pp. 174–175) provides a record-keeping sheet for tracking phonological/phonemic awareness. Additional rows can be included as needed for other expectations or outcomes defined in your local program, framework, or standards.

Considering these skills and strategies discussed in this section, you should be able to clearly identify whether your students generally have needs in these areas and specifically what those needs might be. This is not an exhaustive list of skills and strategies that a student in the emergent phase needs, but these areas capture the key outcomes for this phase. They reflect and can be easily aligned with expectations defined or influenced by recently published CCR. (See Figure 3 on p. 22.) While these cognitive outcomes require much attention, lessons including the use of classroom routines should also be planned with the intent of expanding learners' oral language and world knowledge. Lessons should be conducted to help the learner discover joy and develop a positive identity as a reader and writer. As students demonstrate strong competencies in these key areas, they may be more appropriately addressed as early readers in the next phase of the continuum.

Figure 3: Expected Print Concepts and Phonological Awareness Strategies by Grade (CCR)

	Kindergarten	First Grade
Print Concepts	Demonstrates understanding of the organization and basic features of print Follows words from left to right, top to bottom, and page by page Recognizes that spoken words are represented in written language by specific sequences of letters Understands that words are separated by spaces in print Recognizes and names all upper- and lowercase letters of the alphabet	Demonstrates understanding of the organization and basic features of print Recognizes the distinguishing features of a sentence (e.g., first word, capitalization, ending punctuation)
Phonological Awareness	Demonstrates understanding of spoken words, syllables, and sounds (phonemes) Recognizes and produces rhyming words Counts, pronounces, blends, and segments syllables in spoken words Blends and segments onsets and rimes of single-syllable, spoken words Isolates and pronounces the initial, medial vowel, and final sounds (phonemes) in three-phoneme (consonant-vowel-consonant, or CVC) words (does not include CVCs ending with /l/, /r/, or /x/) Adds or substitutes individual sounds (phonemes) in simple, one-syllable words to make new words	Demonstrates understanding of spoken words, syllables, and sounds (phonemes) Distinguishes long from short vowel sounds in spoken, single-syllable words Orally produces single-syllable words by blending sounds (phonemes), including consonant blends Isolates and pronounces initial, medial vowel, and final sounds (phonemes) in spoken, single-syllable words Segments spoken, single-syllable words into their complete sequence of individual sounds (phonemes)
English Language Arts Standards—Reading: Foundational Skills—Introduction for K–5 from National Governors Association (2010). *The Common Core State Standards.*		

What Skills and Strategies Are Critical for Early Readers and Writers?

When planning for and supporting readers and writers as they are moving from the emergent phase to the early phase, instruction based on routines may need to continue to be planned to review outcomes from the emergent phase. Increasingly, the lessons, however, should start to shift toward outcomes more appropriate for early readers and writers. The learners in this phase need to move to these key additional outcomes:

- **Improve ability to use sound analysis:** Teachers need to target sound-symbol relationships with which the student needs assistance.

Focus shifts to the student's ability to identify and spell words accurately by using initial and ending single consonants, short and long vowel patterns, and rimes. Some of that focus will be on learning the individual sounds certain symbols typically make. Fairly consistent consonant sounds include /b/, /d/, /f/, /h/, /j/, /k/, /l/, /m/, /n/, /p/, /r/, /s/, /t/, /v/, /w/, /y/, and /z/. /W/ and /y/ are consistent consonant sounds, but remember, they also represent vowel sounds, so that can be confusing for some early readers and writers. Symbols that have variable consonant sounds include /c/, /g/, and /x/. Some of that focus will be on teaching common patterns that can be used to figure out new words (e.g., CVC, VCe). And some of that focus will be on teaching common phonograms or anchor words so students can use analogies in figuring out new words. The student will need to be assisted in addressing increasingly more complex sound-symbol relationships. Once single consonant and vowel patterns have been fairly well mastered, more difficult combinations and representations will need some work: consonant digraphs (/ch/, /th/, /wh/, /sh/), initial consonant blends, (/br/, /cr/, /dr/, /fr/, /gr/, /pr/, /tr/, /bl/, /cl/, /fl/, /gl/, /pl/, /sl/, /sc/, /scr/, /sk/, /sm/, /sn/, /sp/, /spl/, /spr/, /st/, /str/, /sw/, and /tw/), ending consonant blends (/ld/, /mp/, /nt/, /nd/, /lt/, /ft/), and digraphs (/ng/).

- Appendix 4 (pp. 176–177) presents a recording sheet to help you stay systematic with the sound-symbol relationships you teach and your students learn. You can add additional rows as needed for other sound-symbol strategies defined by expectations or outcomes in your local program, framework, or standards.
- **Increase sight word vocabulary:** One of the most predictable elements of the English language is the degree of frequency with which a relatively limited number of words are used in print. Leu and Kinzer (2012) remind us that knowing 200 of the most common words on sight will allow students to recognize almost 50 percent of all the words they will encounter when reading. Ten words make up 25 percent of all words in texts: "the," "of," "and," "to," "a," "in," "that," "it," "is," "was." Helping early readers to automatically recognize these words is important in making decisions about instruction. Growing the number of high-frequency words like these that a reader can recognize automatically and a writer can spell without difficulty is an important outcome during this phase. The ultimate goal is to eventually grow the automaticity with which a learner can read and write any word, but beginning with those words that are used with greater frequency is the best place to start. You can create a recording sheet to help you stay systematic with the high-frequency sight words you teach and your students learn by selecting any of the many high-frequency sight lists available to guide you (Leu and Kinzer, 2012; Fry 1980).
- **Ability to analyze through structural analysis:** Another way that words can be analyzed is by using structural analysis.

Linguists estimate for every word we learn, we can figure out six or seven other words using structural analysis (Cunningham and Allington, 2016). Structural analysis involves examining words in terms of their root or base words and attached inflected endings, suffixes, and/or prefixes. It is also called morphemic analysis. Morphemes are the smallest unit of meaning within a word. Morphemic analysis provides students with strategies to analyze longer words for both their pronunciation and meaning. Starting points for structural analysis instruction are easy to identify because of the predictability of the English language. If a word has an ending attached to it, 70 percent of the time it will be -s, -es, -ed, -ing, or -ly. In fact, the four most frequent endings (-s, -es, -ed, -ing) account for 97 percent of suffixed words in printed school English (Honig, Diamond, and Gutlohn, 2000). It is critical that early readers and writers become competent in reading and writing words with these endings.

- Words that have affixes attached to them continue to increase in books as students move through the grades. Most books for early readers will primarily contain words with the common endings discussed above. By third grade, words show up with prefixes and suffixes with significantly greater frequency in texts. These words actually double in frequency in materials for fourth and fifth graders. Often instruction about these structural elements is delayed until readers are older. If instruction for early readers and writers needs to address prefixes and suffixes, it should start with the most common affixes. These are the ones students will most likely encounter when they read and write. Common suffixes beyond the inflected endings can be identified. (See Appendix 5, pp. 178–179.) Similarly, the large number of prefixes learners may need can be narrowed down. Of the 20,000 most commonly used words in English, 4,000—or 20 percent—have prefixes. Fifteen prefixes make up 82 percent of the total usage of all prefixes (White, Sowell and Yanagihara, 1989). Structural analysis also is often used to examine compound words, contractions, and possessives.
- As words grow beyond one syllable, students need to be able to "chunk" the multisyllabic words into meaningful parts to help with pronunciation and determining meaning. This requires spotting patterns that assist in the breakdown of longer words. Students can be taught common syllabication patterns. Hendricks and Rinsky (2007) suggest teaching students the mnemonic CLOVER: Teach about closed syllables, consonant -le syllables, open syllables, double vowel syllables, vowel-consonant-e syllables, and r-controlled syllables. Being able to recognize morphemes that allow the reader to figure out pronunciations and meanings is a critical strategy to move readers forward. It also helps them transform root words into meaningful words as they write. Appendix 5 (p. 179) presents a recording sheet to

help you stay systematic with the teaching of structural elements and analysis strategies you teach and your students learn. Include additional rows as needed for other structural analysis strategies defined by the expectations or outcomes in your local program, framework, or standards.

- **Ability to analyze word meanings through context analysis:** Early readers and writers also need word strategies they can use in the context of real reading and writing. The early reader needs to be introduced to the use of context to monitor the accuracy of known words and figure out new words. Monitoring is the ability to know when a word doesn't make sense. Cross-checking is the ability to use an additional strategy to repair what doesn't make sense with a word that does. Fostering monitoring and cross-checking strategies can start as basic techniques that are addressed as reading is being done. Strategic questioning about whether a word makes sense and/or what other strategies could be tried to figure out a word becomes a starting point for instruction in the use of context. Students can be taught self-regulation systems in which they analyze their word-level strategies. This is described as retrospective miscue analysis (Goodman and Marek, 1996; Moore and Gilles, 2006). In taped readings, students can be shown how to spot a miscue or self-correction and then use a set of questions to guide themselves in analyzing what happened:
    - What was the actual word?
    - What word did I say?
    - Did the word I say make sense?
    - Did I use context to get the meaning?
    - What clues did I use to get the meaning?

- Students who internalize this process will raise their word strategy use to a more metacognitive level and have a greater awareness of how to independently resolve issues related to word strategies.

- In addition to being taught global monitoring and cross-checking strategies, students can be explicitly taught to use context clue patterns to figure out the meanings of unfamiliar words. Artley (1943) first identified nine classic context clue patterns that are found in texts and can be taught more directly. For example, unfamiliar words are often paired with a more common synonym (arid and dry) or antonym (arid, not humid). Unfamiliar words and their definitions are often linked by typographical clues like dashes (magma—hot, melted rock inside the volcano) or parentheses [pumice (rock that has cooled after flowing out of the volcano)]. Figure 4 on page 26 identities the nine context clue patterns with examples. Appendix 6 (p. 180) presents a recording sheet to help you stay systematic with the context clue strategies you teach and your students learn. If your local program has additional expectations or outcomes related to contextual analysis, additional rows can be included to keep track of that instruction.

Figure 4: Categories of Context Clues

Category	Explanation	Think of introducing students to the word *autumn*
Typographical clues	Using typographical marks (parentheses or dashes) to set off an unfamiliar word or its definition	Fall (autumn) is coming.
Structural clues	Using grammatical phrases to link an unfamiliar word to its definition	Autumn, which is another word for fall, is coming.
Direct definitions	Using the explicit pattern of _______ *is* ________	Autumn is one of the four seasons that marks the transition from summer into winter.
Synonyms and antonyms	Pairing of a known word that is a synonym (or antonym) for the unfamiliar word	Fall, or autumn, is coming.
Similes and metaphors	Using a comparative structure to provide insight into an unfamiliar word	The weather in autumn is like cooling off a bowl of soup too hot to sip.
Tone and mood	Using the broader textual clues to provide insight into an unfamiliar word	On an autumn evening when the air was cooler and the dark seemed to come faster, a bit of sadness lingered, a reminder that the summer had ended.
Graphics	Linking the unfamiliar word to a visual explanation	
Inferences	Reading between the lines to figure out the meaning of the unfamiliar word	The leaves are changing, and the weather is getting cooler. It is autumn.
Background knowledge	Using what you know to bring insight into an unknown word	"Autumn...Oh, that's what my aunt always calls *fall*."

With early readers, the focus shifts to the strategies the student is using to unlock and make sense of the texts he or she is reading. Less sophisticated word strategies will probably be more characteristic of students performing at levels near the beginning of this phase. More balanced, automatic strategy use with greater knowledge of sound-symbol relationships, more extensive sight-word vocabularies, the use of structural analysis, and the recognition of context clue patterns will be more characteristic of readers at later levels in this phase. Again, as was stated with the emergent learners, this is not an endless list of skills and strategies that early readers and writers in the emergent phase need, but these areas capture the key outcomes for this phase. They reflect and can also be easily aligned with expectations defined or influenced by recently published CCR. (See Figure 5 on pp. 28–29.) Readers and writers competently and confidently using these word-level strategies are starting to provide evidence that they are moving to the transitional/fluent phase.

EVALUATION IDEA: Using observations and information from oral reading samples, teachers can surface a pattern that reveals what the learner is doing to figure out words. Record errors such as substitutions, omissions, insertions, and assisted or told words. Also note the degree of hesitation, repetition, and self-correction that occurred with words. Then classify each by the type of cues being used by the reader:

- M— **meaning (semantic cues):** Does the error make sense?
- S — **structure or syntax (structural cues):** Does the error sound right grammatically?
- V — **visual (graphophonemic cues):** Does it look like the word on the page?

You can look for patterns to see if the difficult words were high-frequency sight words, tricky due to sound-symbol relationships, confusing because of structural elements, or without meaning in the context. The analysis both reveals what the student can do and what the student needs to be able to do. Look generally at what needs to be worked on, but also dig deeper to see specific needs within that general area. For example, if the student seems to be having difficulty with graphophonemic cues, look at whether the points of difficulty are occurring in the beginning, middle, or end of words. This will help you better target the instruction as you move forward with the plans for your classroom routines.

Figure 5: Expected Phonics and Word-recognition Strategies by Grades (CCR)

	Kindergarten	First Grade	Second Grade
General goal	Know and apply grade-level phonics and word-analysis skills in decoding words	Know and apply grade-level phonics and word-analysis skills in decoding words	Know and apply grade-level phonics and word-analysis skills in decoding words
Sound analysis	Demonstrate basic knowledge of one-to-one letter-sound correspondences by producing the primary sound or many of the most frequent sounds for each consonant Associate the long and short sounds with the common spellings (graphemes) for the five major vowels Distinguish between similarly spelled words by identifying the sounds of the letters that differ	Know the spelling-sound correspondences for common consonant digraphs Decode regularly spelled, one-syllable words Know final -e and common vowel team conventions for representing long vowel sounds	Distinguish long and short vowels when reading regularly spelled, one-syllable words Know spelling-sound correspondences for additional common vowel teams
Sight vocabulary	Read common high-frequency words by sight (e.g., *the, of, to, you, she, my, is, are, do, does*)	Recognize and read grade-appropriate, irregularly spelled words	Identify words with inconsistent but common spelling-sound correspondences Recognize and read grade-appropriate, irregularly spelled words

Figure 5: Expected Phonics and Word-recognition Strategies by Grades (CCR) *continued*

	Kindergarten	First Grade	Second Grade
Structural analysis	Use the most frequently occurring inflections and affixes (e.g., -ed, -s, re-, un-, pre-, -ful, -less) as a clue to the meaning of an unknown word	Use knowledge that every syllable must have a vowel sound to determine the number of syllables in a printed word Decode two-syllable words following basic patterns by breaking the words into syllables Read words with inflectional endings Use frequently occurring affixes as a clue to the meaning of a word Identify frequently occurring root words (e.g., *look*) and their inflectional forms (e.g., *looks, looked, looking*)	Decode regularly spelled, two-syllable words with long vowels Decode words with common prefixes and suffixes Determine the meaning of the new word formed when a known prefix is added to a known word (e.g., *happy/unhappy, tell/retell*) Use a known root word as a clue to the meaning of an unknown word with the same root (e.g., *addition, additional*) Use knowledge of the meaning of individual words to predict the meaning of compound words (e.g., *birdhouse, lighthouse, housefly; bookshelf, notebook, bookmark*)

English Language Arts Standards—Reading: Foundational Skills—Introduction for K–5 from National Governors Association (2010). *The Common Core State Standards.*

Summary

In this chapter, I have laid out critical components to consider in building your foundation to begin the intensification process for your classroom routines. Intensification integrates the use of systematic instruction, explicit instruction, common language, and the gradual release model to power up your existing classroom routines. It involves looking for common patterns across your learners to determine if your primary focus will be on the outcomes for emergent or early learners. Once you have a general focus for your learners, the resources in this chapter will assist you in determining specific intentional teaching points in the critical outcome areas for your students. Building these into your routines will help you intensify your shared writing, shared reading, and word wall routines. In each of the subsequent chapters, I will help you look specifically at a vision of how to intensify each of these routines. As previously stated, let's make sure that the valuable instructional time devoted to these routines is leading to valuable outcomes for all learners.

CHAPTER TWO:

Intensifying Your Shared Writing

> You've got to look back at the old things and see them in a new light.
>
> *John Coltrane*

What Is Shared Writing?

In a balanced literacy program, Fitzgerald (1999) described the need for both "outside in" and "inside out" instructional methods. "Outside in" instructional methods are those in which the decisions of what to learn are made by the teacher and the instruction flows from the teacher to the students. "Inside out" instructional methods are the times when the teacher arranges the instructional context but then follows the leads of the students in making decisions about teaching and learning. Epstein (2007) similarly talks about intentional teaching as the bringing together of adult-guided and child-guided experiences. In the former, the teacher's instruction proceeds toward the teacher's goal but is shaped by the active involvement of the children. In the other, the instruction builds on the actions of the children with teacher support and follows the lead of the students. In applying these principles to writing instruction, three dimensions emerge: writing *for* our students, writing *with* our students, and writing *by* our students. Let's look at each.

Writing *for* our students is usually outside-in, adult-guided instruction. It is sometimes called *modeled writing* or *writing aloud.* I remember the first time I realized the power of writing aloud. I was at our local reading conference and Regie Routman was the keynote speaker. She opened the morning by turning on the overhead projector and started to write on a transparency without speaking. She wrote about how waking up on the shores of Lake Winnebago in Wisconsin that morning reminded her of waking up on summer mornings when she went to camp in upstate New York as a young girl. Within seconds from when the first words flowed from her head to the page, the audience of more than 400 teachers grew silent as they read her thoughts, which continued to fill the page. As they often say, you could hear a pin drop before she was done. You can tell by the technology she was using, it was more than a while ago. Its impact on me has never diminished.

Routman went on to explain the importance of writing aloud—a point that she continued to make in her writings (2000, 2003). Routman wrote aloud without talking. While the reader can learn by watching the writer and reading what was written, the learning would be primarily implicit and indirect. In these cases, the teacher writes a message in front of the students with an expectation that students would learn by observing the teacher's writing behaviors repeatedly over time (Cunningham and Allington, 2016). Any direct, explicit instruction would probably start after the message was written and read. In other descriptions of writing aloud, the teacher models the writing process while thinking aloud in front of the students, verbalizing what is happening as the writing is recorded in a manner that is publicly visible to all students. In these models, the expectation is that students will learn not only by observing the teacher but also through the explicit explanation by the teacher of what is being described. This technique can be used in the drafting stage of the writing process and also to demonstrate and model the planning, revising, and/or editing phases of the process. In the gradual release model, writing aloud would be comparable to the *I do* phase of the model.

Writing *with* one's students can happen in a large group, in a small group, or in an individual conference with the student. These experiences are more often outside-in, adult-guided experiences, especially when they take place in large groups. These are often called *shared writing* experiences. A shared writing experience would move from modeling and demonstrating in front of students to involving students in the writing process through guidance that includes invitation, prompting, monitoring, and coaching through feedback. Routman (2003) labels this a shared demonstration. In this resource, I will use the term *shared writing* to designate the use of these techniques in the large group setting. Wouldn't shared writing also involve writing aloud? Again, purpose will probably drive your decision to use writing aloud instead of shared writing, but yes, most shared writing includes teacher modeling and thinking aloud. In the gradual release model, the shared writing is primarily the *we do* element, but it certainly will contain *I do* elements of modeling and demonstrating.

Many call writing with students in small groups or individual conferences *guided* or *assisted writing experiences* (Dorn and Jones, 2012; Oczkus, 2007). In most guided or assisted experiences, instead of the teacher taking the lead in the writing activity, the teacher follows the lead of the students in small groups or individual conferences, often using writing they created as the catalyst for the instruction. This reflects a more inside-out, child-guided experience. Oczkus (2007) described guided writing as the "bridge between shared writing and independent writing (p. 3)." Keep in mind, no matter what we label these techniques, any of them can inform our thinking when we are working with writers in large groups, small groups, or individual conferences.

Writing *by* students is when students are engaged in the writing process more independently, applying what they have learned through the other dimensions of writing instruction. Independent writing is most reflective of an inside-out, child-guided experience. Writing by students is certainly monitored by the teacher, but it is where teaching for transfer becomes apparent. The teacher stands back as the students provide evidence of increasing self-motivation, regulation, and evaluation during the writing process.

So how does shared writing differ from what some teachers know as the *language experience approach*? While the use of the language experience approach can take many forms, it began with models that primarily involved the teacher recording students' oral language without calling significant attention to the process or mechanics of the writing process as the message was being recorded. The teacher serves as a scribe for students (Pinnell and Fountas, 1998). I used this technique at the end of each day in my first-grade classroom. I had a blank book that we titled the "Class Diary." Every day, as my students were preparing to get ready to leave school, I would ask them, "Does anyone have something for the Class Diary?" My students would share things for me to record in the Class Diary. To start the next day, we would remind ourselves what we did the day before by reading what was recorded in the Class Diary. The power of language experience comes from young children beginning to see the relationship between their oral language and written text (Epstein, 2007). Imagine the joy a child must feel when he discovers that his oral language can be turned into written text. Imagine his excitement as an adult types his words into a computer, prints it out, and reads it back. Can you sense the urgency this would create in a child to have it happen again or eventually try it on his own? For me, the more the large group writing experience is primarily the recording of dictated speech, the closer it is to language experience. The more intentional attention is given to the process or mechanics as speech is being recorded, the closer it is to shared writing. You can see that the line can be a bit blurry. Purpose probably drives the decision of why you would use one approach versus the other, but the distinction between the two may not be that practically significant. Techniques used during language experience approaches and shared writing may overlap and actually help intensify either approach.

So how does shared writing differ from what some teachers call *interactive writing*? For me, these terms are more interchangeable. Interactive writing was also an attempt to make more traditional use of language experience approaches more "interactive" by involving the teacher and the learners in constructing and recording the message together (Pinnell and Fountas, 1998; Routman, 2000). Instead of learners simply saying something to be written down by the teacher, interactive writing gave license to vary from this purist view of language experience. Interactive writing acknowledged the potential additional learning that could take place if the teacher and students worked together in creating the text. For the sake of this book, the terms *shared writing* and *interactive writing* will be used more interchangeably.

So how would the morning message or classroom message fit into this framework? This answer really depends on how the morning message is done. In some classrooms, the message is already written for students as they enter the room or move to the gathering space. Very little is done to intentionally model the writing process, features, or mechanics. The morning message is often used primarily as a shared reading experience. Often the message is read to open the morning activities. It details what is going to happen in that classroom for that day (Adams, et al., 2003; Zarrillo, 2007). In other classrooms, the message is created in front of the students using their language to record news or thoughts (Hayes and Creange, 2001). With minimal attention to the features of print as student language is recorded, this is basically a language experience text. Engaged students can observe the processes as the dictation is recorded and hopefully read back, but what is learned is more incidental than intentional.

If the classroom message is recorded in front of the students, with intentional effort to call attention to the process, features, or mechanics by modeling, demonstrating, offering invitations, prompting, monitoring, and providing feedback, then the classroom message mirrors the best aspects of shared or interactive writing. If features of that message are revisited over time, it grows in intensity. It is this later vision that is at the heart of this chapter. It should be obvious that any existing model of the classroom message can be intensified and moved in a direction that has a more powerful impact in reaching all students.

Why Is Shared Writing a Critical Routine?

In many classrooms, the most efficient use of time and resources is still within the large group setting. You have all your students in one place and you can use the same set of instructional materials across the learners. The large group setting is the most efficient context for providing explanations, models, and demonstrations. The large group setting is also the most efficient context for providing initial practice with the teacher present to monitor and provide support to learners' initial attempts to show knowledge, skills, and dispositions as they learn key literacy outcomes. The large group also puts your diverse group of learners in one setting. Groups provide socially supportive structures for learners to also learn from one another (Fountas and Pinnell, 1996). The shared writing experience embodies all of those advantages.

What Concerns Do Current Theory, Expert Opinion, and Research Raise about Shared Writing Practices?

Besides the issue of intensification, which I have already addressed, three other concerns have surfaced about the use of shared writing experiences: the need for greater engagement, collecting useful data during shared writing instruction, and better integration of the shared writing experience with other parts of the literacy and language arts program.

In regard to engagement, many learners still spend a significant amount of their instructional time in large group settings. While there is nothing inherently disengaging about large group instruction (Kelly and Turner, 2009), engagement is critical for successful large group instruction. As a former first-grade teacher, I was somewhat amazed by how early some students learned to disengage in large group settings. They have discovered that a handful of their classmates will take over the responsibility of raising hands and responding on cue. They have learned quite young that if they just keep their heads down, the teacher will probably call on their classmates, and they can avoid having to think about making a contribution in the large group setting. So, engagement remains a critical concern during shared writing practices. How can students gain from shared writing experiences in the large group setting if they are not engaged during that large group instruction? Planning any shared writing experience needs to be intentional in regard to engagement of all learners during the experience. Research suggests that exemplary teachers who have the greatest impact on traditional literacy performance and achievement measures are able to sustain engagement levels at a 90-90 level: 90 percent of their students were on task 90 percent of the time (Pressley, et al., 2001).

ENGAGEMENT IDEA: Name cards (Opitz and Ford, 2015) are a simple tool for raising levels of engagement during whole class activities. Write the first name of each of your students on a fairly large index card visible enough for them to see from a distance. Print the last name of your students on the back of the same card. Use your name cards to systematically call on students when you need students to respond to a question or independently complete a task. By using name cards, you will automatically involve more students in the interaction. Students will learn quickly that their name can come up on the next card, so they need to raise their levels of engagement. No longer can students just move to the edge of the carpet and assume another student will cover them. The cards can be used to randomly call on students but can also be stacked ahead of time to make sure specific students are intentionally engaged in the shared writing.

One caution in working toward levels of high engagement is to plan your large group lessons to also include processing time. Pacing the lesson quickly may help students stay on task but not really learn what is taught. As DeMeo (2013) points out, for some learners constant attention in a quickly paced lesson can be counterproductive if it precludes time to process internally. Since learning for individuals is always generated internally, build in spaces for thinking. Wait time, turn-and-talks, and other similar techniques allow what is taught to be processed, imprinted, and assimilated.

In regard to evaluation, anything students do throughout the school day can inform our thinking about where they are at in their reading and writing performance. Knowing where the student is at also allows us to better plan for what the student needs next. As Dorn and Jones (2012) pointed out, this "requires us to spend time observing changes that indicate that children are moving in appropriate directions (p. 67)." The concern is that despite the "data" available as students work through the shared writing experiences, very little effort is made to capture the data, analyze it, and use it to inform thinking about what to plan next. I have been in many classrooms where nothing is recorded regarding students' responses or performances during the shared writing experience. Information may be filed away in the teacher's head or heart, but I wonder how often it was used to make subsequent decisions about what to teach. So we must consider how can we gather and use data from the shared writing experience more effectively.

EVALUATION IDEA: Your class list may be one of the most helpful evaluation tools you can use in a large group setting (Opitz and Ford, 2015). Write the names of your students down the left side of a paper and place it on a clipboard you keep close to the gathering space where you conduct shared writing. As students respond to strategic questions and/or complete tasks as independent practice, simple notations can be made next to students' names on the class list. Even simple symbols like a plus sign for a correct response and a minus sign for an inappropriate response recorded over time will start to reveal patterns about students' engagement and competency levels related to the shared writing outcomes. You can also set up a sheet on your tablet to record the information electronically.

Finally, in thinking about integration, the shared writing should be intentionally linked to other elements within the literacy and language arts program. In this resource, I argue to make three common routines (shared writing, shared reading, and word walls) more closely aligned. Then these elements need to be part of a comprehensive literacy program providing a logical flow from one aspect to the next. Eventually, plans should be developed that provide links to content discussed in other subject areas like social studies or science. If elements continue to stand in isolation, the learner will be hampered in her ability to transfer information beyond the contexts in which the concepts were learned.

INTEGRATION IDEA: Consider using the lens of content you are exploring in math, science, or social studies to help you form the heart of your classroom messages (Adams, et al., 2003). Routman (2000) reminds us that the shared writing can also be centered on purposeful classroom tasks. Some examples would include writing an invitation for a class visitor, a thank-you note to a class volunteer, a class newsletter for families, or a class review of a read-aloud book to post on a website.

How Is Shared Writing Intensified for Emergent Readers and Writers?

Shared writing for emergent readers and writers will involve systematic, explicit instruction in the large group setting focused on three critical outcomes: concepts of print, alphabetic knowledge, and phonological/phonemic awareness. The routine uses common language to help emergent students make connections between reading and writing. The routine incorporates a gradual release of responsibility to provide direct explanation, demonstrating, modeling, guided practice, and monitored independent practice. It is rolled out in a five-day sequence with an expectation that each lesson be 15–20 minutes in length. Some of the instructional activities can also be used in subsequent small group settings or left available for students to use as an independent center following the large group lessons. Keep in mind that the sequence provided in this chapter is to illustrate one possible way to intensify this classroom routine for learners in this phase; however, a classroom teacher needs to adapt or modify this vision by staying focused on his or her students' needs within these critical skills and strategies.

Day One: *The Interactive Writing of the Message*

Prior to the start of the five-day cycle, plan a classroom message that could be used for shared writing and the subsequent week of daily activities in the key areas of concepts of print, alphabetic knowledge, and phonological—including phonemic—awareness. Keep your message relatively short (three to four sentences) and plan it with grade-appropriate vocabulary. Look at the sample message below.

> It is fire safety week.
>
> We will have a fire drill.
>
> The fire truck will stop here on Friday.

Consider your students' needs and what you want to explicitly teach related to concepts of print, including the academic language related to reading and writing instruction. (The only concepts of print that can't be taught effectively during shared writing experiences are the book-handling skills and strategies. Those can be addressed as part of the shared reading experiences in the next chapter.) In the lesson sequence provided, the focus is on strengthening voice-print match. Consider also what your students need to know about letters in general or any specific letter names. Notice the focus in the provided lesson sequence is on upper- and lowercase F. Finally, think about what your students need to know to help further develop their phonological/phonemic awareness. Stretching words to hear sounds is the focus in the provided lesson sequence. While the shared reading is primarily a vehicle for literacy instruction, try to build your message with content related to what you might be teaching in subject areas. The focus of the message allows for connections to social studies and science through the lens of fire safety. Try to build joy into your message and experience. The included message attempts to build anticipation about a special school event that week.

Reminders When Planning

- Plan the length of the message, so it can be written in a relatively short amount of time.
- Plan a message mostly using vocabulary that is in the oral and receptive language of your students.
- Plan a message that allows you to explain, demonstrate, model, prompt, monitor, and/or give feedback related to concepts of print your students are still in need of instruction on, support with, or practice in. The good news is that almost any classroom message will give you teachable moments to work on concepts of print.

- Plan a message that allows you to introduce, prompt, monitor, and/or give feedback related to alphabetic knowledge your students are still in need of instruction on, support with, or practice in. Remember, it is hard to teach specific letters if they are not a part of the classroom message. Be intentional about including words spelled with those letters in your message.
- Plan a message that allows you to introduce, prompt, monitor, and/or give feedback related to the use of phonological—including phonemic—awareness your students are still in need of instruction on, support with, or practice in. Remember to think about whether you will be working primarily on word awareness, syllable awareness, onset and rimes, individual phonemes, or some kind of combination. Make sure the classroom message has sentences, longer words, words with clear common rimes, or words with clear individual phonemes to use during your instruction.
- If possible, plan a message that allows for a connection to content being explored in one of your subject areas.
- Plan a message that allows learners to build on what they have experienced with each previous part of the message.
- To make sure you actually record the message you planned, try writing it on a small sticky note so as you write it on the chart paper or whiteboard space, you can make sure you duplicate what you planned.

In writing the planned message, select a gathering place within the classroom where all students can see and hear you as you write the message. In some classrooms, a gathering place might be at a large carpet where the teacher can use chart paper or a large whiteboard to record and work with the message. Sometimes it might work better to leave students at their tables or desks so the teacher can record the writing on a space in front of the classroom. The teacher might also use some projection tool like an interactive whiteboard to record and share the message in a way that can be seen by all students. Just keep in mind that shared experiences are supposed to be in a more intimate setting so all students can clearly see, hear, and benefit from the instruction (Dorn and Jones, 2012).

Start with your first planned sentence (or first part of the message, if longer). Use this sentence for explanation, demonstration, and modeling. This should be the *I do* phase of your lesson. Use think-alouds as you write to make your internal processing public for your students. This allows you to share information as an insider for the reading and writing processes. Concentrate on having students watch you and listen to you during this initial phase. Be very intentional about articulating the concepts of print to which you want to call attention. Also be very intentional about the academic language use related to literacy so students with less experience with those terms become increasingly familiar with them and their meanings. Call attention to the names of letters (especially those with which your students need specific help) as you write words containing those letters. Model phonological/phonemic awareness strategies to create greater awareness of the strategies your students need.

As you move to the second sentence (or middle part of the message, if longer), lessen the amount of explanation, demonstration, and modeling for strategies and skills already presented in the first part. Save additional explanation, modeling, and demonstrating for new concepts that might be encountered in the second sentence. Start to invite the learners in on the writing of the second sentence by having them monitor you, or prompt them to show you what to do. This should be the *we do* phase of your lesson. Use strategic questions to guide the students as they start to practice and apply the concepts previously introduced and modeled. Be very intentional about using questions or prompts that have students applying knowledge about concepts of print, academic language, names of letters, and phonological/phonemic awareness strategies, which are the intentional focus of this lesson.

As you move to the final sentence (or final part of the message), look for opportunities to turn over the writing process to at least some of the learners. Invite students to show you specific concepts of print, academic terms, letter names, or the use of phonological strategies. Move toward the use of monitoring in observing what they can do more independently so that you can also provide specific, appropriate feedback as needed. This would be the start of the *you do* phase of the lesson. This independent practice occurs in a large group under your watchful eye.

The key for effective use of the gradual release model during your routine is being very intentional about your use of language in each part of the lesson. There are subtle differences in teacher language during the *I do*, *we do*, and *you do* phases of the lesson. What you say and ask students to do during each phase needs to reflect these subtle differences. Figure 6 on page 40–41 provides some example language that may be helpful starting points as you reflect on the language you will use. A specific example of how language might sound is illustrated in Figure 7 on page 42.

Figure 6: General Language Examples

	I do Use explanation, demonstration, and modeling	*We do* Use strategic questioning and prompting	*You do* Use monitoring with feedback
Concepts of print	Let me show you... Here's where I start. Here's the way I go. Here's what I do at the beginning of the sentence. Here's what I do between words. Here's what I do when I get to the end of a sentence. Here's what I do when I get to the end of the line.	Tell me... Where do I start? Which way do I go? What do I do at the beginning of the sentence? What do I do between words? What do I do when I get to the end of a sentence? What do I do when I get to the end of the line?	Show me... Where do I start? Which way should I go? What do I do at the beginning of the sentence? What do I do between words? What do I do when I get to the end of a sentence? What do I do when I get to the end of the line?
Alphabetic knowledge	This is a called a letter. This letter is called _____. This is how you make the letter _________.	What do you call this (pointing to a letter)? Yes, a letter. What letter is this? Yes, it is _____. Can you tell me how to make the letter _________?	Show me what we need next. Tell me the name of that. Go ahead and make that.

Figure 6: General Language Examples *continued*

	I do Use explanation, demonstration, and modeling	*We do* Use strategic questioning and prompting	*You do* Use monitoring with feedback
Phonological—including phonemic–awareness	I am going to listen carefully to this sentence and see how many words I hear. I am going to listen carefully to this long word and see how many syllables or parts I hear. I am going to listen carefully to the sounds at the end of this word and say what I hear. I am going to listen carefully to these words and see if their ending parts are the same. I am going to see if they rhyme. I am going to listen carefully to this word and say the sounds I hear in this word. I am going to listen carefully to these words and see if there are any matching sounds in these words. I am going to add a sound to this word and make it into a new word. I am going to segment and say the individual sounds in this word. I am going to blend these individual sounds to make a word. I am going to change a sound in this word to make a new word.	Let's listen carefully to this sentence and see how many words we hear. Let's listen carefully to this long word and see how many syllables or parts we hear. Let's listen carefully to the sounds at the end of this word and say what we hear. Let's listen carefully to these words and see if their ending parts are the same and if they rhyme. Let's listen carefully to this word and say the sounds we hear in this word. Let's listen to these words and see if there are any matching sounds in these words. Let's add a sound to this word and make it into a new word. Let's segment and say the individual sounds in this word. Let's blend these individual sounds to make a word. Let's change a sound in this word to make a new word.	How many words do you hear in this sentence? How many syllables or parts do you hear in this long word? What sounds do you hear at the end of this word? Tell me two words that have the same ending parts and rhyme. Say the sounds you hear in this word. Say the matching sounds in these words. Add this sound to this word and make it into a new word. Segment and say the individual sounds in this word. Blend these individual sounds to make a word. Change a sound in this word to make a new word.

Figure 7: Specific Language Example

Lesson Phase	Focus of the Phase	Sample Teacher Talk
Part One: *I do*	Explanation, modeling, and demonstrating	When we write, we usually go from left to right like this....
Part Two: *We do*	Strategic questioning and prompting	Watch me, friends. I just got to the end of this line. See if I go to the right place next... Did I? How did you know? Help me friends. I just got to the end of this line. Where do I go next? How did you know?
Phase Three: *You do*	Monitoring and providing feedback	Who would like to show us where we go next? Do you agree with your friend? How did you know?

Upon completion of the shared writing, do a quick rereading of the message. Remember, the more formal rereading and assisted reading of the message will take place on day two of the routine. This rereading is mainly a way to put the message back together and leave the learners with a holistic final experience with the text.

End each day by engaging the students in a simple self-evaluation of their work behaviors during the shared writing experiences. (i.e., thumbs-up, thumbs to the side). Finish by explicitly stating a "lesson link" to the next lesson in the sequence. In this case, the writing of the message will be followed by the rereading, so a lesson link would leave the learners thinking about making reading-writing connections on the next day.

Reminders When Writing

- Pace the lesson quickly to stay within the 15- to 20-minute time frame.
- As you write the first part of the message, focus on teacher explanation, demonstration, and modeling (*I do*).
- As you write the second part of the message, focus on using teacher prompts and strategic questions to allow students to show you what they are learning while you are all together in the large group (*We do*).
- As you write the final part of the message, look for opportunities to invite students to "take over" the writing process and show you what they know and are learning. This allows you to observe, monitor, and provide feedback while you are together in the large group (*You do*).
- When you consider what concepts of print to call attention to, refer to the guide provided on pages 18–19 and Appendix 1 (pp. 170–171).
- When you consider what academic language to use, refer to the guide on page 18 for terms.
- When you consider what alphabetic concepts to call attention to, refer to the guide on pages 18–19 and Appendix 2 (pp. 172–173) for additional skills and strategies.
- When you consider what phonological/phonemic strategies to call attention to, refer to the guide on pages 20–22 and Appendix 3 (pp. 174–175) for additional skills and strategies. Remember, strategies in these areas are primarily auditory in nature.
- To make sure you actually remember your teachable moments as you write the message, jot down small reminders on sticky notes so you see them as you're writing.

ENGAGEMENT IDEA:
Dorn and Jones (2012) recommend giving each student a whiteboard, a marker, and some magnetic letters so everyone can be involved in individual problem solving while the message is being written collectively.

Day Two: *Shared and Assisted Reading of the Message*

Now that the classroom message has been created and recorded, it can be used as a text for rereading and assisted reading. Day two of the shared writing cycle is designed to help emergent readers see the connections between the writing processes on day one and the reading process on day two. The reading activities should focus on the same aspects of concepts of print, academic language, alphabetic knowledge, and phonological—including phonemic—awareness strategies that were brought to the attention of the learners on day one.

Reminders When Planning the Reading

- Plan the lesson so the reading activities and instruction can stay within a 15- to 20-minute time frame.
- Plan the reading instruction to allow you an opportunity to explain, demonstrate, model, prompt, monitor, and/or give feedback related to concepts of print that your student were introduced to on day one during the writing process.
- Plan the reading instruction to allow you an opportunity to review, prompt, monitor, and/or give feedback related to alphabetic knowledge your students were introduced to on day one during the writing process.
- Plan the reading instruction to allow you an opportunity to review, prompt, monitor, and/or give feedback related to phonological—including phonemic—awareness strategies your students were introduced to on day one during the writing process.
- Prepare small sticky notes to place on or near the classroom message to remind you of any important teaching points you want to remember during the reading process.

In reading the classroom message, return to your gathering place within the classroom where all students would be able to see and hear you as read the message. For the gradual release, you can structure the lesson in one of two ways. You can divide the message into parts—the first part is *I do*, the second part is *We do*, and the third part is *You do*. Or, with a relatively short message, you can do three readings—the first reading is *I do*, the second reading is *We do*, and the third reading is *You do*. In either case, during the *I do* phase of the reading, the teacher takes the lead using explanation, modeling, and demonstrating, focusing on sharing your information as an insider for the reading processes. Use think-alouds as you read to make your internal processing public for your students. Concentrate on having them watch and listen to you during this initial phase. Be very intentional about reviewing the concepts of print to which you called attention during day one. Be very intentional about repeating the academic language previously used, so students get more exposure to those terms. Also call attention to the letters on which you previously focused on day one. Finally, remodel previous phonological/ phonemic awareness strategies demonstrated on day one.

As you move to the second phase of the reading or the *we do* part of the lesson, reduce your explanation, demonstration, and modeling. Move toward what some call *assisted reading*. Invite the learners in on the second reading of the message by either following your lead or following their lead, monitoring and promoting as needed. Guide students as they start to practice and apply the concepts previously introduced and modeled within the reading process. Be very intentional about using questions or prompts as you read that have students applying knowledge about concepts of print, academic language, names of letters, and phonological/phonemic awareness strategies within the context of this second reading.

As you move to the third phase of the lesson—*I do*—intentionally look for opportunities to turn over the reading to at least some of the learners. Invite students to show you specific concepts of print, academic terms, letter names, or the use of phonological strategies as they read the message on their own. This will allow you to more closely monitor and observe what the students can do more independently. This also allows you to provide specific, appropriate feedback about the reading process as needed. Again, it provides a chance for students to engage in independent practice in the large group under your watchful eye.

Upon completion of the third reading, you may want to end the day with a final choral reading by taking the lead, so students are leaving the gathering space with a successful, fluent final reading of the text in their heads. Like on day one, end with a simple self-evaluation of behaviors and explicitly provide a lesson link to the next lesson in the sequence. In this case, the writing and reading of the message will be followed by more specific attention to important concepts of print on day three.

Reminders When Reading

- Pace the readings quickly to stay within the 15- to 20-minute time frame.
- As you do the first reading, focus on teacher explanation, demonstration, and modeling *(I do)*.
- As you do the second reading, assist or guide the reading with you taking the lead as needed. Use teacher prompts and strategic questions to allow the students to show you what they have learned while you are all together in the large group *(We do)*.
- As you do the third reading, look for opportunities to invite students to "take over" the reading and show you what they know and are learning. This allows you a chance to observe, monitor, and provide feedback while you are all together in the large group *(You do)*.
- When you consider what concepts of print to call attention to, include concepts of print modeled during the writing process on day one.
- When you consider what academic language to use, focus on reviewing any terms used during the writing process on day one.
- When you consider what alphabetic concepts to call attention to, consider reviewing the letters taught during the writing process on day one.

- When you consider what phonological/phonemic strategies to call attention to, consider reviewing the strategies taught during the writing process on day one.
- Be ready to follow appropriate leads from your students that may vary from previously introduced skills and strategies.

Day Three: *Intensifying Instruction toward Outcomes Related to Concepts of Print*

Over the next three days, the focus will shift toward cognitive outcomes in the three key areas of need for emergent readers and writers. Day three of the shared writing cycle is designed to help emergent readers work on specific concepts of print and academic language. This instruction should be as closely linked to the concepts of print and academic language that were part of the focus on day one when the message was written and day two when the message was read back.

You can always start with another reading of the text, but move quickly into the focus for the day. This day is set aside to focus systematically and explicitly on concepts of print. The lesson will be grounded in the text of the classroom message but does not have to be limited to that text. Other samples and examples from other texts can be used to show a concept of print in a variety of contexts.

Remember the critical, specific outcomes in this area that emergent readers and writers need to become proficient at (Clay, 1993):

- Sentence directionality: Where texts (sentences) start and which way they go (move from top to bottom and left to right)
- Return sweep: At the end of a line, the reader/writer returns to the left side of the page
- Word directionality: Words are written left to right
- Spacing: Spaces are needed to isolate words but not letters
- Voice-print match: Each written word matches an oral word
- Monitoring: Knowing when a sentence, word, or letter is not right (out of order, mixed up, or reversed)
- Punctuation: The meanings of periods, commas, question marks, exclamation points, and quotation marks

One way to review concepts of print and academic language is to engage students in a scavenger hunt through the classroom message. You can count the number of sentences (calling attention to features that create sentences); you can count words in a sentence or in the entire classroom message (calling attention to features that create words); and you can count letters in a word, letters in a sentence, or even letters in the whole text (calling attention to features of letters). You can look for punctuation marks like periods, commas, question marks, exclamation points, and quotation marks. Another way of calling attention to the features of print

ENGAGEMENT IDEA: When using searching, tallying, and comparing activities during concepts of print instruction, prepare a scavenger hunt sheet for each student. (See Appendix 7, p. 181.) This sheet invites students to attempt the count first and then provides a place to record the collective effort to secure the correct count. Sheets can actually be marked (numbers, letters, color dots) to differentiate tasks for different students. For example, some students can be counting the sentences while others count the words or letters.

EVALUATION IDEA: Paper trails are created anytime students are asked to write down responses on scratch paper, worksheets, journal pages, etc. to keep them involved in the large group activity. These activities raise levels of engagement and provide opportunities to collect data both on individual students as well as collectively to get a sense of how students are doing. Any paper trail gives you information about the performance on the task, additional competencies (like how students wrote their numbers on the scavenger hunt sheets), and levels of engagement during the task.

(sentences, words, and letters) is using comparative activities. Invite students to find the longest or shortest sentences, counting the words in each. Students can also find the longest or shortest words, counting the letters in each. Tallying activities can also engage students in exploring concepts of print. Students can be asked to find any words that occur more than once or the word that occurs most. Be creative. Revisit the text in any manner that allows you and your students an opportunity to explore and examine the various concepts of print using the appropriate academic language as you do that.

Upon completion of the third day, end with another simple self-evaluation of behaviors and explicitly provide a lesson link to the next lesson in the sequence. In this case, the attention to concepts of print will flow into work on letters on day four. Remember, it is important to remind your students that what was learned about these concepts of print in this lesson can be used when they are working on their independent reading and writing.

Reminders When Teaching Concepts of Print

- Plan the lesson with a clear focus and short length to fit within a 15-minute time frame.
- Plan the lesson with links to concepts of print that were previously introduced when the message was written and reread (days one and two).
- Consider the expectations of your curriculum and the needs of students. Plan the lesson to allow you to explain, demonstrate, model, prompt, monitor, and/or give feedback related to concepts of print your students are still in need of instruction on, support with, or practice in.
- To make sure you actually address teachable moments, try writing reminders on small sticky notes so you can stay focused on what you planned.
- Start with a rereading of the classroom message. Remember, you can invite students in with a choral reading or assisted reading. Stop a few times to insert some attention to concepts of print during this quick read.
- Following the reading, address the identified concept(s) of print for this lesson. Explain, demonstrate, and model the concept first *(I do)*. Then invite students in with strategic questions and prompting as you guide practice of the concept with the students *(We do)*. Leave time for students to show understanding of the concept independently *(You do)*. Be prepared to probe responses.
- Be responsive and follow appropriate leads from students that may surface additional concepts of print from the interactions but that haven't been planned. Record those moments to help reflection for future lessons.
- Involve students in the self-evaluation level of engagement before transitioning from the shared writing experience. End with an intentional link to reading and writing with which students will be involved away from the shared writing.
- Plan for independent work away from the shared writing that will allow students to practice and apply what was learned during the shared writing.

Day Four: *Intensifying Instruction toward Outcomes Related to Alphabetic Knowledge*

On day four of the sequence, the focus shifts to the cognitive outcomes related to alphabetic knowledge. This instruction should be closely linked to concepts that were introduced when the message was written and read back. Alphabetic knowledge includes outcomes that are both conceptual (i.e., What is a letter?) and knowledge based (i.e., This letter is *m*). Alphabetic concepts and knowledge are critical for students to find success with phonics and spelling instruction later on.

Start with another reading of the text, but move quickly into the focus for the day: alphabetic knowledge. Remember that the emergent reader and writer is working toward outcomes such as the following:

- understanding what a letter is
- understanding that letters form words
- understanding that letters stand for sounds
- recognizing letters (i.e., Which letter is the *b*?)
- identifying letters (i.e., Which letter is this?)
- matching letters (i.e., Which two letters are the same?)
- writing letters
- distinguishing between uppercase (capital) and lowercase (small) letters
- knowing when to use uppercase (capital) and lowercase (small) letters
- knowing what features distinguish one letter from another
- knowing that letters can appear in slightly different forms (fonts) but are the same letters

One difficult challenge with these outcomes—especially recognizing, identifying, and printing letters—is that the student needs to be able to do that for each letter of the alphabet, both in uppercase and lowercase forms. It is critical to work on those letters your students are having the most difficulty recognizing, identifying, or printing. Choose a focus that makes sense for a quick lesson. As stated before, make sure the message you have written provides you with opportunities to work on those letters.

Think about preparing strategic questions you want to ask if the students need involvement in recognition ("Let's see if we can find the letter *w* in our classroom message"), identification ("What letter is this?" while pointing to a *w*), visual matching ("Find another letter that looks like this" while pointing to a *w*), or printing ("Let's write the letter *w*."). You can have individual letter cards ready to go and invite students to come up and name the letter in isolation, find the match in the classroom message, or provide a model for printing. Remember to always probe beyond an accurate answer ("How did you know that was a match?"), challenge a

INTEGRATION IDEA:
Counting, graphing, and comparing quantities are easy math concepts to integrate with concepts of print and alphabet and phonological awareness activities. The number of words in different sentences, letters in words, or sounds we hear in words can be recorded on simple graphs, providing many opportunities to discuss which is the most, more, fewer, and fewest, as well as questions that involve mathematical operations like "How many more?" or "How many fewer?" (Hayes and Creange, 2001).

right answer ("How did you know it wasn't this one?"), or try inquiring about an inappropriate answer ("Tell me how you figured out your answer."). Probing one student's response will help all students better notice and use the features of letters.

Upon completion of the fourth day, end with another simple self-evaluation of behaviors. Start to engage students in looking at their behaviors over the past few days. Provide an explicit lesson link to the final lesson in the sequence. In this case, the work on letters will flow into phonological/phonemic strategies on day five. Remember, it is important to remind your students that what they learned about letters today can be used when they are working on their independent reading and writing.

ENGAGEMENT IDEA: For many of the letter activities, students might stay engaged if they can look for letters in their own copy of the classroom message. Make copies of the message for each child, and place the copies in a plastic page. Each child can point to or mark the letters on their copy. Always have the materials ready to go, so setup doesn't consume valuable instructional time. Since the back of the copies are blank, students can flip the page over and have a ready-to-go space for making letters during practice in the lesson. Remember, even when penmanship is the not the intended outcome, students working on recognizing letters and identifying their names may learn them by not only seeing the letter and hearing the name but also by involving kinesthetic/tactile senses in the learning process. If penmanship is the focus, you could also slip a traditional sheet of lined printing paper behind the classroom message in the plastic page so when students flip the message over, they will see lined paper on which to practice. They can also use their fingers as they "write letters in the carpet."

Reminders When Teaching Skills Related to Alphabetic Knowledge

- Plan the lesson with a clear focus and short length to fit within a 15-minute time frame.
- Plan the lesson with links to alphabetic knowledge that were previously introduced when the message was written and reread (day one and two) or connected to the concepts of print addressed on day three.
- Consider the expectations of your curriculum and the needs of students. Think about the content you need to cover, such as broad concepts about letters or specific knowledge about certain letters. Determining this will help you decide which parts of the classroom message will support your instruction.
- Once you know the content to cover, consider which strategies your students need support: recognition, identification, matching in isolation, matching with context of words, and/or printing.
- Plan the lesson to allow you to explain, demonstrate, model, prompt, monitor, and/or give feedback related to the alphabetic skills based on the degree of instruction, support, or practice students may need. To make sure you address teachable moments, write reminders on small sticky notes placed near the message.

- Be responsive and follow appropriate leads about additional alphabetic knowledge concepts or skills from students that may surface from the planned interactions. Record those moments to help reflection for future lessons.
- Start with a rereading of the classroom message. Remember, you can invite students in with a choral reading or assisted reading. Stop a few times to insert some attention to alphabetic knowledge during this quick read.
- Following the reading, address the identified alphabetic skills for this lesson. Explain, demonstrate, and model the skill first *(I do)*. Then invite students in with strategic questions and prompting as you guide practice of the skill with the students *(We do)*. Leave time for students to show understanding of the skill independently *(You do)*. Be prepared to probe responses.
- Involve students in the self-evaluation level of engagement before transitioning from the shared writing experience. End with an intentional link to reading and writing with which students will be involved away from the shared writing.
- Plan for independent work away from the shared writing that will allow students to practice and apply alphabetic knowledge learned during the shared writing.

Day Five: *Intensifying Instruction toward Outcomes of Phonological/Phonemic Awareness*

On day five of the sequence, the focus shifts to the cognitive outcomes related to phonological/phonemic awareness. These are primarily auditory activities that start with broad phonological strategies (word awareness, syllable awareness, rhyming) and move toward more narrow phonemic awareness strategies to help students stretch, isolate, and blend specific phonemes. This instruction should be closely linked to any strategies that were introduced when the message was written and read back earlier in the week.

Start with a final reading of the text, but move quickly into the focus for the day: phonological/phonemic awareness. Decide on a focus for your instruction based on the needs of your students and the expectations of your curriculum. Consider whether you will be attending to broader phonological strategies (word awareness, syllable awareness, onsets and rimes) or narrower phonemic awareness strategies related to individual phonemes within words. Also decide what strategy you want to work on: matching, identifying, adding, removing, segmenting, blending, or manipulating sound units. In Figure 8 on pages 52–53, four potential activities are outlined for each level of sound unit (words, syllables, onset and rime, phonemes). They include the following:

- **Secret Boxes** [also sometime referred to as Elkonin (1963) boxes] can be used to help learners segment sounds by isolating each individual sound and actually pushing "the sound" into the box. This can be done with fingers or simple manipulatives (chips).

- **Turtle Talk** models for learners how to stretch out sounds. By speaking slowly and drawing out the sound units, the teacher can help students learn that sentences or words are made up of separate sound units and these separate sound units can be pushed back together to form real sentences or words. Segmenting competencies will be important as students continue their work with spelling strategies.
- **Blenders** can be used to help students learn how to take distinctly separate sound units and blend them into real sentences or words. Instead of just drawing out the sounds like in Turtle Talk (duuhoooogguuh), Blenders start by separating the sound units (d...o...g) and asking learners to put them in their blender and turn them into real words (or sentences). Blending competencies will be important as students continue their work with sound analysis strategies.
- **Transformers** model how to manipulate sound units in sentences or words. Transformers can include deleting, adding, or changing a sound unit. This sort of manipulation is usually more difficult for some students. Keep in mind additions, subtractions, and changes at the beginnings of sentences and words may be the easiest way to get started. Ending transformations may also be a bit easier for students. Medial changes may be the most difficult.

Upon completion of the fifth day, students can be engaged with a self-evaluation of behaviors by looking back on the entire week. Provide an explicit review of what was learned this week (concepts of print, alphabetic, and phonological awareness strategies) since this is the final lesson in the sequence. As previously stated, always remind your students that what they learned this week can be used when they are working on their independent reading and writing.

ENGAGEMENT IDEA: For many of the phonological awareness activities, individual whiteboards (or a comparable surface) in the hands of each learner will raise the engagement levels. For Secret Boxes, each student can draw the appropriate number of boxes on their surface and push their fingers or a manipulative into each box as the words, syllables, chunks, or sounds are said. In Transformers, students can actually try to draw a picture illustrating the new word that is made after subtracting, adding, or changing a sound to the first word—for example, making *hat* into *bat*. Be sure to have the materials ready to go so setup doesn't consume most of your instructional time. One way to make a very affordable set of markable surfaces is to put a white sheet of paper in a plastic page.

Reminders When Teaching Strategies Related to Phonological/Phonemic Awareness

- Plan the lesson with a clear focus and short length to fit within a 15-minute time frame.
- Plan the lesson with links to phonological/phonemic awareness strategies that were previously introduced when the message was written and reread (day one and two), connected to the concepts of print addressed (day three), and connected to the alphabetic skills addressed on day four.
- Consider the expectations of your curriculum and the needs of students.
- Think about what level of sound units you need to address (words, syllables, onsets and rimes, or individual phonemes). The level of sound units you choose will help you decide which sentences or words to use to provide instruction.
- Consider the strategies you want the students to use with that sound unit: matching, identifying, isolating, segmenting, blending, adding, removing, or manipulating the sound units. The strategies selected will help you determine what activities you might use: Secret Boxes, Turtle Talk, Blenders, or Transformers.
- Plan the lesson to allow you to explain, demonstrate, model, prompt, monitor, and/or give feedback related to the phonological/phonemic awareness strategies based on what instruction, support, or practice students may need.
- To make sure you actually address teachable moments, try writing reminders on small sticky notes placed near the message so you can stay focused on what you planned.
- Start with a rereading of the classroom message. Remember, you can invite students in with a choral reading or assisted reading. Stop a few times to insert some attention to phonological/phonemic awareness during this quick read.
- Following the reading, address the identified phonological/phonemic awareness strategies for this lesson. Explain, demonstrate, and model the skill first (*I do*). Then invite students in with strategic questions and prompting as you guide practice of the skill with students (*We do*). Leave time for students to show understanding of the skill independently (*You do*). Be prepared to probe responses.
- Involve students in the self-evaluation level of engagement before transitioning from the shared writing experience. End with an intentional link to reading and writing with which students will be involved away from the shared writing.
- Plan for independent work with the phonological/phonemic awareness strategies away from the shared writing that will allow students to practice and apply what was learned during the shared writing.

Figure 8: Phonological/Phonemic Awareness Activities

	Word Awareness	Syllable Awareness	Onset and Rimes	Phonemic Awareness
Secret Boxes	Pick a sentence from the class message with clearly separable words. Draw one box for each word in the sentence on a blank surface. Say the sentence and see if students can push each separate word into the corresponding box.	Pick a longer word from the message with clearly distinguishable syllables. Draw one box for each syllable. Say the syllables and see if students can push each syllable into the corresponding box.	Pick an anchor word from the message (embed one from the three most common phonograms). Draw two boxes. Say the word and separate the onset from the rime and see if students can push each part into the corresponding box.	Pick a word from the message with clearly distinguishable phonemes. Draw one box for each phoneme (sound). Say the word and see if students can push each sound into the corresponding box.
Turtle Talk	Pick a sentence from the class message. Tell your students you are going to talk like a turtle and say the sentence really slowly without breaks between the words. Invite them to separate the turtle's words and say the sentence in an appropriate manner.	Pick a longer word from the class message. Tell your students you are going to talk like a turtle and say the word really slowly, stretching out the syllables. Invite them to segment the syllables and then say the word in an appropriate manner.	Pick an anchor word from the class message. Tell your students you are going to talk like a turtle and say the word really slowly, stretching out the onset and the rime. Invite them to segment the two parts and then say the word in an appropriate manner.	Pick a word from the class message. Tell your students you are going to talk like a turtle and say the word really slowly, stretching out the individual sounds. Invite them to segment the sounds and then say the word in an appropriate manner.
Blenders	Pick a sentence from the class message. Say the sentence with the words excessively separated. Invite students to put the words into their blenders so they can blend the words together and say the sentence in a more appropriate manner.	Pick a longer sentence from the class message. Say the sentence with the syllables excessively separated. Invite students to put the syllables into their blenders so they can blend the syllables together and say the word in a more appropriate manner.	Pick an anchor word from the class message. Say the word with the onset and rime excessively separated. Invite students to put the parts into their blenders so they can blend the parts together and say the word in a more appropriate manner.	Pick a word from the class message. Say the word with the sounds excessively separated. Invite students to put the sounds into their blenders so they can blend the sounds together and say the word in a more appropriate manner.

Figure 8: Phonological/Phonemic Awareness Activities *continued*

	Word Awareness	Syllable Awareness	Onset and Rimes	Phonemic Awareness
Transformers	Pick a sentence from the class message. Invite students to think about the sentence but to add, take away, or substitute one word and say the changed sentence.	Pick a longer word from the class message. Invite students to think about the word but to add, take away, or substitute one syllable and say the changed word.	Pick an anchor word from the class message. Invite students to think about the word but to substitute new onsets and say the changed word.	Pick a word from the class message. Invite students to think about the word but to add, take away, or substitute one sound and say the changed word.

How Is Shared Writing Intensified for Early Readers and Writers?

Shared writing for early readers and writers will also involve systematic, explicit instruction in the large group setting, but focus will shift to four critical outcomes at the word level: sound analysis strategies, high-frequency sight vocabulary, structural or morphemic analysis strategies, and context clue strategies. Again, intentional effort will be made to use common language to help early students make connections between reading and writing, especially between decoding words and encoding (or spelling) words. As with the previous intensification procedures, the routine will be rolled out in a five-day sequence with an expectation that each lesson would be 15–20 minutes in length. It will incorporate a gradual release of responsibility to provide direct explanation, demonstrating, modeling, guided practice, and monitored independent practice. The word activities introduced can also be used in small group settings or left for students to work on independently at a station or center. Remember that the sequence provided illustrates one possible way to intensify this classroom routine for early readers and writers; however, it should be adapted or modified for your students' needs within these critical skills and strategies.

Day One: *The Interactive Writing and Rereading of the Message*

Prior to the start of the five-day cycle, plan a classroom message that could be used for shared writing and the subsequent week of daily activities in the key word study strategies: sound analysis (phonics), sight word recognition, structural or morphemic analysis, and the use of context clues. These lessons should further help students use graphophonemic (visual), syntactic (structural and grammatical), and semantic cues (meaning based) as they search, monitor, and correct words in the context of real reading and writing.

Keep your message relatively short (four to five sentences) and plan it with grade-appropriate vocabulary. In planning your message, think about what your students need to know in each of these four areas of word identification strategies. Start with considering what sound analysis or phonics strategies you need to teach. Make sure you plan your message to provide teachable moments related to the teaching of individual sound-symbol relationships, phonograms, and/or sound-symbol generalizations. Make sure those teachable moments will help you focus on specific sound-symbol relationships that are still confusing for your students. Use the guide on pages 22–23 in Chapter One to help you determine the specific instructional needs in this area.

Then consider what high-frequency vocabulary words you would need to focus on in order for your students to expand the number of words they know on sight. The good news is that almost any classroom message you plan to write will probably contain at least some high-frequency sight words. It is hard to write a message without them; however, you may need to be more intentional to embed high-frequency sight words your students are still having trouble recognizing. Again, refer to a readily available list of high-frequency sight words, preferably within your local program, to assist your instructional decision making in this area.

The third thing to consider is embedding words that can be analyzed through their structures or morphemes. These are words in which it is possible to look at root or base words, suffixes (including inflected endings), and prefixes. Certain categories of words, like compound words, possessives, and contractions, can also be analyzed through structure. For early readers and writers, they will encounter the inflected endings more frequently than others. Again, many grammatically correct sentences will contain words with inflected endings; however, you may need to be more intentional to embed a word that will allow for the specific structural analysis strategy with which your students need help. In this area, use the guide on pages 24–25 in Chapter One to help you determine specific instruction.

Finally, the message needs to be planned so students can learn how to use context clues to identify an unfamiliar word. The message should be constructed so that most students will know most words. But in order to work on context clues, at least one word needs to be a less familiar word. If it is a word that students might be unfamiliar with, make sure it is a word that students will at least understand conceptually. They may not know this specific label, but they know the thing it is labeling. Beck, McKeown, and Kucan (2002) have identified these as Tier Two words. The students may not know the new word (e.g., *fortunate*), but they understand the concept behind the new word (e.g., *lucky*). These words are often important for comprehension, might have multiple meanings, and transcend a variety of contexts. They are the words that mature language users use, providing them with more specific language to describe specific concepts. As Jane O'Connor's fictional character Fancy Nancy might say, they are the *fancy* way of saying more common, ordinary (Tier One) words.

To introduce a word that might be new to your students, make sure to place it within a context in which it can be identified using surrounding words. This can be quite tricky because the message needs to be written using one of the nine typical context clue patterns (p. 26), especially since the goal is to get students familiar with these patterns. The guide on page 25 in Chapter One can be used to help you determine specific instructional needs related to contextual analysis.

Reminders When Planning the Message

- Plan the length of the message so that it can be written and read back in a relatively short amount of time.
- Plan a message mostly using vocabulary that is not only in the oral and receptive language of your students but can be read by most students.
- Plan a message that allows you to explain, demonstrate, model, prompt, monitor, and/or give feedback related to sound analysis (phonics) strategies your students are still in need of instruction on, support with, or practice in. Make sure you include words that allow you to teach specific sound-symbol relationships your students need to address the most. It's not just about teaching sound analysis strategies, but teaching the sound analysis strategies your students need.
- Plan a message that allows you to introduce, prompt, monitor, and/or give feedback related to high-frequency sight words your students are still in need of instruction on, support with, or practice in. Remember, it is hard to teach those words if they are not a part of the classroom message.
- Plan a message that allows you to introduce, prompt, monitor, and/or give feedback related to the use of structural analysis strategies your students are still in need of instruction on, support with, or practice in. Remember to think about the structural elements with which your students need support. Make sure the classroom message has words that contain those structural elements for you to use during your instruction.
- Plan a message that allows you to introduce, prompt, monitor, and/or give feedback related to the use of context clue strategies your students are still in need of instruction on, support with, or practice in. You need to embed at least one unfamiliar or less familiar word within one of the typical nine context clue patterns so you can explain, model, and demonstrate how to use those patterns to figure out new words. Vary the patterns. As students become competent with one, move to another one.
- Plan a message that allows for a connection to content being explored in one of your subject areas.
- To make sure you actually record the message you planned, try writing it on a small sticky note so as you write it on chart paper or whiteboard space, you can make sure you duplicate what you planned.

Writing the planned message can follow similar guidelines to what was previously shared in discussing emergent readers and writers. The main thing to keep in mind is that all students need to be able to clearly see, hear, and benefit from the instruction. The writing of the message can follow a similar sequence. Start with your first planned sentence (or first part of the message, if longer). Use this sentence for explanation, demonstration, and modeling as part of the *I do* phase of your lesson. Use think-alouds as you write to make your internal processing public for your students, especially as you intentionally provide information about word identification strategies, including sound, sight, structure, and context.

With the second sentence (or middle part of the message, if longer), start to invite the learners in on the writing by having them monitor your use of word identification strategies or prompting them to show you what they can do with the same word identification strategies. The *we do* phase of your lesson allows you to guide the students as they start to practice and apply the strategies you are focusing on. Be very intentional about using questions or prompts that have students applying knowledge about sound, sight, structure, and context strategies that will be the intentional focus of this cycle of lessons.

With the final sentence (or final part of the message), let at least some of the learners take over the writing process. In this *you do* phase of the lesson, let them show you what they can do more independently, so you can provide specific, appropriate feedback as needed. This starts the students' independent practice in the large group under your watchful eye.

Once the message is constructed, early readers and writers will benefit from a quick rereading to experience the whole text after dealing with its parts while it was written. It is still important to build in self-evaluation techniques and lesson links as was discussed for emergent readers and writers. Always make sure the learners can see how what was learned during the shared writing can be used in their other reading and writing contexts.

Reminders When Writing

- Pace the lesson quickly to stay within the 15- to 20-minute time frame.
- As you write the first part of the message, focus on teacher explanation, demonstration, and modeling *(I do).*
- As you write the second part of the message, focus on use of teacher prompts and strategic questions to allow the students to show you what they are learning while you are all together in the large group *(We do).*
- As you write the final part of the message, look for opportunities to invite students to "take over" the writing process and show you what they know and are learning. This allows you a chance to observe, monitor, and provide feedback while you are all together in the large group *(You do).*

- When you consider what sound analysis strategies to call attention to, focus on those with which your students need support, including any of the following: specific sound-symbol relationships (single consonants, single vowels, consonant blends, consonant digraphs, vowel digraphs, diphthongs, etc.); common phonograms (see list on p. 59); and patterns or generalizations (CV, VC, CVC, VCe, VVC, etc.). Remember, your choices are not limited to this list. (Refer to the guide on pp. 22–23 and Appendix 4 on pp. 176–177.)
- When you consider what high-frequency sight words to call attention to, focus on those with which your students need support, including any that might be identified for students at a specific grade level by your curriculum. If not specifically identified by your curriculum, find a high-frequency sight words list (Dolch, Fry, etc.) and work your way through that list. Remember to focus on those words that students still struggle with when you listen to them read aloud or when they are writing.
- When you consider what structural analysis strategies to call attention to, focus on those with which your students need support. Consider starting with inflected endings. Then add common suffixes and/or prefixes as you see students needing them. Attention to other categories of words that can be analyzed by structure (contractions, compounds, and possessives) can be integrated as needed. (Refer to the guide on pp. 23–24 and Appendix 5 on pp. 178–179.)
- When you consider what context clue strategies to call attention to, systematically introduce each of the nine common patterns. (Refer to the guide on pp. 25–27 and Appendix 6 on p. 180.)
- To make sure you actually remember your teachable moments as you write the message, jot down small reminders on sticky notes so you see them as you write.

Day Two: *Intensifying Instruction toward Outcomes of Teaching Specific Sound Analysis Strategies and Graphophonemic Cues*

Over the next four days, the focus will shift toward cognitive outcomes in the four key areas of word identification strategies needed by early readers and writers: sound analysis, sight vocabulary, structural analysis, and context clues. Day two of the shared writing cycle is designed to help early readers and writers work on specific strategies related to sound analysis or phonics. Remember to link to any instruction that was introduced on day one when the message was written and reread.

Start with a quick reading of the text. Highlight words and strategies that will be the focus of sound-symbol instruction following the reading. You might model or highlight how you use sound analysis strategies to figure out a few of the words in your message. For example, you can even intentionally insert a miscue and show how you use a sound-based strategy to cross-check and correct the miscue.

Move quickly into the focus for the day—systematic and explicit instruction on sound analysis. The lesson should be connected to the text of the classroom message but does not have to be limited only to that text. Other samples and examples can be brought in to teach sound analysis strategies in a variety of contexts.

Remember, the specific outcomes in this area that early readers and writers need to become proficient. You can focus on outcomes in three critical areas: specific sound-symbol relationships, common phonograms or common rimes, and consistent vowel-consonant generalizations.

Specific sound-symbol relationships: As you plan the message you will teach, consider specific sound-symbol relationships with which your early readers struggle the most. Being able to decode the consonant sounds in words often gets the readers close enough that they can unlock the whole word, so start with single-consonant sound-symbol relationships (/b/, /d/, /f/, /h/, /j/, /k/, /l/, /m/, /n/, /p/, /r/, /s/, /t/, /v/, /w/, /y/, /z/). /W/ and /y/ are consistent consonant sounds, but remember, they also represent vowel sounds, so that can be confusing for some early readers and writers. Then look at symbols that have variable sound relations, especially /c/, /g/, and /x/. Once these individual sound-symbol relationships have been mastered, consider consonant combinations, especially initial blends (/br/, /cr/, /dr/, /fr/, /gr/, /pr/, /tr/, /bl/, /cl/, /fl/, /gl/, /pl/, /sl/, /sc/, /scr/, /sk/, /sm/, /sn/, /sp/, /spl/, /spr/, /st/, /str/, /sw/, and /tw/) and initial digraphs (/ch/, /th/, /wh/, /sh/). Additional ending blends (/ld/, /mp/, /nt/, /nd/, /lt/, /ft/) and digraphs (/ng/) may need to be introduced as well since these often differ from those in the initial positions. Vowels can be trickier because they are less consistent in their sound-symbol relationships. The five vowel letters or combinations represent 19 different sounds. Short and long vowel sounds might be easier starting points. Other, more complex sounds might be addressed later (schwa, consonant-controlled, diphthongs, and unique digraphs).

Many different instructional activities can be modified and used during day two of the shared writing cycle. For example, you can modify the concepts used in a print scavenger hunt with the classroom message. This sound analysis helps students see and hear specific sound-symbol relationships. (See Appendix 8, p. 182.)

INTEGRATION IDEA:
When one of the 37 common phonograms are taught, the anchor words should be placed on your word wall, so students are constantly reminded of a word they know that could be used to unlock other words they need.

Common phonograms or common rimes: As you plan the message you will teach, intentionally embed an anchor word that contains one of the 37 most common phonograms. (See Figure 9, p. 59.) By learning these phonograms or common rimes (clusters of sounds) with an analogy strategy (substituting one consonant sound for another), early readers and writers will be able to unlock more than 500 of the most common words they will encounter as they read and write. Others have identified additional rimes beyond these. Fox (2014) identified 50 common rimes that could extend this initial instruction. These phonograms are best learned when they are taught as a part of learning an anchor word. The best anchor words are those that are more memorable because they are "content" words and easily accessible to the students in their receptive vocabulary (Gaskins, et al., 1996).

Figure 9: Phonograms

In addition, nearly 500 words can be derived from the following 37 rimes:

-ack	-ame	-at	-ell	-ight	-ink	-op	-ump
-ain	-an	-ate	-est	-ill	-ip	-or	-unk
-ake	-ank	-aw	-ice	-in	-ir	-ore	
-ale	-ap	-ay	-ick	-ine	-ock	-uck	
-all	-ash	-eat	-ide	-ing	-oke	-ug	

Find the anchor word in the classroom text. Isolate the anchor word from the text. Create the word with magnetic letters, with letter cards, or on a whiteboard, so you can isolate the rime of the anchor word. One way to do this is have the anchor word written on an index card and then actually cut the first consonant sound(s) away to explicitly show students the two parts. Once the rime has been isolated, show students that you can use part of the word you know to help you figure out other words you might not know. Show how when you replace the initial consonant sound with others and add it to the part you know, it makes a new word. Some refer to this as "making and breaking" words. Remember, in initial attempts of this strategy, form new words that will be in the oral language of the students and easily accessible in terms of meaning as they represent concrete items versus abstract concepts. For example, in the lesson sequence included on pages 71–72, you will see that the message was intentionally written with an anchor word *spring*, using the common phonogram *-ing*. It became the springboard to making *ring*, *king*, and *sing*.

ENGAGEMENT IDEA: When making and breaking words while teaching students how to use common phonograms to figure out new words, give each of the students a four-box grid. (See Appendix 9, p. 183.) Guide the students in writing the anchor word in the first box. When you model how to form a new word by adding a new consonant sound to the rime of the anchor word, students add that word to their grids. After working together, substituting another consonant to the rime to make a third word, they should add that to the third box on their grids. End the lesson by guiding the students through a more independent attempt to form the fourth word and add it to the final box on their grids.

EVALUATION IDEA: While the grid activity creates a paper trail you can use to evaluate students' performance on working with phonograms, you can add an additional layer to the level of understanding of the process by asking students to independently add an illustration to show the meaning of the word written in each box. This will allow you to see if students could actually read back and understand the words they created on the grid.

Consistent vowel-consonant generalizations: Teaching generalizations can be tricky because so many of them have so many exceptions. Think about the old rule often taught children: "When two vowels go a-walking, the first one does all the talking and says its name, and the second one is silent." That rule works in fewer than 50 percent of the words in which it can be applied. The rule is a bit more consistent in more common words. This is especially true for the words early learners are most likely to encounter in reading or need in writing. But many early readers and writers will also encounter words that are exceptions to the rules with some of the first words they will see in their reading and writing (*said, friend, been, their*).

So why teach phonics rules if they are so unreliable? Some experts have pointed out that even when the rule doesn't work, it often will get a student close enough to the correct word that the student can use backup strategies to figure out the right word (Stahl, 1992). Simple strategies like teaching students to flip a vowel sound if the word doesn't sound right after applying a rule (Boushey and Moser, 2014) can be taught as backup strategies. Students can be taught to try the short sound if the long sound doesn't work or to try the long sound if the short sound doesn't work. The following might be the most useful phonics generalizations to teach early readers and writers:

- CVC generalization = usually short vowel
- VC generalization = usually short vowel
- VCe generalization = usually long vowel (with silent *e*)
- VVC generalization = usually long vowel
- CV generalization = usually long vowel

When planning the shared writing message, intentionally embed words that allow for teachable moments and learning opportunities about these high-utility patterns. The patterns can be taught directly to students using samples or examples embedded in the classroom message. Be prepared with other examples you can use to guide the practice of students recognizing and using the patterns to identify other words.

You can also structure a more analytical approach to teaching about these patterns. In this case, you may want to embed more than one example of the pattern in your message. Pull those words out of the message and list them with other examples as needed. Use the following sequence:

1. Say each word.
2. Look closely at each word. Guide students to discover the visual pattern in the words.
3. Say each word again, listening carefully to the sounds in the words. Guide students to discover similarities in the way they sound.
4. Help students connect the visual pattern to the sound pattern.

5. Provide a few more examples to practice.
6. Provide an outlier so students know they need to cross-check, sometimes with an additional strategy.

Reminders When Teaching Sound Analysis

- Plan the lesson with a clear focus and short length to fit within a 15-minute time frame.
- Plan the lesson with links to sound analysis that were previously introduced when the message was written and reread on day one.
- Consider the expectations of your curriculum and the needs of students. Plan the lesson to allow you to explain, demonstrate, model, prompt, monitor, and/or give feedback related to sound analysis your students are still in need of instruction on, support with, or practice in. If your curriculum is silent on these strategies, consult the expectations identified by the CCSS. (See Figure 5 on pp. 28–29 or Appendix 4 on pp. 176–177.)
- To make sure you actually address teachable moments, try writing reminders on small sticky notes so you can make sure you focus on what you planned.
- Start with a rereading of the classroom message. Remember, you can invite students in with a choral reading or assisted reading. Highlight words or strategies during this quick read that will connect to the sound analysis instruction that will follow.
- Following the reading, address the identified sound analysis instruction for this lesson. Explain, demonstrate, and model the strategies first (*I do*). Then invite students in with strategic questions and prompting as you guide practice of the strategies with the students (*We do*). Leave time for students to show an independent understanding of the strategy (*You do*). Be prepared to probe responses and be responsive to unexpected needs that surface.
- Involve students in the self-evaluation level of their engagement before transitioning from the shared writing experience. End with an intentional link to reading and writing with which students will be involved away from the shared writing.
- Plan for independent work with sound analysis strategies away from the shared writing that will allow students to practice and apply what was learned during the shared writing.

Day Three: *Intensifying Instruction toward Outcomes of Teaching Specific High-frequency Sight Vocabulary*

Day three moves attention to sight vocabulary. As was previously discussed, one of the most predictable aspects of the English language is the relatively low amount of words that are used with the greatest frequency. The master of these vocabulary words will facilitate students' reading and writing. These words occur with such great frequency that, without them, reading and writing would shut down rapidly. Day three of the shared writing cycle is designed to help early readers and writers work on specific high-frequency sight words. Remember to link to any instruction introduced on day one when the message was written and reread or connected to the sound analysis instruction conducted on day two.

Start with a quick reading of the text. Highlight high-frequency words that will be the focus of instruction following the reading. You might model or highlight how you use visual strategies to figure out some of the sight words in your message. You can even intentionally insert a miscue on a sight word and show how you use a visually-based strategy to cross-check and correct the miscue.

Move quickly into the focus for the day—systematic and explicit instruction on high-frequency words. The lesson should connect to the text of the classroom message but does not have to be limited only to that text. Other samples and examples can be brought in to teach high-frequency words to transfer use in a variety of contexts.

Remember the specific outcomes in this area that early readers and writers need to become proficient at. It's not just about focusing on high-frequency words. It's about working on the high-frequency words your students need help with.

Many different instructional activities can be modified and used during day three of the shared writing cycle. Since these are words you want students to recognize on sight, focus on activities that strengthen visual recognition. For example, in the lesson sequence provided on pages 73–74, the key high-frequency words for the classroom message (*and, is, it, see, the, we*) were isolated on a list. Numbered lists are a good way to focus on visually recognizing words. The list can be read forward and backward. The list can be read in many different voices. The teacher can call out a number and the students can call out the word next to the number. The teacher can say a word and the students can show the number next to it by flashing a corresponding number of fingers. Writing the list in alternating colors may allow some children to track the words on the list more effectively.

Words can be targeted with more explicit instruction as well. One technique to explicitly teach words in this manner is the Look-Say-Cover-Write-Check (Ellery, 2014):

1. Look: Call attention to the visual features of the word, studying the sequence of its letters and other noticeable features.
2. Say: Verbally say the word, spell the word, and talk about the word.
3. Cover: Students cover up the word.
4. Write: Students take the word from visual memory and write it down.
5. Check: Students uncover the word and then go letter by letter to see that they wrote the word accurately.

Students can be given a practice sheet such as the one in Appendix 10 (p. 184). Using techniques, like these, are easy for students to do away from the shared writing context. Use techniques that can also be tools to use in small groups with partners and individually.

One way for bringing the strategies focused on day one and day two together is to ask students to use a Sight Word and Sound Grid (Figure 10 below) in which to place words learned while making and breaking words using common phonograms into short phrases or sentences. This will allow students an opportunity to practice both strategies.

Figure 10: Sight Word and Sound Grid

It is spring.	He is king.
We see a ring.	We will sing.

Reminders When Teaching High-frequency Sight Vocabulary

- Plan the lesson with a clear focus and short length to fit within a 15-minute time frame.
- Plan the lesson with links to the high-frequency sight vocabulary words that were highlighted on previous days.
- Consider the high-frequency sight vocabulary words that have been identified by the expectations stated in your curriculum. Plan the lesson to allow you to provide maximum practice with the sight words your students are in need of instruction or support with. If your curriculum is silent on these words, consult one of the many high-frequency lists available to guide you.
- Write down the specific sight words on small sticky notes so you can focus on those words.
- Start with a rereading of the classroom message. Remember, you can invite students in with a choral reading or assisted reading. Highlight those sight words that will connect to the instruction that will follow.
- Following the reading, address the identified sight words for this lesson.
- Involve students in the self-evaluation level of engagement before transitioning from the shared writing experience.
- End with an intentional link to reading and writing with which students will be involved away from the shared writing.
- Plan for independent work with sight vocabulary away from the shared writing and that will allow students to practice and apply what was learned during the shared writing.

INTEGRATION IDEA: I was recently reminded of one of my favorite ways to call attention to a hard-to-learn, high-frequency sight vocabulary word. Save a clear plastic name badge holder from a professional development meeting you attend. Write the difficult high-frequency sight word clearly on a blank index card and slip that in the name badge holder. Wear the word so that your students can see it. Keep reminding or asking them what the word is throughout the day. If the name badge holder is clear on both sides, you can also put one on the flip side and review two tricky words throughout the day. In one classroom, the teacher secured enough name badge holders so each child could wear one. Each holder contained a different high-frequency sight word that had been introduced. Instead of using the child's name, the students had to call on each other by the name of the sight word they were wearing.

Day Four: *Intensifying Instruction toward Outcomes of Teaching Specific Structural Analysis Strategies and Syntactic Cues*

Day four shifts attention to the use of strategies for structural or morphemic analysis. Students' ability to use these strategies becomes increasingly important as they become more competent in their abilities to figure out shorter one- or two-syllable words and grow an increasingly expanding sight word vocabulary. While those two outcomes might be more critical for early readers and writers, structural analysis is also critical for these students. Certain structural elements of our language require understanding to successfully negotiate reading and writing demands. For example, as stated previously, the inflected endings are needed grammatically for numbers, tenses, or comparisons (-s, -es, -ed, -ing, -ly, -er, -est). These are encountered during the beginning steps into reading and writing. Day four of the shared writing cycle is designed to help early readers and writers work on specific structural analysis strategies. Remember to link to any instruction that was introduced on the previous days.

Start with a quick reading of the text. Highlight any words that will be the focus of structural analysis instruction following the reading. You might model or highlight how you use structural analysis strategies to figure out a few of the words in your message. You can even intentionally insert a miscue and show how you use a syntactic or structural-based strategy to cross-check and correct the miscue. Try this with words that won't sound right grammatically and will require a structural change to an ending to sound right in the sentence.

Move quickly into the focus for the day—systematic and explicit instruction on structural elements of words. The lesson should connect to the text of the classroom message but does not have to be limited only to that text. Other samples and examples can be brought in to teach the structural elements of words and show the strategies that can be used to help with longer words in a variety of contexts.

Many different instructional activities can be modified and used during day four of the shared writing cycle. In the lesson outlined on pages 74–76, it was decided to focus on introducing singular and plural forms of words. Each student was given a plurals counting sheet. (See Appendix 11, p. 185.) The teacher can post an enlarged version of a similar sheet near the shared writing experience. The teacher can use nouns in the message (*days*, *birds*, *flowers*) as well as words learned on other days (*king*, *ring*) as the words to analyze for structure. When each word is dissected, strategic questioning leads learners to classify the word as representing singular (1) or plural (2). Once it is decided which column the word should be assigned to, the learners can then discuss how the word can be transformed to fit the other column. By leaving additional lines, students can be encouraged to find other samples and examples from their reading and writing experiences away from the shared writing experiences.

INTEGRATION IDEA: Always look at words previously taught on other days in the cycle (or in previous cycles) to pull samples and examples to work with in introducing new concepts. This builds in review, which can raise more words to an automatic level of recognition.

Making and breaking words also works for structural analysis, though the focus would shift to morphemes from phonemes. Morphemes are units of meaning. Start with an anchor word that can be used as a root word and upon which additional prefixes or suffixes can be added. For example, a word like *light* can get transformed into *lights*, *lighted*, and *lighting*. See Figure 11. Asking students to add a graphic to each box will allow you to see the level of understanding students have when endings are added to a root word.

Figure 11: Morphemic Making and Breaking Word Grid

light	lights
lighted	lighting

Reminders When Teaching Structural Analysis

- Plan the lesson with a clear focus and short length to fit within a 15-minute time frame.
- Plan the lesson with links to any structural analysis strategies highlighted on previous days.
- Consider the structural elements that have been identified by the expectations stated in your curriculum. Plan the lesson to allow maximum practice with the structural elements for which your students are in need of instruction, support, or practice. If your curriculum is silent on these strategies, consult the expectations identified by the CCSS. (See Figure 5 on pp. 28–29 or Appendix 5 on pp. 178–179.)
- Write down the specific sample words you will use for instruction on small sticky notes so you can make sure you focus on those words.
- Start with a rereading of the classroom message. Remember, you can invite students in with a choral reading or assisted reading. Highlight words that will connect to the structural analysis instruction that will follow.

INTEGRATION IDEA: To help make connections, look at your word wall words. Find good example root words. Add common endings to those root words (-s, -es, -ed, -ing, -ly, -er, -est) and post them so students can see those, along with the more common root words. Select words initially that do not offer exceptions to the rules. With some endings (-ed, -ing), you may want to select examples where the ending is added without a change to the root word, where the final consonant is doubled on the root word, and where the final -e is dropped before adding the ending to the root word.

- Following the reading, address the identified structural analysis strategies for this lesson.
- Involve students in the self-evaluation level of engagement before transitioning from the shared writing experience.
- End with an intentional link to reading and writing with which students will be involved away from the shared writing.
- Plan for independent work with structural analysis strategies away from the shared writing that will allow students to practice and apply what was learned during the shared writing.

Day Five: *Intensifying Instruction toward Outcomes of Teaching Specific Context Clue Patterns and Strategies and Semantic and Syntactic Cues*

Day five shifts attention to the use of context clues. Start with a quick reading of the text. Highlight any words that will be the focus of context clue instruction following the reading. You might model or highlight how you use context clue strategies to figure out a few of the words in your message. You can even intentionally insert a miscue and show how you use a semantic-based strategy to cross-check and correct the miscue. Try this with words that won't make sense and will require changing to a word to make sense in the sentence.

Move quickly into the focus for the day—systematic and explicit instruction on context clues. The lesson should connect to the text of the classroom message but does not have to be limited only to that text. Other samples and examples can be brought in to teach the context clue strategies and help with unfamiliar words in a variety of contexts.

Many different instructional activities can be modified and used during day five of the shared writing cycle to focus on context clues. The easiest to plan is to use cover-ups. Cover-ups involve putting something (sticky notes, marking tape) over a few content words in the classroom message. While students may try to remember the words from the classroom message that are now covered up, they can also be asked to think of other words that would make sense and sound right in the key sentence. For example, in the classroom message about spring on pages 76–78, the class message stated, *We see flowers and birds*. The children saw the message with the words *flowers* and *birds* covered up. They were invited to generate other words that would make sense in the sentence.

ENGAGEMENT ACTIVITY: When working with sentence completion activities to practice context clue strategies and the use of semantic cues, provide each student with a self-illustrated page (Appendix 12, p. 186) so they can complete the sentence with words either selected from the classroom message, from available brainstormed alternatives, or on their own. These individual pages can be illustrated and gathered to combine into a class predictable book based on the pattern. The pattern also gives the readers additional practice with some of the key high-frequency sight words worked on previously.

As readers grow increasingly competent, their need will shift toward being able to figure out unfamiliar words and their meanings. As previously discussed, there are nine typical context clue patterns that can actually be explicitly taught to early readers and writers (p. 26). On a systematic basis, one of these can be embedded into the classroom message to provide a teachable moment on day five of the cycle. In teaching these patterns, prepare the lesson using a gradual release model. Start by telling and/or showing how to recognize the pattern and how to use the pattern to figure out the unfamiliar word. Prepare a second example, so you can practice recognition and use of the pattern to figure out another unfamiliar word. Prepare a third example to use for independent practice with the students in the large group setting. Growing awareness of these patterns can be connected to what students are seeing in their reading away from the shared writing experience.

Reminders When Teaching Context Clues

- Plan the lesson with a clear focus and short length to fit within a 15-minute time frame.
- Plan the lesson with links to any context clue strategies that were highlighted on previous days.
- Consider the context clues that have been identified by the expectations stated in your curriculum. Plan the lesson to allow you to provide maximum practice with the context clue strategies for which your students need the most instruction, support, or practice.
- Write down the specific sample words you will use for instruction on small sticky notes so you can make sure you focus on those words.
- Start with a rereading of the classroom message. Remember, you can invite students in with a choral reading or assisted reading. Highlight those words that will connect to the context clue instruction that will follow.
- Following the reading, address the identified context clue strategies for this lesson. Decide whether you are going to focus on semantic cues, which are doable with almost any message (using a technique like cover-ups), or on one of the specific context clue patterns. The latter requires having the pattern embedded in the message and the preparation of additional examples for use in guided and independent practice phases within the lesson.
- Involve students in the self-evaluation level of engagement before transitioning from the shared writing experience.
- End with an intentional link to reading and writing with which students will be involved away from the shared writing.
- Plan for independent work with context clue strategies away from the shared writing that will allow students to practice and apply context clue strategies learned during the shared writing.

EVALUATION IDEA: After completion of the five-day cycle, students will be very familiar with the message. Prepare individual "Swiss cheese" versions of the message with certain parts missing. Leave out certain sound-symbol relationships, sight words, structural elements, and content words—especially those that were the focus of instruction during the five-day cycle. (See Figure 12 for ideas.) Ask students to reconstruct the message by filling in the "holes." A quick review of the reconstructions will let you know about individual student needs and students' collective needs so you can use that data to inform your thinking as you plan a similar cycle for subsequent weeks. (See Figure 13.)

Figure 12: Ideas for Creating "Swiss Cheese" Messages

For graphophonemic cues
Leave out specific:

- initial and ending sounds
- blends and digraphs
- vowel sounds
- vowel patterns
- common rimes

For sight words
Leave out specific:

- high-frequency sight words

For structural elements
Leave out specific:

- common inflected endings
- high-utility suffixes and prefixes
- common "chunks" or syllables
- parts of contractions and compounds
- syntactic elements (discuss what would sound right grammatically)

For context-based elements
Leave out specific:

- content words and discuss what would makes sense

Figure 13: "Swiss Cheese" Message

______ day__ are __arm.

We ______ ____rds and

flower__. It __ spr______.

Sample Week of Lessons for Shared Writing (Early Readers and Writers)

The lessons in this sequence are based on this classroom message:

> The days are warm.
>
> We see birds and flowers.
>
> It is spring.

Lesson Plan: *Day One*

Shared Writing (Early Readers and Writers)

1. Take attendance using name cards: "Everyone stand up. Watch for your name. Sit down when you see it. You can try to read the other students' names, but keep the answer in your head."
2. State purpose: "This week, I am going to ask you to help me show how what we are learning about our words in reading can help us in our writing. We will also learn how what we know about words in our writing can help us with our reading. This will help us get better at both our reading and writing. I think reading and writing are so important, and this will help us be the best readers and writers we can be!"
3. Model and demonstrate: "I have a message I want to write for you. I will get it started and then you can help me with the rest. Before I write my first sentence, I want to think about the words I need: *The days are warm.* I want my words that I write to match the words I just said so it sounds right and makes sense. I need four words."
4. Model writing: *The days are warm.*

   [The] "Let's start with the first word, *The.* Now that's a hard word to sound out, but we see it a lot when we read and use it a lot when we write. We need to remember what it looks like: *T-h-e.* When I put it in my brain, I try to remember what it looks like. I also capitalized *The* because it is the first word of the sentence."

   [days] "Let's leave a space and work on our second word, *days.* That is an easy word to get started: /d/. But for the /ā/, I need to remember it is a tricky spelling: *ay.* And it is also a word we see a lot when we read and use a lot when we write, so it is important to remember that. And since it is more than one *day,* I need to add an s."

   [Repeat modeling in a similar think-aloud style for *are* and *warm.*]

   "That's the end of my sentence, so I will put a period here. Now remember when you write, it's good to reread what you wrote so you can see if it sounds right and makes sense. I will use my trusty microphone and reread and listen if it sounds right and makes sense: *The days are warm.* Yes, that sounds right and it makes sense."

5. Guided practice: "Now I am going to ask you to help me with the next sentence. Give me a thumbs-up if you think you can help me with the next sentence. First, before I write, I want to think about the words I need: We see birds and flowers. Let's count how many words we need. I will help you learn the words. Whisper to a partner how many words we need (five). Show me that many fingers."

6. Guided writing with teacher leading: *We see birds and flowers.*

   [We] "What should I leave before I work on the first word, *We*? (Space.) That's an easy word to remember because we see it a lot when we read and use it a lot when we write. Turn and tell your partner what letter I need to start the word. (/W/.) Raise your hand if you know. On the count of three, let's all say it: /W/. What do you hear next? (/ē/.) Raise your hand if you know what I need to remember since it is the first letter of the sentence." (Call on a student. It needs to be capitalized.)

   [see] "What should I leave before I work on the next word, *see*? (Space.) Now that's an easy word to get started. It starts with /s/. Turn and tell your partner what letter it starts with. Raise your hand if you know. On the count of three, let's all say it: s. You can hear the next sound, /ē/, but remember, it is spelled with two e's."

   [Repeat guided practice with students in a similar style for *birds*, *and*, and *flowers*.]

   "That's the end of my sentence, so what will I put here? A period. Now remember when you write, it's good to reread what you wrote so you can see if it sounds right and makes sense. Let's pick volunteers to use our microphones, and we will reread it with them: *We see birds and flowers*. Let's check to see if it sounds right. If it sounds right, give me a thumbs-up. Let's check to see if it makes sense. Reread (trade off microphones). If it makes sense, give me a thumbs-up."

7. Independent practice:

   Guided writing with teacher monitoring individual students:
   It is spring.

   "I am going to need some helpers to write our last sentence. These are the words I will need: *It is spring.*" Put out three sticky notes on the message—one for each word. Use name cards to invite helpers to come forward. Have a volunteer rehearse on the teacher whiteboard and then write on the sticky note. Invite other children to watch and check and then signal agreement.

   [It]: Pick a volunteer using name cards. Have the student rehearse on the whiteboard. Write on a sticky note. Probe why the student did what she did. Invite other children to check. Signal agreement. Point out *It* is an important word we see a lot in our reading and use a lot in our writing, so it is important to remember what it looks like.

   [is]: Pick a volunteer using name cards. Have the student rehearse on the whiteboard. Write on the sticky note. Probe why the student did what he did. Invite other children to check. Signal agreement. Point

out *is* is an important word we see a lot in our reading and use a lot in our writing, so it is important to remember what it looks like.

[spring]: Pick a volunteer using name cards. Have the student rehearse on the whiteboard. Write on a sticky note. Probe why the student did what she did. Invite other children to check. Signal agreement.

"That's the end of my sentence, so tell your neighbor what I will put here." Use name cards to pick a volunteer to add the period. "Now, remember when you write, it's good to reread what you wrote so you can see if it sounds right and makes sense. Let's pick volunteers to use our microphones and we will reread it with them: *It is spring.* Let's check to see if it sounds right. If it sounds right, give me a thumbs-up. Let's check to see if it makes sense." Reread (trade off microphones). "If it makes sense, give me a thumbs-up." Reread the whole message.

8. Self-evaluation: "Let's rate how well you worked today. Put your hands in your lap. If you worked your hardest, put three fingers in your lap. If you worked pretty hard today, put two fingers in your lap, and if you are going to try to work better tomorrow, put one finger in your lap. On the count of three, show me your fingers. One, two, three." (Probe why some students rated themselves that way.)
9. Lesson link: "Remember, you can use some of the tricks we used today to figure out words in your reading and writing. Tomorrow, we are going to use our message to learn some secrets about learning words. Give a thumbs-up if you will be ready for that!"

Lesson Plan: *Day Two*

Shared Writing (Early Readers and Writers)

Focus on Sound Strategies (Graphophonemic Cues)

1. Take attendance using name cards: "Today, boys and girls, watch for your name and raise your hand when you see it so I know you are here. Remember, everyone is trying to learn. You can try to read the other students' names, but keep the answer in your head until others have had a chance."
2. State the purpose: "Yesterday, I told you I am going to ask you to help me with a special message. This message shows how what we are learning about our words in reading can help us in our writing and how what we know about words in our writing can help us with our reading. Raise your hand if you are working to get better at reading and writing. Wow! I think reading and writing are so important and this will help us be the best readers and writers we can be!"
3. Reread: "When I write something, I try to reread it to see if there is anything else I want to add to what I wrote. Yesterday, I wrote the first sentence, and you helped me with what you know about words to write the second sentence. Then a few of our friends helped me by writing the third sentence on their own. I am going to use my name cards to pick two people who can use our special microphones to help us reread what we wrote yesterday." Use name cards to select two

readers. Have them stand by the message. Lead them in rereading and invite other students to read along: *The days are warm. We see birds and flowers. It is spring.* Probe the first student: "Does our message make sense?" Probe the second student: "Does our message sound right?"

4. Sound work (phonogram -ing, using *spring* as the anchor word): "Today I have a special sheet for you to help make some new words. Put your name at the top. (Model.) Today I want to share a secret about reading and writing words. If you know one word, you can use the sounds and letters of part of that word to help you learn new words. We just learned this word: *spring*. Let's write that in the first box of our grid. (Model.) Now watch this, boys and girls. I am going to use this part of *spring—ing—*to help me make *ring*. I have *ing*, so all I need to do is add /r/ at the beginning. Now don't say it out loud, but whisper to your neighbor what letter makes that sound. Put your hand on your head if you know it. Let's use the name card to call on someone. (Respond.) Let's add r to the beginning of the *ing*. Now we have *ring*. Let's write *ring* in our second box. Now I am going to use this part of *spring* and *ring—ing—*to help me make *king*. I have *ing*, so all I need to do is add /k/ at the beginning. Now don't say it out loud, but whisper to your neighbor what letter makes that sound. Put your hand on your head if you know it. Let's use the name card to call on someone. (Respond.) Let's add *k* to the being of the *ing*. Now we have *king*. Let's spell that in our third box. Now I am going to use this part of *spring*, *ring*, and *king—ing—*to help me make *sing*. I have *ing*, so all I need to do is add /s/ at the beginning. Now don't say it out loud, but whisper to your neighbor what letter makes that sound. Put your hand on your head if you know it. Let's use the name card to call on someone. (Respond.) Let's add s to the beginning of the *ing*. Now we have *sing*. Let's write that in our last box."

   "Let's check to see if we really know these words." Display *spring*, *ring*, *king*, and *sing*. Hold up a picture of a ring. Have students point to it on their sheet. Use a name card to select a student to clothespin it to the display word. Repeat using a picture of a king. Then ask students to raise their hands if they remember what the last word is. Use a name card to call on a student. "Boys and girls, I don't have a picture of that, but we can do it. Let's sing *sing...SING*!"

5. Self-evaluation: "Let's rate how well you worked today. Put your hands in your lap. If you worked your hardest, put three fingers in your lap. If you worked pretty hard today, put two fingers in your lap, and if you are going to try to work better tomorrow, put one finger in your lap. On the count of three, show me your fingers. One, two, three." (Probe why some students rated themselves that way.)

6. Lesson link: "Remember, you can use what we learned today about using a word we know to figure out how to sound out or spell new words in your reading and writing. We learned *spring*, and we used it to help us with *ring*, *king*, and *sing*. Tomorrow, we are going to use our message to learn some more secrets about learning words. Raise a high five in the air if you will be ready for that!"

Lesson Plan: *Day Three*

Shared Writing (Early Readers and Writers)

Focus on Sight Vocabulary (Visual Cues)

1. Take attendance using name cards: "Yesterday, boys and girls, we learned how if you know one word like *spring*, you can use it to help you sound out or write other words like *ring*, *king*, and *sing*. Today when I show your name, I am going to show you one of our new words and see if you can remember it from yesterday. (Use flashcards for *spring*, *ring*, *king*, and *sing*.) Remember, everyone is trying to learn. You can try to read the other students' names, but keep the answer in your head, silently say the word I am showing, and let them first have a chance to say it."

2. Restate purpose: "Yesterday, you showed me what you are learning about our words in reading can help us in our writing and how what we know about words in our writing can help us with our reading. We also learned a secret about words. You can use sounds from a word you know to help you figure out how to read or write a word you are still learning. Today, we will learn another secret about words that will also help us get better at reading and writing. Raise your hand if you are working to get better at reading and writing. Wow! I think reading and writing are so important and will help us be the best readers and writers we can be!"

3. Reread: "It's always good to reread our message. It helps us get better at our words. I am going to use my name cards to pick a helper who can use our special microphone to help us reread what we wrote yesterday. (Use name cards to select a reader. Have him stand by the message. Lead him in rereading and invite other students to read along.) Now I am going to give you something special. I am going to give you a copy of the special message. When you see your name, come up and I will give you a copy of your special message, and then sit down and use a quiet voice to see if you can practice reading it on your own. (Model and then use name cards to distribute individual copies.) Now that everyone has a copy, eyes on me. Let's all read it together." (Use the pointer while students read from their copies.)

4. Sight word work (focus on key sight words *and*, *is*, *it*, *see*, *the*, *we*): "Today I want to share a new secret I know about words. There are some words we see over and over again in our reading and we spell them over and over again in our writing. These words are so important that we should remember what they look like, so we can read and spell them as fast as we can. We have some of these words in our special message. Let's look for them in your copy of the message, and then I will have someone use our special magnifying glass to see if she can spot them in the big class message."

   [and] "Let's see if we can find the word *and*. *And* is used a lot in reading and writing. Can you find *and* in your message and put your finger on *and*? Let's pick someone to come up and use the magnifying glass to show us where *and* is on our class message. (Use

name cards.) Let's all see if she can find *and*. (Probe student after finding the word.) How did you know that was *and*? Let's say the letters as we remember the word: *a-n-d, and*!"

[*is*] "Let's see if we can find the word *is*. *Is* is used a lot in reading and writing. Can you find *is* in your message and put your finger on *is*? Let's pick someone to come up and use the magnifying glass to show us where *is* is on our class message. (Use name cards.) Let's all see if he can find *is*. (Probe student after finding the word.) How did you know that was *is*? Let's say the letters as we remember the word: *i-s, is*!"

(Repeat process for *it*, *see*, *the*, and *we*.)

"Let's check to see if we really know these words." Collect the individual messages. Sit in a circle. Place flashcards with the sight words on them in the middle of the circle. Use name cards to call on students to find the word you say. After all have had a turn, have each student say the word and collect the card.

5. Self-evaluation: "Let's rate how well you worked today. Put your hands in your lap. If you worked your hardest, put three fingers in your lap. If you worked pretty hard today, put two fingers in your lap, and if you are going to try to work better tomorrow, put one finger in your lap. On the count of three, show me your fingers. One, two, three." (Probe why some students rated themselves that way.)
6. Lesson link: "Remember, you can use what we learned today about remembering what a word looks like to read or spell important words in your reading and writing. We learned that *and*, *is*, *it*, *see*, *the*, and *we* are very important because we use them over and over again, so we need to remember what they look like to help us. Maybe when you are reading your books today, you will find some of these words. Tomorrow, we are going to use our message to learn another secret about learning words. Give me a one-hand clap if you will be ready for that!"

Lesson Plan: *Day Four*

Shared Writing (Early Readers and Writers)

Focus on Structural Analysis (Inflected Endings/ Syntactical Cues)

1. Take attendance using name cards.

"Over the past few days, boys and girls, we have been learning secrets about how to figure out words. We learned if you know one word like *spring*, you can use it to help you sound out or write other words like *ring*, *king*, and *sing*. (Show flashcards for these words.) Then we learned that some words are used over and over again, so if we remember what they look like, we can use those words in our reading and writing. These words include *and*, *is*, *it*, *see*, *the*, and *we*.

(Show flashcards for *and, is, it, see, the*, and *we*.) Now, I have put these words on a list. (Show list of sight words.) Let's say the words on the list. (Practice the words on the list in a couple different ways.) Today, when I show your name, I am going to call out a number and see if you can read the words we practiced yesterday. Remember, everyone is trying to learn. You can try to read the other students' names, but keep the answer in your head, silently say the word next to the number, and let them first have a chance to say it."

2. Restate purpose: "We keep learning secrets about words. These secrets help you figure out how to read or write words. Today, we will learn another secret about words that will also help us get better at reading and writing. Raise your hand if you are working to get better at reading and writing. Wow! I think reading and writing are so important, and this will help us be the best readers and writers we can be!"

3. Reread: "Every day, it's always good to reread our message. It helps us get better at our words. I am going to use my name cards to pick a helper who can use our special microphone to help us reread what we wrote." (Use a number count and spell out a name to select a reader. Have her stand by the message. Lead her in rereading and invite other students to read along.)

4. Structural word work (focus on singular and plural with words like *king, ring, birds, days*, and *flowers*): "Today, we are going to learn a new secret about words. Sometimes you can start with a word you know and add an ending so the new word makes more sense and sounds better. Sometimes you can start with a word you know and take away an ending to also make a new word to make more sense and sound better. I have a special word sheet to help you learn how to do that." (Pass out copies of Appendix 11 on p. 185, whiteboards, and pencils. Prior to the start of the lesson, secure or make two copies of a picture of a king, ring, bird, and flower.)

   [king] Model how *king* means one *king*. Write the word under the "1" column. Have students write along with you.

   [kings] Show two *king* pictures. Talk about how we have to change *king* to *kings* so it makes more sense and sounds better. Model how to write *king* and add *s* to make it plural.

   [ring] Use name cards to have a student help with *ring*. Show one *ring* picture. Ask if it means *one* or *two or more*. Write it under the "1" column.

   [rings] Use name cards to have a student help with *rings*. Show two *ring* pictures. Talk about how we have to change *ring* to *rings* so it makes more sense and sounds better. Ask if it means *one* or *two or more*. Write *ring* and then add *s* to make it plural.

   Now use some words from the class message:

   [birds] Use name cards to have a student help with *birds*. Ask if it means *one* or *two or more*. Write it under the "2" column.

[bird] Use name cards to have a student help with *bird*. Talk about how we have to change *birds* to *bird* so it makes more sense and sounds better. Cut *s* away from *birds*. Ask if it means *one* or *two or more*. Write *bird* under the "1" column.

[flowers] Use name cards to have a student help with *flowers*. Ask if it means *one* or *two or more*. Write it under the "2" column.

[flower] Use name cards to have a student help with *flower*. Talk about how we have to change *flowers* to *flower* so it makes more sense and sounds better. Cut *s* away from *flowers*. Ask if it means *one* or *two or more*. Write *flower* under the "1" column.

[days] Use name cards to have a student help with *days*. Ask if it means *one* or *two or more*. Write it under the "2" column.

[day] Use name cards to have a student help with *day*. Talk about how we have to change *days* to *day* so it makes more sense and sounds better. Cut *s* away from *days*. Ask if it means *one* or *two or more*. Write *day* under the "1" column.

"Let's check to see if we really know these words. I will call out a word, and you see if you can find it on your sheet. After you find it, put your finger on it. Listen very carefully at the end to see if it is one or two or more."

5. Self-evaluation: "Let's rate how well you worked today. Put your hands in your lap. If you worked your hardest, put three fingers in your lap. If you worked pretty hard today, put two fingers in your lap, and if you are going to try to work better tomorrow, put one finger in your lap. On the count of three, show me your fingers. One, two, three!" (Probe why some students rated themselves that way.)
6. Lesson link: "Remember, you can use what we learned today about remembering how to make a word mean *one* or *two or more* when you read or spell important words in your reading and writing. Maybe when you are reading your books today, you will find some words that mean *one* and some that mean *two or more*. Tomorrow, we are going to use our message to learn one more secret about learning words. Give me a fingernail clap if you will be ready for that!"

Lesson Plan: *Day Five*

Shared Writing (Early Readers and Writers)

Focus on Context Clues (Semantic and Syntactic Cues)

1. Take attendance using name cards and word cards.
2. (Start in a circle.) "This week, boys and girls, we have been learning secrets about how to figure out words. Let's see if we can use those secrets to figure out our words. First we learned if you know one word, you can use the sounds and letters of it to figure out other words. (Move around the circle, and have the first student say the word *spring*. Then move around the circle to try *ring*, *king*, and *sing*. Show flashcards for *spring*, *ring*, *king*, and *sing*.) Then we learned that some words are used over and over again, so if we remember what they

look like, we can use those words in our reading and writing. (Continue to move around the circle showing flashcards for *and, is, it, see, the*, and *we*.) Yesterday we learned if you know one word, you can sometimes add an ending to make it sound better and make sense." (Move around the circle and show flashcards for *king, kings, ring, rings, birds, bird, flowers, flower, days*, and *day*.)

3. Restate purpose: "We keep learning secrets about words. These secrets help you figure out how to read or write words. Today, we will learn another secret about words that will also help us get better at reading and writing. But first, let's play our word card game to see if you really are learning your words. I will show a name card and that person can find a word she knows." (Probe how she knew.)
4. Reread: "Let's sit in our special spots so we can reread our message. Every day, it's always good to reread our message. Rereading helps us get better at our words. I am going to use my name cards to pick a helper who can use our special microphone to help us reread what we wrote." (Use a number count and spell out a name to select a reader. Have him stand by the message. Lead him in rereading and invite other students to read along.)
5. Context clue word work (focus on thinking about what makes sense and sounds right within a sentence frame): "Today, we are going to learn a new secret about words. Sometimes you can use the words around other words in a sentence to figure out a word that makes sense and sounds right. Let's look at this sentence. Our story is about spring. Read this sentence with me: *We see birds and flowers*. But what if I covered up *birds*? And what if I covered up *flowers*? Can you think of any other things we see in spring that would make sense and sound right in this sentence?" (Use name cards to call on a few students until enough examples are generated. Probe to reinforce the plural and singular strategy from day four. Write word choices on sticky notes.)

   "Boys and girls, I am going to let you write your own spring sentence with words that sound right and make sense. You can use some of the words we came up with on our message board, or you can write using your own spring words. (Model with a framed sentence.) Once you have made a spring sentence that sounds right and makes sense, you can add an illustration. (Model with a framed sentence page. Pass out framed sentence pages, whiteboards, and pencils.) Let's check our sentences by sharing them." (Use name cards to call on a few students to share.)
6. Self-evaluation: "Let's rate how much we learned all week. Put your hands in your lap. If you worked your hardest all week and learned a whole lot about words, put three fingers in your lap. If you worked pretty hard all week and learned some new things about words, put two fingers in your lap. If you worked somewhat hard all week and at least learned a little about words, put one finger in your lap. On the count of three, show me your fingers. One, two, three!" (Probe why some students rated themselves that way.)

7. Lesson link: "Next week, we will take what we have learned about words and write a new class message. Until then, use the secrets we learned about words this week to help you with your reading and your writing."

Final Thoughts about Intensifying Your Shared Writing Routine

In this chapter, you have looked extensively at how to intensify your shared writing routine, focusing on the use of a classroom message. This common routine still has an important role to play in literacy and language arts programs for young readers and writers. I hope this chapter has provided you with ways to intensify your use of the shared writing experience to increase its power in reaching more students with what they need to help them grow as independent, strategic readers and writers. If your students are primarily emergent readers and writers, the shared writing experience can be adapted to meet their needs related to concepts of print, alphabetic knowledge, and phonemic awareness. As students grow in their competence and confidence, the same routine can be modified to address skills and strategies related to sound-symbol relationships, high-frequency sight words, structural and morphological elements, and context clue patterns. A sequenced set of lessons for the early phase of reading development was provided to give you insights and ideas on how to move forward as you develop similar plans for your students.

CHAPTER THREE: Intensifying Your Shared Reading

> The shared reading of carefully selected material provides special opportunities for convincing children that they can be readers and writers.
>
> *Margaret Mooney*

What Is Shared Reading?

For one generation of students, reading instruction was focused on reading about a family of characters, story after story, in their basal reading series. I was one of those students. I can remember being taught to read in elementary school by using stories featuring Dick and Jane and their family and friends. But for another generation of students, their early reading experiences were defined by a washerwoman and three animals. Many of these students were introduced to Joy Cowley's favorite character Mrs. Wishy-Washy and her three farm animals—the cow, pig, and duck. Students first encountered Mrs. Wishy-Washy when their teacher shared a Big Book with a predictable story capturing the antics of her disobedient animals. For this generation of students, Big Books dominated their early childhood and primary classrooms. Teachers shared these Big Books to teach needed literacy skills and strategies to all students in a large group setting. So where did this idea come from? Many trace its origins to New Zealand literacy expert Don Holdaway. Holdaway (1979) developed the shared reading experience, or what he called the "shared book experience," as a way for teachers to finally bridge the gap between the use of read-alouds and small group reading instruction. His inspiration actually came from research on students who learned to read before coming to school. He was especially interested in examining the interactions with print these early readers usually had with a significant adult in the home setting.

In a "to, with, and by" framework of literacy activities related to reading (Mooney, 1990), the read-aloud is defined as reading *to* students, shared and guided reading are defined as reading *with* students, and independent individualized reading is defined as reading *by* students. All are critical experiences in a balanced reading program. Swartz, Shook, and Klein (2002) point out that shared reading "occurs when someone who is already a proficient reader (the teacher) reads with someone who is still learning to read (the student) (1)." Shared reading is often distinguished from guided reading by the size of the group in which it is most often conducted. Shared reading is typically conducted in the large group and guided reading is typically conducted in small groups.

Shared reading is also distinguishable by the degree of teacher support during the instructional activity. Swartz, Shook, and Klein remind us the three activities of reading aloud, shared reading, and guided reading all employ different levels of teacher supports. Reading aloud uses the most teacher support, shared reading uses less, and guided reading usually uses the least amount of the three. Shared reading is an activity in which the teacher leads the instruction for the students. As was stated with shared writing, shared reading activities are usually outside-in (Fitzgerald, 1999) and adult-guided (Epstein, 2007). By contrast, guided reading should be more inside-out and child-guided. The best forms of guided reading start with the intentional plans of the teacher but quickly follow the lead of the students (Ford, 2016). Finally, shared reading usually focuses on the use of an enlarged text in the large group setting, so it can be seen by all students. Guided reading usually involves the use of smaller-sized texts in the hands of each student. [For a good summary of the differences between shared and guided reading, see Hornsby (2000).]

Swartz, Shook, and Klein (2002) conclude that there are six key characteristics of shared readings:

- the teacher and students read the text together;
- all students can see the text;
- the teacher provides multiple levels of support;
- the teacher models various reading behaviors;
- there are a variety of instructional opportunities; and
- the lesson has a focus on discussing how to understand what is read.

So shared reading is basically reading with your students in a large group setting using an enlarged text with the teacher intentionally taking the lead as students are invited into the text to learn about skills, strategies, and behaviors. It forms the bridge between reading to students through the use of a read-aloud and reading with students using guided reading in small groups. Burkins and Yaris (2016) conclude:

> *Shared reading combines the auditory engagement factors of the read-aloud, the visual engagement factors of following along in the text, the emotional pull of an excellent text, and the cognitive lure of productive effort. Shared reading presents one of the richest and most inviting opportunities to offer students guided practice in increasingly difficult texts (53).*

So what's the difference among read-alouds, shared reading, and what some educators call "interactive read-alouds"? It should be noted that the use of read-alouds is critical in classrooms (Fox, 2013; Layne, 2009), but the read-aloud is often done with more of an aesthetic focus with limited intentional instruction accompanying it. Boyles (2009) observed that the read-aloud is used to typically provide enjoyment but not to provide instruction. Students definitely benefit from the language, words, structures, and thoughts they are exposed to through read-alouds, but learning is more implicit than explicit. Combs (2002) states that the read-aloud allows the student to enjoy and think about a text read by someone else. In contrast, "shared reading engages students more directly as participants in the reading (70)." Burkins and Croft (2010) state that, in shared reading, "teachers scaffold students by explicitly teaching them how to strategically use the text to support reading (14)."

The interactive read-aloud was also developed to add a more intentional focus to the more passive read-aloud experience and directly involve the learners during the experience (Rog, 2003). In many ways, it invites the learner in to be more "interactive" in exploring the text. Johnson and Keier (2010) distinguish the interactive read-aloud from the traditional read-aloud by observing that the text is read with a clear instructional purpose and is often accompanied by the teacher leading the students in discussing the text before, during, and after the reading. Clearly, recommended frameworks like this suggest more than a typical read-aloud. An interactive read-aloud involves more intentional positioning of the text for instructional purposes.

So how is the interactive read-aloud different from a shared reading? As described previously, the interactive read-aloud does often resemble the shared reading—used in a large group, involving the use of teacher-led instruction, and inviting the students to interact with the texts to learn some skill, strategy, or behaviors to use when reading other texts. Boyles (2009) suggested that the interactive read-aloud often differs from the shared reading in its narrowness of focus. She described the interactive read-aloud as inviting students to react to the text "in any way that feels right for them." The shared reading, on the other hand, "is usually organized around one clear, focused objective (xvi)." That clearly, however, is not the case in the framework described above. Perhaps another difference in the use of these terms is that a shared reading often involves a text that is enlarged for all students to see. Interactive read-alouds may involve more traditionally-sized texts and may focus on aspects that need to be heard but not always seen. In the end, the attempts to distinguish interactive read-alouds from shared readings may be more semantic than practical. The line between them is clearly blurry. In this chapter, the term "shared reading" will be used predominantly, though the insights and ideas discussed may also influence the use of interactive read-alouds.

Why Is Shared Reading a Critical Routine?

I said that Holdaway (1979) drew some of his inspiration for the shared reading experience from his observation and research of conditions that lead children to learn to read before they formally entered school. He was particularly interested in how a significant family member or adult seems to interact with a child when the adult reads aloud to the child. The child is physically drawn close to the adult, so he or she can look carefully at the print and the illustrations when the book was read. The adult would often stop and point out things about the text. So would the child. The adult would also stop and ask the child questions about the text. The child would also stop and ask questions of the adult. The first reading of the text was often followed by a second (or third) repeated reading of the text, usually requested by the child. Following the reading, the text was often left available for the child to explore independently at another time. The child would often try to emulate the reading behaviors of the adult on his or her own, with each attempt providing more and more satisfaction and sophistication. The child's reading competency started to grow. What inspired Holdaway, others (Jett-Simpson, 1984) began to promote as the "Lap Technique" in their work with families to build an important literacy foundation for children at home. The Lap Technique was just what its name implied. Adults were taught the importance of placing their child on their lap and how to interact with the child as a favorite book was shared.

Holdaway wondered how the benefits of the home reading experience could be transferred to the classroom. How could you provide that intimate reading experience in certain home environments that seemed to be so beneficial for many children in the classroom? As Zarrillo (2007) asked: How can a teacher "attempt to achieve with a group of children what has long been accomplished when an adult shares a picture book with one child (14)?" That might be especially critical to reach students who have not benefited from those experiences in their homes. Cutting (1989) observed: "For children who have not had many books read to them, shared reading provides immediate access to experiences other children may have taken for granted (34)." Since the size of any teacher's lap would always limit the number of children who could sit with the teacher at one time, Holdaway proposed the text would have to be enlarged so all children could see it if they sat at the feet of the teacher in a gathering space. Emergent readers especially needed to be able to see the print, so when the words are spoken by an adult, the students can see they are coming from a specific place on the page and not just from the illustrations (Combs, 2002). Since Holdaway's idea preceded the publication of commercial Big Books, these texts were first created by the teacher. Using popular rhymes, chants, songs, or patterned stories, the teacher would replicate the texts on large sheets of paper with print written in a size that was observable by all children. Sometimes large classroom charts were used. Other times, lines of print on sentence strips were placed in large pocket charts. But in order to teach book handling skills and strategies, teachers often created their own Big Book versions. Many times, teachers would ask students and parent helpers to add illustrations to the texts (Cutting, 1989). Eventually, commercial companies saw the popularity of the enlarged texts and started to publish similarly formatted texts for teachers to use. These Big Books soon found their way into many classrooms. Today, technology allows projection of texts in multiple ways. With all of these tools and techniques, teachers finally found a way to expand their "laps" so more children could climb on and have that intimate experience with the text.

The popularity of Big Books led to many trade books being reformatted to enlarged versions, but this often ignored one other critical element of Holdaway's technique. Holdaway intentionally selected the use of a text that could easily enter the oral language of the children after being read repeatedly by the teacher. Knowing that repeated reading of texts has always shown tremendous instructional value (Rasinski, 1990), shared readings often focused on the repeated readings of short, familiar rhymes, chants, or songs. Stories written with easily accessible patterns (such as *Brown Bear, Brown Bear, What Do You See?*) were also featured in shared readings (Combs, 2002). When these texts were made available to the children, they laid a foundation for future attempts to read the text independently. Enlarged texts without these easily accessible features often fell short in their ability to transfer the reading attempts from the teacher to the child. Some may be quick to point out that familiar, patterned, predictable texts suggested for shared readings by Holdaway only led to memorized readings by students when they worked on the texts independently. They say the children "aren't really reading. They just memorized it." But research suggests that memorized reading is a common stage emergent readers pass through on their way to more conventional reading behavior (Sulzby, 1985). As soon as those emergent readers pick up a text from shared reading and start interacting with it, the teacher can start to provide scaffolded instruction in moving the children from where they are at to where they need to be. It is both the size and the nature of the text that make it more appropriate for shared reading.

Holdaway believed that many of the interactive techniques used between families and children around stories and books are the best techniques to use in shared readings between teachers and students. The type of interaction often seen between older family members and young children at home during story times begins with simple "What's this?" and "What's that?" questions as concept books about things like colors, shapes, numbers, and animals were being shared. These interactions also include predictive questions being asked about what is going to happen next in simple narrative stories, including common folktales and fairy tales, as well as the joining and filling in of repeated parts in predictable, patterned stories.

The power of the shared reading experience as a critical routine comes when it effectively captures the key features of the storybook reading some children experience outside the school setting. It is a critical routine because it allows the novice to learn from the expert who provides a model of strategic, fluent, expressive reading as meaning is being made. It takes place in a socially supportive group setting where everyone can learn from each other and sometimes the expert even learns from the novices. It allows for intentional planning and ongoing responsive teaching through explicit instruction, invitations, interactions, prompting, probing, and feedback. It allows for the use of teacher think-alouds, so the experts can publicly reveal what they know about how reading works in front of the learners (Oczkus, 2010). The teacher can make thought processes transparent (Burkins and Croft, 2010). Shared reading leads readers toward independent reading explorations in which they can transfer what was learned to grow their competencies and confidence. It can serve as a bridging activity for students with greater needs in language development or moving toward new language systems (Cutting, 1989; Saunders-Smith, 2009). Intensifying shared reading is one way to make sure it achieves these important goals.

What Concerns Do Current Theory, Expert Opinion, and Research Raise about Shared Reading Practices?

There is always concern when an important classroom routine is done so often that it becomes unchanged. One of the major concerns about the use of shared reading is that it is often conducted in a similar manner every time it is used. In fact, some have observed that many shared book experiences are conducted more like traditional reading practices, including whole group, round-robin reading (Hoffman, et al., 1998; Burkins and Yaris, 2016). Rarely are the plans adjusted to meet the changing needs of students, though emergent and early readers clearly have variations that would suggest the need to use shared readings in different ways. Similarly, the demands of different texts, ranging from narrative stories to informational reports, featured in shared readings would also require different types of lessons. One of the goals of intensification is to bring greater intentionality when planning the shared reading routine to better address the needs of the students by considering the demands of the text.

It's interesting to see that when Mooney (1990) originally discussed shared reading, she suggested that invitations to students to participate in the reading "should come from the book itself or from the way the reader reads the book rather than by any planned or overt direction (26)." But since then, people have advocated for more intentionality. Burkins and Croft (2010) stated shared reading needs to be instructionally dense.

Swartz, Shook, and Klein (2002) remind us, "[p]lanning is an important part of getting the full value from a lesson using shared reading (2)." Others argue that the main focus of shared reading should be the explicit instruction of skills and strategies (Richardson, 2016; Boyles, 2009). It is clear from these experts shared reading needs to be planned instruction that considers the needs and strengths of the children to validate their existing knowledge and lead them to new learning (Dorn and Jones, 2012). Learning is not automatic by just using a shared reading experience. The teacher needs to know where his or her students are at, where they need to move toward, and that planning the use of the shared reading to bridge those two points is critical.

Shared reading also shares three concerns with shared writing experiences: the need for greater engagement, collecting useful data during shared reading instruction, and better integration of the shared reading experience with other parts of the literacy and language arts program. The concerns about engagement in a large group setting don't simply disappear just because we are using a Big Book or an enlarged text with the students (Richardson, 2009). The shared reading experience must intentionally address the issue of engagement. Saunders-Smith (2009) reminds teachers that the challenge in any whole group lesson is the teacher and the students all have to attend to the same single task. While the teacher and many students are able to do that, some of the students may be attending but not to the intended task. Working toward the higher engagement levels (90 percent of the students on task 90 percent of the time) of high-impact classrooms (Pressley, et al., 2001) is still an important goal. Some of the students will be highly engaged during any large group activity. Others may be more engaged during shared writing activities but less so during shared reading experiences. For other students, engagement may be better during shared reading than shared writing experiences. And don't forget, some—hopefully the fewest in number—may not be very engaged during any whole group activity. If the shared reading activities are to impact all students, especially those who need the help the most, then students need to be engaged during the instruction. Obviously when a child is reading with a family member on a lap, engagement is less of a problem; but in a classroom, engagement is always a concern. Boyles (2009) recommends the first step in an effective shared reading experience is "getting students to care (xv)." One way to foster engagement and focus in young learners is to keep the lessons short. Richardson (2016) suggests a length of 10–15 minutes. In the sequence I will describe, the lessons are designed for a slightly longer session but no more then 15–20 minutes. In their Shared Reading Procedural Checklist and Self-Assessment, Swartz, Shook, and Klein (2002) recommend that when a teacher reflects on any shared reading lesson conducted, the question of how engagement was sustained should always be asked.

ENGAGEMENT IDEA: Interactive guides (Opitz and Ford, 2015) can be developed to heighten engagement of whole group instructional activities, such as shared reading experiences. Interactive guides are simple graphic organizers that can be created by dividing a blank sheet of paper into a specific number of boxes based on the number of times the teacher is going to ask students to stop and process before, during, or after the shared reading. Instead of discussions being primarily oral and often involving only a handful of students, every student would have an interactive guide and a means to contribute to the discussion. If the teacher starts with the question, "What do you think we are going to read about today?," instead of a few hands going up and one or two students being called on, every student would be invited to write their guess in box number one. Emergent readers can even be allowed a write or draw an option and be encouraged to spell the best they can. If the teacher follows up with, "Tell me what you already know about that topic," all students can jot down something in box number two. After a picture walk, the teacher can ask all students to "Write down one thing you learned about the topic from the picture walk in box number three." Finally, the teacher might use box number four to encourage students to self-evaluate: "How well did you think you worked during the shared reading today?" The interactive guide provides a paper trail during the shared reading experience that can also be a good additional source of assessment information. (See Appendix 13, p. 187.)

In addition to engagement, assessment is another concern with the current practice of shared reading. If anything students do throughout the school day can inform our thinking about what to plan next to meet their needs, then that will be true for time spent during shared reading. But like shared writing, very little effort is made to capture data during shared reading experiences. If data are not captured, how can they be analyzed and used to inform our thinking about what to do next? Allington (2012) concludes successful use of shared reading experiences requires the teacher to pay attention to students' responses to be able to adapt future lessons based on those responses. In looking at a 10-step process in getting started with shared reading (Swartz, Shook, and Klein, 2002), the teacher is clearly told to have an instructional focus and to select a text to support that purpose. The lesson is designed to address, revisit, and practice that focus, but in no step is the teacher told to record information about how the students performed in regard to that focus. These experts do talk about the importance of observing students during the shared reading and the observations should be systematic and recorded. But in multiple photographs of the teacher conducting the lesson, the teacher is never seen recording any information about the students while the lesson is being conducted, even when the children are clearly in front of the group performing the expected reading behaviors. It suggests important data are to be filed away again in the teacher's head or heart. Like shared writing, teachers need to consider how to gather and use data from the shared reading experience more effectively.

The final area of concern shared reading shares with shared writing is related to integration. Like shared writing, shared reading should be intentionally linked to other elements within the literacy and language arts program. It is particularly important to align the sequences of shared reading and shared writing if students are to see the important connections between the two processes. Students need to be explicitly reminded that what they learn during reading helps them during writing and what they learn during writing helps them during reading. Once these elements are aligned, students will benefit from a smooth flow from these to other aspects of a comprehensive literacy program. "The power of the shared reading is enhanced by opportunities to connect it to other elements in a balanced literacy framework (Swartz, Shook, and Klein, 2002, p. 6)." Saunders-Smith (2009) agrees. Whole group instruction is most appropriate for creating awareness, initiation, demonstration, and modeling but must be further explored in small groups and in individual activities. Burkins and Croft (2010) recommend that planning for shared readings always considers reinforcing or practicing the skills taught. Can links be made to the read-aloud, guided reading, independent reading, and independent writing? If elements are not well integrated, the learner will be hampered in his or her ability to transfer information beyond the shared reading experiences.

One additional area of concern about the pedagogy of shared readings is often seen in the fundamental debates about explicit versus implicit instruction (Zarrillo, 2007; Dow and Baer, 2012). Does evidence support one approach as a more effective means for impacting the performance and achievement of the learners? Shared readings, especially those using texts such as poems, rhymes, chants, songs, and patterned stories, often follow a *top-down* teaching framework. Top-down approaches follow a whole-to-part sequencing (Dorn and Jones, 2012, Combs, 2002; Ford, 1996). First, a text is chosen that can be easily placed into the head of the learner through repeated readings of the whole text. Sometimes, the text is chosen because it is already in the heads of the learner. It may be a verse or chant they have already learned through oral language activities. Once the text is in the heads of the learner, then instruction is focused on making a connection between the words in the learner's head and words on the page. The focus typically begins with a smaller "chunk" of the text, such as a stanza or page. Then, instruction focuses on text at the sentence or line level. Learners are invited to revisit the text, recognizing, identifying, matching, and monitoring lines of texts from the reading. Learners begin to recognize features of the print at this level. Lines are then broken down into phrases, and learners must focus more carefully on working with phrases of texts from the reading, using an increasingly finer degree of visual discrimination in looking at features of print. Phrases are then broken down into individual words. This requires an even more sophisticated degree of visual discrimination as students begin to learn about features of words through their activities. Finally, words are broken down into their word parts with a focus related to features about graphemes, phonemes, and morphemes.

Direct instruction needs to find a logical home within a shared reading lesson (Burkins and Croft, 2010). There is nothing inherent in the shared reading experience that precludes the inclusion of systematic explicit instruction. As seen in the top-down sequence, there are many opportunities for explicit instruction. This is especially true when the lessons flow all the way through to focus on features related to sounds, letters, and other word parts, but often shared readings focused on the "wholes" and aren't sustained long enough to bring attention to the needed smaller parts. When the smaller parts (phonemes, graphemes, and morphemes) are attended to, they often don't receive the systematic instruction they warrant. The concern is that direct, explicit skill and strategy instruction is often not done with the frequency and intensity it requires. This means for many learners, the acquisition of the critical tools needed to be successful readers would be learned through embedded, implicit instruction versus explicit instruction. In contrast, more *bottom-up* approaches that started with these smaller parts and then moved toward the wholes seemed to focus more systematically on critical skills and strategies. The critique of bottom-up approaches, on the other hand, is usually they never pay off in allowing learners to experience the joy of the whole reading experience. Intensification techniques are designed to make sure that systematic, explicit instruction is used during the shared reading while also allowing learners to experience the positive outcomes that draw readers to texts in the first place.

It is interesting to note research done on the shared reading experience in New Zealand showed significant gains for children in reading and listening comprehension and the ability to use English with second language learners (Elley and Mangubhai, 1983). Research done in the United States (Reutzel, Hollingsworth, and Eldredge, 1994; Eldredge, Reutzel, and Hollingsworth, 1996) has shown that even a 10-minute shared reading experience, when contrasted to another classroom practice like 20 minutes of round-robin reading in a whole group setting, had "statistically superior impacts on all measures of reading proficiency... especially on the reading performances of average and struggling readers (Allington, 2012, p. 114)." So whether the learning was more from explicit or implicit instruction during the shared reading, research suggested students did gain necessary skills and strategies.

How Is Shared Reading Intensified for Emergent Readers and Writers?

Combs (2002) identifies some instructional literacy activities as *extensive* reading activities and others as *intensive* reading activities. Extensive reading activities use primarily the same activity with different texts over an extended period of time. Reading aloud in classrooms is often done this way. Intensive reading activities involve repeated engagement with the same text over an extended period of time. Keep in mind that the repeated readings children seek at home with their favorite storybooks provides an intensive reading experience. It leads to the revisiting of a text that leads to the continual discovery of new understanding about print. This is what should be achieved with the intensification of the shared reading experience. In this case, continued involvement with the same text on repeated occasions allows the reader to notice an increasing number of new details about the text over time. Every time the text is revisited, it allows for a closer inspection. This sets up another opportunity to learn new things about how print works. I argue this was important in structuring the shared writing routine. I am going to recommend the routine of shared reading is also structured in a similar intensive manner.

To align with shared writing, shared reading for emergent readers and writers will also involve systematic, explicit instruction in the large group setting focused on three different critical outcomes: concepts of print, alphabetic knowledge, and phonological/phonemic awareness. Academic language included during the shared writing will be used in shared reading experiences to further help students make connections between reading and writing. The shared reading routine will also incorporate a gradual release of responsibility model to provide direct explanation, demonstrating, modeling, guided practice, and monitored independent practice. Like others who have written about shared reading (Boyles, 2009), a five-day sequence of 15- to 20-minute lessons is used so it can parallel what is done during the shared writing experience. Use instructional activities that can also be completed in small group settings, such as guided reading, or left available for students to use in an independent center following the large group lessons. As previously stated, the sequence described is just one vision of how to intensify shared reading for emergent readers and writers. Teachers should feel free to adapt or modify the presented plans to better meet the needs of their students and achieve these critical outcomes.

Day One: *Preparing for Initial Reading of the Text*

Keep in mind that the use of shared reading is not an end in and of itself. While families can always sustain the joys of the interaction around a family story time experience, in a classroom, the shared reading is being used to move children toward becoming independent strategic readers who find and sustain the joys of reading on their own. Planning needs to consider where the students are at (data from assessments) and where the students need to be (expectations identified from the curriculum). One reason why shared reading is such a powerful classroom routine is it can be used to address many teaching points (Swartz, Shook, and Klein, 2002). But remember, it isn't just about including a teaching point; it's about including a teaching point that is needed by the learners to move them forward as confident and competent readers. Having an instructional purpose will help with the selection of the text. With the shared writing experience, the teacher creates the text with the students. Teachers can also create the texts they use for shared reading. Holdaway (1979) did this in his development of the shared book experience.

INTEGRATION IDEA: For shared reading texts, familiar rhymes, chants, and songs may be very good vehicles with which to start. In my first-grade class, our opening activities always included the singing of a fun action song like "Mrs. O'Leary's Cow," "Head, Shoulders, Knees, and Toes," or "The Grand Old Duke of York." To introduce these songs, I created a song sock. This was a decorated white knee sock. Inside I placed chips with the names of different action songs on them. Each day, a student would come up to the song sock and pull out one of the chips. The song on the chip would be introduced for the day. Once all the songs had been introduced, the chips were returned to the song sock to be chosen and sung repeatedly throughout the year. Once the songs had been sung a few times, they were very familiar to the students, which makes their transfer to text formats very conducive for shared reading experiences.

In many classrooms, the teacher has access to enlarged texts and does not usually have to make the text. The teacher can select an available text for the shared reading experience. In some commercial programs, the decision of what text to use may have already been determined. If not, the teacher controls the selection of the text. Since the text can come from a variety of sources as well as in a variety of formats, selecting an appropriate text can be challenging. There are numerous considerations when selecting the text but two considerations rise to the top of the list: purpose (what outcome you are trying to achieve) and audience (who the students participating in this lesson are). Again, text selection depends on knowing your curricular expectations and the needs of your students. The text should have enough challenges but also sufficient supports, so the students can enter the reading (Hornsby, 2000). Burkins and Yaris (2016) recommend the level of the text should probably be one or two levels above the guided reading levels of most students but below the level of difficulty of books chosen for traditional read-alouds. The following are considerations for selecting a shared reading text:

1. Does the text facilitate instruction toward the critical general outcomes for emergent readers and writers—concepts of print, alphabetic knowledge, and/or phonological awareness?
2. Does the text facilitate instruction for the specific outcome you want to achieve during this lesson (e.g., a specific concept of print, letter name, and/or phonological awareness strategy)?
3. Can the print within the text be seen by all students when used in a large group?
4. Is the text presented in a standard manner (large type, ample white space between words and sentences, consistent placement on each page, clearly separate from supportive illustrations, whole sentences that flow from left to right and top to bottom, etc.)?
5. Is the text at a level that can be accessible for most readers with teacher support? (Remember, a read-aloud text can be at a higher level than the learners' reading levels, but a shared reading text needs to be closer to the instructional level of the learners.)

6. Are most of the vocabulary words and language structures within the text reflective of the words and syntax of the learners with whom it is being used?
7. Does the shared reading text lend itself to alignment with the shared writing text?
8. Does the text allow for important interaction and discussion focused on making meaning?
9. When possible, does the text provide content that is easily understood by the students, with links to instruction in other subject areas?
10. Does the genre or format of the text best serve the instructional goals of the lesson?
11. Can the text sustain the interest and engagement of the learners?

Once the text has been selected, it is important to think about how to physically present it. Classroom organization is critical in conducting effective shared reading experiences. Keep in mind the setting for the shared reading must allow for that intimate interaction with the text to reach the feeling of family storybook reading experiences. The text is the primary focus of the lesson, so feature it in a way that is accessible for all. That means all students need to be able to see and hear the text. Make sure to consider the size of the print, the angle of the book, and potential glare factors in positioning the text for all to see (Burkins and Yaris, 2016). As with shared writing, a gathering place within the classroom where all students can see and hear may work the best. Without a space like that, your only choice may be to leave students at their tables or desks. If that precludes access for all, move the text around the classroom as it is shared. Many teachers can provide access by using some projection tool that will allow the text to be seen by all students as it is being read. Fortunately, many teachers also can secure digital versions of the texts they want to use in shared reading experiences, making the projections even more convenient to use in classrooms.

In shared reading, the first day of the five-day instructional cycle is used to set up the text for subsequent readings and explorations by the students. If the shared reading text needs to be created, day one of the shared reading cycle focuses on recording the words of the text in a book or chart format. If this is the case, day one of the shared reading process mirrors creating a classroom message during day one of the shared writing experience. If the shared reading text is already created and available for use, day one of the shared reading experience is focused on making a plan to get ready to read the selected text. Just like day one of shared writing focuses on making a plan for writing the class message, day one of the shared reading cycle is focused on strategies that are helpful for making a plan to read the class text. Swartz, Shook, and Klein (2002) point out proficient readers have ways of organizing their thinking before starting to read a text, so they can effectively make meaning as they read the new text. Buehl (2013) also called this "preparing for the learning," which concentrates on two main strategies: activating and focusing. Day one of the shared reading cycle is used to teach emergent readers and writers about these preparation strategies. In other words, day one is the pre-reading stage of the cycle. It is the day used to *frontload* the story to help the students build a foundation for subsequent successful interactions with the text. Frontloading typically has five key goals:

1. activate schema, especially where background knowledge exists;
2. build additional background knowledge where knowledge is limited;
3. address anticipated skill and strategy needs;
4. set a purpose for reading; and
5. generate interest in reading.

Teachers must determine how much support they will need to give during the frontloading, so students can enjoy and handle the demands of the text being shared (Swartz, Shook, and Klein, 2002). Recently, some experts have cautioned about providing too much frontloading prior to the reading of the text. The teacher has done so much of the work before the reading, the students have little work to do during the reading of the text (Burkins & Yaris, 2016). Instead of creating a sense of urgency in the readers, a sense of exhaustion sets in. Remember, the end goal is not frontloading. The end goal is a successful, enjoyable reading experience that will cause students to want to seek the experience again.

Many activities can be used to frontload a shared reading experience, but often there is an overreliance on a limited number of techniques. A common recommendation is to conduct an oral discussion of the cover followed by predictions of what will follow (Zarrillo, 2007; Swartz, Shook, and Klein, 2002). Unfortunately, the overuse of this technique is one way the shared reading routine has become dull. Another problem is this pre-reading discussion often falls into a discourse pattern that experts call I-R-E: the teacher INITIATES a discussion usually by asking a question; one or two students RESPOND, usually with one word or short phrases; and then the teacher EVALUATES the response with some simple praise like "Good answer!" In planning shared reading activities, we want to intentionally break out of this pattern. Himmele and Himmele (2011) talk about the use of total participation techniques to redefine the discourse flow in whole group settings. These can range from the use of better questions (higher-order, strategy-embedded, open-ended questions to encourage more complex responses) to increasing teacher wait time (flash one-two-three fingers before calling on anyone), from turn-and-talks (share with your partner before you share in the large group) to choral response cards (students flash "yes" or "no" cards based on a question and then defend responses). Techniques like these will help break the I-R-E discourse pattern and make the shared reading less routinized.

EVALUATION IDEA: Shagoury (2016) observed, "recording language gives teachers a chance to re-hear conversations in their classrooms (1)." If you want to analyze and improve classroom discourse patterns, consider recording one of your shared reading experiences. Opitz and Ford (2015) developed an analysis guide to use in examining your classroom interaction pattern. You can evaluate dimensions like wait time, use of questioning, nature of student responses, frequency of probing, and degree of prompting. Shagoury recommends to keep your focus narrow, transcribe segments you want to share with others, download recordings to be listened to at more convenient times (during the school commute), and consider if segments can be played back to students to involve them in the analysis.

One way to intensify the common technique of discussing the cover and making predictions is to invite your learners to look carefully at the cover of the text. Give the learners a short time limit and a direction to try to remember everything they can about what is on the cover. Prepare a blank sheet you can use to cover up the cover of the text. At the end of the time, cover up the cover. Then invite learners to be ready to tell you what they saw on the cover. Allow them a chance to turn and talk with a partner first before soliciting contributions in the large group. Once learners have had enough time to share with partners, invite learners to share what they remembered in the whole group. As students describe things from the cover, record the ideas that are shared, making a numbered list on the blank sheet of paper used to cover up the cover. Recording those ideas provides a great opportunity to borrow any of the techniques used during shared writing to record language. You can call explicit attention to concepts of print, letter names, and phonological strategies as you try to capture what the students remembered. You can also highlight or add any key words or phrases you know will be a part of the shared reading text. You can address vocabulary needs as you complete the frontloading activity to set a firmer foundation for subsequent readings.

Once the list is created, you can use it for an initial shared reading experience as you guide the class in reading it together. A numbered list provides an easy text for emergent readers to explore with guidance. Create the numbered list using alternating colors to make it easier for emergent readers to track with their eyes as they read. The list can be read up and down, fast and slow, softly and loudly, and in different fun voices. The list can be read chorally by all, or the whole group can be divided into two groups, with each group assigned a different color. Students can respond with a word or phrase when the teacher calls out a number, or students can flash a number next to a word or phrase the teacher calls out. By the time you are done doing a few of these fun activities together, these ideas and the language related to them will be useful to students as they explore the text more independently.

Eventually, the cover sheet can be removed and compared to the actual cover. New ideas and words can be added to the list for additional exploration. When students are offered invitations to predict what will happen or be learned during the shared reading, most will be better prepared to offer thoughtful responses. This alternative to a traditional discussion will help address the key goals of frontloading. Students will have activated existing knowledge and even added more background knowledge before reading the text. You will have opportunities to address skills and strategies in those discussions. Everyone will have a purpose to read to see if their predictions are close or on track. And if done with a bit of joyous effort, students should be more interested in participating in the subsequent shared reading experiences.

Reminders When Teaching the Pre-reading Phase of Shared Reading

- Plan the lesson so that the introduction can stay within a 15- to 20-minute time frame.
- Consider the key goals of frontloading in planning the introduction of the text.
  - Activate existing background knowledge that students can bring to the text.
  - Build additional background knowledge needed to make sense of the text.
  - Anticipate and address any skills or strategies, including vocabulary, that may be needed by the students to meet demands of the text.
  - Set an explicit purpose for the reading that will follow.
  - Generate interest—a sense of urgency—in wanting to read the text.
- Consider alignment between the day one instruction in shared reading and the day one instruction in shared writing.
- Plan the lesson to intentionally avoid the typical discourse pattern of whole group discussion (i.e., I-R-E).
- Frame questions as open-ended, strategy-embedded, and higher-order questions to encourage deeper, more sophisticated thinking.
- Integrate engagement techniques that encourage total participation (e.g., turn-and-talks, choral responses.)
- Use shared writing techniques during the frontloading (e.g., recording oral responses on a chart) that allow you to seize additional teachable moments during the lesson. Guide the reading back to any text created with the students.
- Be ready to use teaching opportunities to address key outcomes related to the instruction of concepts of print, alphabetic knowledge, and phonological/phonemic awareness that will follow on subsequent days.
- Involve students in the self-evaluation of their engagement and performance before transitioning from the shared reading experience.
- End with an intentional link between the activities in shared reading and strategies that can be used by students in independent reading and writing.

Day Two: *Shared and Assisted Reading of the Message*

Day two of the shared reading instructional cycle should build on the sense of urgency created through the frontloading on day one. Day two should celebrate the text that is going to be shared. You want students to enjoy the experience of reading the text, so you can create momentum that carries from the shared reading to other reading activities within the classroom. Day two of the shared reading should be used to help students have an intimate experience with the text that closely resembles family storybook reading. Use caution in seeing the shared reading text as only a tool to use in conducting skill and strategy instruction. Let students become familiar and friendly with the text first. Then it can be revisited for further explorations to foster understandings about concepts of print, alphabetic knowledge, and phonological/phonemic awareness. There are three days left in the sequence that can be used for additional skill and strategy instruction. The cognitive outcomes are important, but it is also important for emergent readers to see reading as a pleasurable experience (Combs, 2002).

In the initial reading of the shared reading text, return to your gathering place within the classroom where all students would be able to see the text and hear you as you read the text. Start with a review of strategies used during the pre-reading stage on day one. Remind students what background knowledge they need to bring to the page. Restate the purpose for today's reading to get students to refocus. Review any information that was recorded on a chart to help students see the connection between day one and day two. Then start the reading. For the gradual release, it might be best to structure the lesson with a shorter text using three repeated readings of the text. Let the first reading serve as the *I do* phase of the gradual release, the second reading as the *we do* phase, and the third reading as the *you do* phase of the lesson.

The first reading is a chance for the teacher to introduce students to the text with "a full dramatic punch (Zarrillo, 2007, p. 14)." It's the phase of the reading that involves teacher modeling and demonstrations to show how to read the text by sharing it in a way that will excite students. As was the case in reading the classroom message during the shared writing experience, the main job of students is watching and listening to you during this initial reading. You can invite students to try to read along with you in their heads (Mooney, 1990), but you should use this opportunity to take the lead. This is a chance for the teacher to share information about the reading process using think-alouds to make thinking public for the students. Exercise some restraint in using your think-alouds during the first reading. Avoid having your attempts to teach interfere with students' attempts to enjoy the text during their first time encountering it. Remember, some use of think-alouds can also focus on more aesthetic stances as you read the story. Think about language like: "I really like what the author did in the next part" or "That line really made me laugh." You can use think-aloud language to show readers how to enjoy texts as well as how to use cognitive strategies. You don't have to avoid making cognitive connections during the first reading. There may be reasons to link to concepts of print, academic language, alphabetic knowledge, and phonological/phonemic awareness strategies to review what was previously introduced or to set up instruction that will follow on subsequent days. Just find a balance that allows for enjoyment before framing the text as primarily a tool for skill instruction.

After the first reading, provide a chance for students to think about what was read and offer a reaction to it. Let the students take the lead with a more natural reaction, unsolicited or constrained by a standard set of teacher questions. This honors Mooney's (1990) original recommendation that invitations to students to participate in the reading "should come from the book itself ... rather than by any planned or overt direction (26)." This does not have to be extensive, but you do want to enhance the experience by allowing students a chance to respond to what was just read. As work with the text continues, opportunities will surface to discuss more formally the meaning of the text, the author's intent, and connections to other readings, and as well as to share beyond their personal experience (Swartz, Shook, and Klein, 2002).

As you move to a second reading of the text, move to the *we do* phase of the lesson. Reduce your explanation, demonstration, and modeling. Use more of a choral reading of the text or what was previously called an "assisted reading." Invite learners in on the second reading of the text. They can either follow your lead or you can follow their lead, monitoring and prompting as needed. Hornsby (2000) recommended encouraging students to come in and out of the reading as they can. Students can attempt to read along with you in a variety of ways, depending on their abilities. Allow for different approximations of reading, ranging from some students reading right along with you to others mouthing the words to themselves as you say them (Mooney, 1990). The nice thing is the large group context is a safe place to practice. Any missteps are barely noticed by others. I compare it to singing in a school concert. Most of us feel comfortable singing along in the choir, but very few of us want to be the soloist. That's a high-risk setting where any attempts are definitely more noticeable to others. The second reading provides opportunities to naturally apply strategies previously introduced. Be ready to use questions or prompts that invite students to apply knowledge about concepts of print, academic language, names of letters, and phonological/phonemic awareness strategies within the context of the second reading.

As you move to the third repeated reading of the text—the *I do* phase of the lesson—intentionally look for opportunities to turn over the reading to the learners. This could happen in a variety of ways. You can take the lead and then let the students fill in words, phrases, lines, sentences, or sections on their own. Students can chorally read the text on their own while you monitor and support the reading as needed. Different students or groups of students can read different assigned parts, or individual students can be invited to read the text on their own. The third reading is also a better time to make connections to the critical cognitive outcomes. You will be able to more closely monitor and observe what the students can do independently during the third reading. Then you can provide specific, appropriate feedback about these skills and strategies as needed. Again, it provides a chance for students, in the large group, to engage in independent practice of skills previously introduced on day one or during shared writing under your watchful eye. These opportunities can also inform your thinking about instructional connections to make to concepts of print on day three, alphabetic knowledge on day four, and/or phonological/phonemic awareness strategies on day five.

Celebrate the text with a final choral reading. Take the lead so students are leaving the gathering space with a successful, fluent final reading of the text in their heads. One way to encourage the revisiting of the text is to invite students to come back to the gathering space and practice reading the Big Book when they have independent work time (Swartz, Shook, and Klein, 2002). Some teachers actually include the Big Book stand or area as a learning station or center (Stead, 2009; Richardson, 2009). Students can be given permission to use the texts and tools used by the teacher during shared reading on their own time individually or with partners. If you have ever watched students revisit a Big Book area under these conditions, what you most often see is students echoing the language and actions of the teacher. It's a good way to evaluate our teaching as they mirror what they have often seen and heard us do! Finish the day by using simple self-evaluation techniques to engage students in looking at their behaviors during the readings of the text before transitioning, and then provide an explicit link to the next lesson in the sequence. In this case, the shared reading will be followed by more specific attention to important concepts of print and academic language on day three.

Reminders When Doing the Initial Shared Reading of the Text

- Link to issues and ideas surfaced during the pre-reading phase of the lesson related to activating and focusing strategies from day one.
- Pace the readings quickly to stay within the 15- to 20-minute time frame.
- As you do the first reading, focus on teacher explanation, demonstration, and modeling (*I do*), but keep think-alouds to a minimum to focus on enjoyment of the text. Remember, think-alouds can be used to show students how you are enjoying the text.
- With the second reading, take the lead as needed (*we do*). While in the large group, be ready to seize teachable moments using teacher prompts and strategic questions. These allow students to show you what they can do.
- As you do the third reading, look for opportunities to invite students to take over the reading and show you what they know and are learning (*you do*). This allows you a chance to observe, monitor, and provide feedback while all are together in the large group.
- Consider connections you can make to cognitive outcomes and expectations (concepts of print, alphabetic knowledge, and phonological/phonemic awareness) to review concepts and strategies

addressed on day one. Keep these to a minimum during the first reading, and increase attention to them during the second and third readings.

- Consider connections you can make to cognitive outcomes and expectations (concepts of print, alphabetic knowledge, and phonological/phonemic awareness) to review concepts and strategies aligned with shared writing instruction. Again, keep these to a minimum during the first reading, and increase attention during the second and third readings.
- Be responsive and follow appropriate leads from students that may surface additional instructional opportunities from the interactions but haven't been planned. Record those moments to help reflection for future lessons.
- Involve students in the self-evaluation of their engagement and performance before transitioning from the shared reading experience. End with an intentional link to reading and writing with which students will be involved away from the shared reading.
- Plan for independent work away from the shared reading that will allow students to practice and apply what was learned during the shared reading. Remind students they can visit the shared reading space and this text during their independent work time.

Day Three: *Intensifying Instruction toward Outcomes Related to Concepts of Print*

Like shared writing, the next three days of the intensification cycle for shared reading will shift focus toward specific cognitive outcomes in the three critical areas of need for emergent readers and writers. Day three of the shared reading cycle is designed to help emergent readers work on specific concepts of print and academic language related to literacy activities and tasks. As you plan for day three, be very intentional about which specific concepts of print will be the focus during the rereading of the shared text. Consider what the expected outcomes are in this area as identified in your curriculum, but also adjust those expectations based on what you know your students need. Also reflect on what connections can be made to any concepts of print explored during the pre-reading phase of the lesson on day one and the first reading of the text on day two. More importantly, efforts should be made to align the concepts of print work done during the shared reading with the concepts of print work done during the shared writing experience. For example, if you focused on the voice-print match during the shared writing lesson, focus on voice-print match during this phase of the shared reading cycle. As you plan your lesson to focus on critical outcomes in concepts of print and academic language, remember that the guide in Chapter One (p. 18) and the reminders in Chapter Two (p. 46) may help you if your local curricular supports are silent on these concepts, skills, and strategies.

Zarrillo (2007) reminds teachers the shared reading experience has the potential to teach all of the concepts of print. One difference between the shared reading and the shared writing is the shared reading experience—when it involves an actual enlarged text such as a Big Book—is more appropriate to address book-handling skills and related academic language. Since the created shared writing text is usually not in a book format, the shared reading offers a better opportunity to model book-handling strategies. These include starting at the beginning, finding the first page to start reading, holding the book right side up, and reading page after page to the end of the book. Since the teacher is using a real book, these strategies can be modeled. With a real book in the teacher's hands, it is easier to introduce, explain, and use academic terms like *front, back, cover, title, author, illustrator, title page, copyright, illustration, page*, and *page number.* Be sure to consider the need to address these strategies and terms, which may not have been addressed during the shared writing experience. Remember that concepts of print and academic language actually become increasing sophisticated as texts become increasingly more complex. Informational texts have a number of nonfiction features students need to learn to negotiate, from captions to headers and footnotes to glossaries. The academic language related to features like those and many others will eventually need to be learned by readers and writers at other developmental phases as well. Since it is hard to embed these in shared writing messages that a teacher creates, it will be important to use shared reading experiences with enlarged texts to teach these sophisticated aspects of texts. In addition, traditional ways of dealing with text may not always work when the readers encounter a post-modern picture book that challenges conventions as it uses print to present its story. Some texts are not always read top to bottom. In Andrew Clements' *Double Trouble in Walla Walla*, one two-page spread contains words that are actually presented and read in circular fashion. Some texts are not always read from front to back. In Richard Byrne's *This Book Just Ate My Dog!*, the reader is actually instructed to turn the book on its side to read a note and then to shake the book to release the captured characters. Instruction regarding book-handling skills may start simply with more conventional texts, but they also may need to be revisited when new and unconventional features show up in texts.

Day three would start with a rereading of the text. You always want to revisit the initial reading of the text because the material will now be familiar to students. This leads to more fluent reading attempts. Reading a text fluently offers more enjoyment than struggling with a new text. Students can better sense what it feels like to read with proficiency, growing their confidence (Swartz, Shook, and Klein, 2002). Quickly move into systematic and explicit instruction on concepts of print. The concept of print lesson should be grounded in the shared reading text but does not have to be limited to that text. You can be prepared to use other samples, and examples from other texts can be used to show a concept of print in a variety of contexts.

ENGAGEMENT IDEA:
Some commercial big books come in sets with multiple copies or with access to smaller, reproducible versions of the book. Each student (or at least groups of students) can be given a copy of the book to explore during shared reading activities like the scavenger hunt. Instead of needing to have all eyes on the large text while noticing and counting features, eyes can be directed to the small texts, which should make involvement with these activities easier, thus increasing engagement levels.

The scavenger hunt used during the shared writing (Appendix 7, p. 181) can also be modified for the shared reading. Students can be engaged to review concepts of print and academic language by conducting a similar scavenger hunt through the shared reading text. Like with the shared writing, students can count with the teacher how many sentences they find in the shared reading text (reviewing features of sentences), words in a sentence or in the entire shared reading text (reviewing features of words), and letters in a word, a sentence, or even the whole shared reading text (reviewing features of letters). The shared reading text is another opportunity to look for punctuation marks like periods, commas, question marks, exclamation points, and quotation marks. Remember, even if the shared reading text doesn't contain an example, students get as much practice looking for something not there as they do counting things that are in the text. You can assign different punctuation marks to student groups. Then slowly review the text, asking each group to tally when they see their punctuation mark. Compare results within and across groups at the end. Remember, other comparative activities and tallying exercises can be used with the shared reading to provide additional practice and review in showing understanding of concepts of print related to sentences, words, and letters. In planning a scavenger hunt for shared reading, consider alignment with the tasks students were asked to do during the shared writing. You will save time if directions can be kept to a minimum and raise engagement levels if students feel confident about being able to complete the task. You can actually create a scavenger hunt sheet that can be prepared with two columns—one can be filled out during the shared writing and the other can be filled out during the shared reading. There are many ways a shared reading text can be creatively used to provide students an opportunity to explore and examine the various concepts of print using the appropriate academic language.

EVALUATION IDEA: Bring a basket of smaller, appropriate-level trade books or guided reading books to the gathering space. Students can select a text from the basket to demonstrate understanding of taught concepts and strategies using a new book. The assessment can take place across students in the large group. Each student can use their book to collectively show responses to key questions. For example, you can ask all students to "find your title page" or "put your finger on the last word in your book." A quick glance around the room will let you know who is on track and who might need some additional review. Keep your class list handy so you can note any major concerns to address with individuals later. You can also dismiss students from the gathering area individually by asking them to show an understanding of a concept of print and/or academic term with one of the books from the basket. These exit questions can be tailored to individuals to assess specific items, which can also be recorded on the class list.

The day three lesson would again end with another simple self-evaluation of behaviors and an explicit lesson link to the next lesson in the sequence. Like with shared writing, the next day in the shared reading cycle will focus attention on alphabetic knowledge. Always remind your students that what was learned about concepts of print in this lesson can be used when they are working on their independent reading and writing.

Reminders When Teaching Concepts of Print

- Plan the lesson with a clear focus and short length to fit within a 15-minute time frame.
- Consider the expectations of your curriculum and the needs of students. Plan the lesson to allow you to explain, demonstrate, model, prompt, monitor, and/or give feedback related to concepts of print your students are still in need of instruction on, support with, or practice in.
- Plan the lesson with consideration of links to concepts of print that were previously introduced during days one and two of the shared reading text.
- Plan the lesson to align with the concepts of print lesson that was taught during (or will be taught on) day three of the shared writing experience.
- To make sure you actually address teachable moments, try writing reminders on small sticky notes that you place within the text so you can stay focused on what you planned.
- Start with a quick rereading of the shared reading text. Remember, you can invite students in with a choral reading or assisted reading. As appropriate, stop to attend to concepts of print during the rereading.
- Following the rereading, address the identified concept(s) of print skills or strategies for this lesson. Explain, demonstrate, and model the concept first *(I do)*. Then invite students in with strategic questions and prompting as you guide practice of the concept with the students *(we do)*. Leave time for students to show understanding of the concept independently *(you do)*. Be prepared to probe responses.
- Be responsive and follow appropriate leads from students that may surface additional concepts of print from the interactions but haven't been planned. Record those moments to help reflection for future lessons.
- Involve students in self-evaluation of their performance and engagement levels before transitioning from the shared reading experience. End with an intentional link to the next lesson in the shared reading experience that will be focused on alphabetic knowledge.
- Plan for independent work in reading and writing that will allow students to practice and apply what was learned during the shared reading.

Day Four: *Intensifying Instruction toward Outcomes Related to Alphabetic Knowledge*

For consistency between the shared reading and shared writing, day four of the shared reading sequence shifts to cognitive outcomes related to alphabetic knowledge. Be very intentional about the alphabetic concepts on which you will focus during the rereading of the shared text. Choose a focus that makes sense for a quick lesson, but make sure the text you are using can support that focus. Consider what expected outcomes related to alphabetic knowledge are identified in your curriculum, but also adjust those expectations based on what alphabetic knowledge your students need additional instruction and practice in. In identifying that focus, reflect on what the connections can be to any alphabetic concepts explored during the pre-reading phase of the lesson on day one, the first reading of the text on day two, and/or any alphabetic concepts surfaced during day three, even though the focus was on concepts of print. Finally, make an effort to align the alphabetic work in the shared reading with the alphabetic work done during the shared writing experience. For example, if you focused on recognition, identification, and matching of the upper- and lowercase letter F during the shared writing lesson; continue to focus on reviewing that letter during day four of the shared reading cycle. Just remember, like the message you created for shared writing, make sure the text you have selected for shared reading provides you with opportunities to work on those identified letters. It's hard to work on specific letters if the letters are not in the text. As you plan your lesson to focus on critical outcomes in this area, remember the alphabetic knowledge guide in Chapter One (pp. 18–19) and the reminders in Chapter Two (pp. 48–49) may help you if your curricular supports are silent on the alphabetic knowledge you need to develop so students can find greater success with phonics and spelling instruction.

The same strategic questions that were used during shared writing can be used during shared reading. In fact, the use of similar questions when working on alphabetic concepts during shared reading and shared writing should help students see more connections across their reading and writing. Remember these key types of questions:

- ❑ Recognition = "Let's see if we can find the letter F in our shared reading."
- ❑ Identification = "What letter is this?" (pointing to an F in the shared reading)
- ❑ Visual Matching = "Find another letter that looks like this." (pointing to an F in the shared reading)
- ❑ Printing = "Let's write the letter F." (show an F in the shared reading)

The same techniques and tools used during shared writing should be integrated in the shared reading alphabetic knowledge work. Individual letter cards used during the shared writing can be used during the shared reading since they are ready to go. Students can be invited to come up and name the letter on the card in isolation, find the match in the shared reading text, or use the model to show how it is printed. Teachers should continue to probe beyond an accurate answer ("How did you know that was a match?"), challenge a correct answer ("How did you know it wasn't this one?"), or inquire about an inappropriate answer ("Tell me how you figured out your answer."). Asking questions like these in a large group during shared reading will allow one student's response to help all students better notice and use the features of letters.

Marking up a shared reading text may be more difficult than marking up a classroom message during shared writing. Usually shared reading texts are commercial resources and need to be maintained in their original forms from year to year. Tools are available that allow teachers and students to mark texts without leaving permanent results. Highlighting and corrective tape can be used to mark a letter but easily removed afterward. Wikki Stix are made to stick to paper, can be used to circle and underline print, and can then be easily removed without a trace. "Windows" can be purchased or made and used to frame elements of print. Business envelopes with clear windows to display a recipient's address can be trimmed to provide a tool that can be used by students to frame parts of print. When placed over a letter, the window isolates the letter without leaving a permanent mark. A piece of plastic the size of the page of the enlarged text can always be placed over the real page so marks on the page are left on the piece of plastic and not on the book. One obvious advantage to projected texts—especially ones that can be used with interactive whiteboards or similar technology—is they allow teachers and students to mark up the text without fear of leaving behind something permanent.

After working with the shared reading for four days, end the lesson with self-evaluation that asks students to look at their behaviors over the past few days. Also provide an explicit lesson link to the final lesson in the sequence. In this case, work on alphabetic knowledge with the shared reading text shifts to work on phonological/phonemic strategies. Make sure students leave the shared reading knowing they can use what they have learned about letters today in their independent reading and writing. Keep in mind one of the main reasons for calling attention to the way letters work within a text created by an author used for shared reading is so students will have new insights to use in their independent reading and writing (Fountas and Pinnell, 1996).

Reminders When Teaching Skills Related to Alphabetic Knowledge

- Plan the lesson with a clear focus and short length to fit within a 15-minute time frame.
- Consider the expectations of your curriculum and the needs of students. Think about the content you need to cover, such as broad concepts about letters or specific knowledge about certain letters. Determining this will help you decide which parts of the shared reading text will best support the instruction.
- Plan the lesson with consideration of links to alphabetic knowledge lesson that was previously introduced during the pre-reading phase and initial reading of the shared reading text (days one and two) and/or connected to the concepts of print addressed on day three.
- Plan the lesson to align with the alphabetic knowledge lesson that was taught during (or will be taught on) day three of the shared writing experience.
- Once you know your content, consider which strategies your students need support with: recognition, identification, matching in isolation, matching within context of words, and/or printing of letters.
- Plan the lesson to allow you to explain, demonstrate, model, prompt, monitor, and/or give feedback related to the alphabetic skills based on the degree of instruction, support, or practice students may need.
- To make sure you actually address teachable moments, try writing reminders on small sticky notes that you place within the enlarged text, so you can stay focused on the alphabetic knowledge you planned.
- Start with a rereading of the classroom message. Remember, you can invite students in with a choral reading or assisted reading. As needed, stop to insert some attention to alphabetic knowledge during this quick read.
- Following the reading, address the identified alphabetic skills for this lesson. Explain, demonstrate, and model the skill first (*I do*). Then invite students in with strategic questions and prompting as you guide practice of the skill (*we do*). Leave time for students to show understanding of the skill independently (*you do*). Be prepared to probe responses.
- Be responsive and follow appropriate leads about additional alphabetic knowledge concepts or skills from students that may surface from the planned interactions. Record those moments to help reflection for future lessons.
- Involve students in the self-evaluation level of engagement and performance before transitioning from the shared writing experience. End with an intentional link to day five of the shared reading cycle, which will be phonological awareness strategies.
- Plan for independent work away from the shared reading that will allow students to apply alphabetic knowledge learned during the shared reading experience.

Day Five: *Intensifying Instruction toward Outcomes of Phonological/Phonemic Awareness*

The alignment of the shared writing and shared reading continues on day five with the focus shifting to the cognitive outcomes related to phonological/phonemic awareness. The shared reading provides another opportunity for intentional instruction using auditory activities to focus on broad phonological strategies (word awareness, syllable awareness, rhyming) or moving toward narrow phonemic awareness strategies to work with specific phonemes. Choose a focus that makes sense for a quick lesson, but make sure the shared reading text allows you to address that specific phonological/phonemic strategy. Consider outcomes related to phonological/phonemic awareness identified in your curriculum, but use assessment data to inform your thinking about what strategies your students need additional instruction in and practice with. This instruction should be closely linked to any strategies addressed during the first four days of the shared reading experience. It should connect to the instruction in phonological and phonemic awareness done during the shared writing experience. For example, if you focused on stretching words to hear individual phonemes during the shared writing, it would make sense to review that strategy during day five of the shared reading cycle. For that to happen, the shared reading text needs to be able to provide you with opportunities to work on that strategy. You need to be able to springboard from the text to the instructional focus of the day. As you plan your lesson to focus on critical outcomes in this area, remember the phonological and phonemic awareness guide in Chapter One (pp. 20–22) may help if you are unsure of what would be most helpful to teach to continue students' growth as readers and writers.

The day should start with a final reading of the shared reading text. Since this text has been explored and practiced all week long, students can be encouraged to take the lead in the rereading of the text. Once the text has been reread, move quickly to the phonological/phonemic awareness focus for the day. Consider the needs of your students and the expectations of your curriculum. Decide if attention will be given to broader phonological strategies or narrower phonemic awareness strategies. Identify what strategy you will use, such as matching, identifying, adding, removing, segmenting, blending, or manipulating sound units. The four potential activities described for each level of sound unit can be used to support instruction during shared reading as they were for shared writing. (See Chapter Two, pp. 49–50.)

Reminders When Teaching Strategies Related to Phonological/Phonemic Awareness

- Plan the lesson with a clear focus and short length to fit within a 15-minute time frame.
- Consider the expectations of your curriculum and the needs of students. Think about the content you need to cover related to phonological/phonemic awareness strategies. Determining this will help you decide which parts of the shared reading text will best support the instruction
- Plan the lesson with links to phonological/phonemic awareness strategies that were previously introduced during the pre-reading phase and initial reading of the shared reading text (days one and two), the concepts of print addressed on day three, and/or the alphabetic skills addressed on day four.
- Think about what level of sound unit you need to address (words, syllables, onsets and rimes, or individual phonemes). Knowing the level of sound unit will help you decide which sentences or words to use from the shared reading text to provide instruction.
- Consider the strategies you want the students to use with that sound unit: matching, identifying, isolating, segmenting, blending, adding, removing, or manipulating the sound units. The strategies selected will help you determine what activities you might use: Secret Boxes, Turtle Talk, Blenders, or Transformers.
- Plan the lesson to allow you to explain, demonstrate, model, prompt, monitor, and/or give feedback related to the phonological/phonemic awareness strategies based on what instruction, support, or practice students may need.
- To make sure you actually address teachable moments, try writing reminders on small sticky notes placed in the text so you can stay focused on the phonological and phonemic awareness instruction you planned.
- Start with a rereading of the text. Students should be very familiar with the text by day five, so let them take the lead in the rereading of the text. Stop the students a few times to insert some attention to phonological/phonemic awareness during this quick read.
- Address the identified phonological/phonemic awareness strategies for this lesson. Explain, demonstrate, and model the skill first (*I do*). Invite students in with strategic questions and prompting as you guide practice of the skill (*we do*). Let students show independent understanding of the skill (*you do*). Be prepared to probe responses.
- Involve students in the self-evaluation of their performance levels throughout the week before transitioning from the shared reading experience. End with an intentional link to a new shared reading with which students will be involved during the next week.
- Plan for independent work with the phonological/phonemic awareness strategies away from the shared reading that will allow students to practice and apply what was learned during the shared reading.

How Is Shared Reading Intensified for Early Readers and Writers?

The shared reading experience for early readers and writers needs to be seen as an intensive reading experience (Combs, 2002). One text will be used during the five-day cycle and revisited each day with a slightly different lens, so it can be a context for a connected study of word identification strategies. Closer readings of the text can be done if it is read multiple times throughout the week. The repeated readings will help early readers and writers discover new things about word strategies with each visit to the text. Systematic instruction can be planned by springboarding off those different readings.

To align with shared writing, shared reading for early readers and writers will also involve systematic, explicit instruction in the large group setting focused on critical outcomes related to word-analysis strategies: sound analysis (phonics), high-frequency sight words, structural or morphemic analysis, and the use of context clues. Common academic language used in the shared writing experience will be used in the shared reading experience to further help early readers and writers make important connections between reading and writing. The shared reading routine is developed with a gradual release of responsibility structure to provide direct explanation, demonstrating, modeling, guided practice, and monitored independent practice. A five-day sequence of 15- to 20-minute lessons is used so it can parallel what is done during the shared writing experiences. Shared reading lessons should adapt the use of instructional techniques modeled and used during the shared writing experiences whenever possible. These instructional activities should also give consideration to activities that can be used in small group settings, such as guided reading, or be left for students to use independently following the large group lessons. As previously stated, the sequence described in the next section is just one vision of how to intensify shared reading for early readers and writers. Any teacher should always feel free to adapt or modify the presented plan, especially to better meet the needs of students to achieve these critical word-analysis outcomes.

Day One: *Preparing for Initial Reading of the Text*

As with emergent readers, shared reading with early readers depends on the selection of an appropriate text to use in the large group setting. For some teachers, the text has been predetermined because of the use of a required commercial program or identified within a curricular framework that must be followed. In those cases, the selection of the text is quite easy—use what is expected or assigned! If this is the case, your main task is to get very familiar with the text and the suggested lesson that accompanies it. By knowing the text inside out, you will be better able to address the specific focus of the lesson; but more importantly, you will be able to go beyond the lesson to intentionally address or respond to other needed word-analysis strategies. If the text is not predetermined and the choice is up to the teacher, the decision about what text to use becomes easier once you've determined two critical things: purpose (what outcome you are trying to achieve) and audience (what students are participating in this lesson). A teacher who knows curricular expectations and the needs of students should be able to narrow down the texts that will best serve the curriculum and the students.

Modifying criteria suggested for selecting texts for emergent readers, the following are some things to consider in selecting the text to feature during a shared reading with early readers:

1. Does the text facilitate instruction toward the critical general outcomes for early readers—sound analysis, high-frequency sight words, structural analysis, and context clue patterns?
2. Does the text facilitate instruction for the specific outcomes you want to achieve during this lesson (e.g., a specific sound-symbol relationship, word family, or phonics generalization; specific high-frequency sight words; specific prefixes, roots, suffixes, or inflected endings; or a specific context clue pattern)?
3. Can the print within the text be seen by all students when used in a large group, even as it is presented in more complex formats?
4. Is the text at a level that can be accessible for most readers with teacher support?
5. Are most—but not all—of the vocabulary words and language structures within the text reflective of the words and syntax of the learners with whom it is being used? (To teach about word-analysis clues, you need a text that might contain a few more challenging words to serve as teachable moments during instruction.)
6. Does the shared reading text lend itself to alignment with the shared writing text?
7. Does the text allow for important interaction and discussion focused on making meaning?
8. When possible, does the text provide content that is easily understood by students with links to instruction in other subject areas?
9. Does the genre or format of the text best serve the instructional goals of the lesson?
10. Can the text sustain the interest and engagement of the learners?

Once your instructional focus has been determined and the text has been selected, day one of the shared reading cycle can be divided into two parts: frontloading and initial reading of the text. Since the whole class activity needs to be quickly paced and kept within a limited timetable, select a frontloading activity that allows for moving rapidly into the reading of the text. One activity that meets the key goals of frontloading the text while providing many opportunities to begin calling attention to word-analysis strategies is a vocabulary technique developed by Cunningham, Hall, and Cunningham (2000) called the Rivet technique. It can be done fairly quickly, allowing you to move rapidly into the reading of the text. The teacher looks through the text and selects four to six key vocabulary words to explore that will also start to introduce the text to the readers. The words are presented to the students by using lines for each of the words (see Figure 14). The teacher creates a numbered list, and next to each number are blank spaces for each letter in one of the key words. For example, the class poem featured in the sample lessons (p. 125) was introduced using a Rivet chart featuring four key words: *caterpillar*, *chrysalis*, *leaf*, and *butterfly*. Students can also create a similar Rivet chart to use during the instruction.

Figure 14: Rivet Chart

1. ___ ___ ___ ___ ___ ___ ___ ___ ___ ___ ___

2. ___ ___ ___ ___ ___ ___ ___ ___ ___

3. ___ ___ ___ ___

4. ___ ___ ___ ___ ___ ___ ___ ___ ___

The teacher guides students in trying to figure out the words by giving clues as the spaces are filled in. As the students are trying to figure out the words, clues can be given about sound-symbol relationships, visual patterns, structural elements, and word meanings. This allows for many teaching opportunities to lay a foundation for future word-analysis strategies instruction on subsequent days. The activity can be quickly paced and include discussions of word meanings and related content. This will also activate schema, build background knowledge, generate interest, and provide an opportunity to define a purpose for the subsequent reading of the text.

Reminders When Preparing for the Initial Reading of the Text

- Strategically select the text or become familiar with an assigned text.
- Plan the length of the lesson so the frontloading and initial shared reading can be completed within a 20-minute time frame.
- In planning the frontloading, keep in mind the need to:
    - activate and/or build background knowledge;
    - address skills and strategies needed to meet the demands of the text;
    - create a purpose for subsequent reading; and
    - generate interest in the text and the instruction to follow.
- Think about how to divide the reading of the text in three parts.
- Plan a lesson that lays a foundation for future instruction to allow you to explain, demonstrate, model, prompt, monitor, and/or give feedback related to sound-analysis (phonics) strategies your students

are still in need of instruction on, support with, or practice in. Make sure the shared reading text has words that allow you to teach specific sound-symbol relationships your students need to address the most. Plan a lesson that lays a foundation for future instruction to allow you to introduce, prompt, monitor, and/or give feedback related to high-frequency sight words your students are still in need of instruction on, support with, or practice in. Make sure the shared reading text contains these specific high-frequency sight words.

- Plan a lesson that lays a foundation for future instruction to allow you to introduce, prompt, monitor, and/or give feedback related to the use of structural analysis strategies your students are still in need of instruction on, support with, or practice in. Remember to think about the structural elements with which your students need support. Make sure the shared reading has words that can be used to teach those structural elements.
- Plan a lesson that lays a foundation for future instruction to allow you to introduce, prompt, monitor, and/or give feedback related to the use of context clue strategies your students are still in need of instruction on, support with, or practice in. Analyze the text to determine if at least one unfamiliar or less familiar word in the text uses one of the nine typical context clue patterns so you can explain, model, and demonstrate how to use those patterns to figure out new words.
- Plan a lesson that allows for a connection to content being explored in other subject areas.
- To make sure you actually seize teachable moments within the shared text, try writing reminders on small sticky notes and place them within the text so you can address those moments as the text is shared.

Following the frontloading, the teacher should move into reading the text as quickly as possible. Consider how to present the text in three phases. Depending on the length of the shared reading, consider what was discussed in working with emergent readers and writers. If the text is relatively short, you might plan three repeated readings. If the text is longer, you may want to divide the text into three sections. If it takes too much time to frontload and share the entire text, consider where you can stop on day one. Be strategic about stopping at a point that will leave your students wanting more and be eager to return to the text on the following day.

Start with the first reading or first part of the text. Use this part of the text for explanation, demonstration, and modeling as part of the *I do* phase of your lesson. Use think-alouds sparingly, primarily as a way to reveal word-analysis strategies related to sound, sight, structure, and context. You can do this by intentionally inserting a miscue as you read and then articulating how you monitored and repaired the miscue. Other times, you might actually make a natural miscue during your oral reading, which will allow you an opportunity to talk about the error and how you caught and fixed it. Figure 15 on page 111 provides some sample language you can modify. Just remember that if students are encountering this text for the first time, you want the presentation to be enjoyable and engaging. Use restraint in inserting too many think-alouds or teachable moments that might minimize enjoyment of the text.

Figure 15: Language for Thinking Aloud about Miscues

- ❑ What did I notice about the word I missed?
- ❑ Did it look like the word on the page?
- ❑ Did it sound right when I said the sentence?
- ❑ Did it make sense in the sentence I read?
- ❑ Did I correct the word?
- ❑ Did I need to correct the word?
- ❑ What strategy did I use to first recognize the word?
- ❑ What strategy did I use to correct the word?
- ❑ What strategy did I use to make sure the word was correct?

In the second reading or the second part of the text, start to invite learners in on the shared reading of the text. This is the *we do* phase of the lesson. It allows you to guide the students as they start to practice and apply critical strategies. Let students monitor your use of word identification strategies, or prompt them to show you what they can do with the same word identification strategies. Be very intentional about using questions or prompts that have students applying knowledge about sound, sight, structure, and context strategies that will be the intentional focus of this cycle of lessons. Again, these can be teachable moments that are intentionally inserted or may just happen more naturally as often happens when someone reads.

With the third and final reading or third part of the reading, consider how to have some of the learners take over the shared reading. In this *you do* phase of the lesson, let them show you what they can do more independently so that you can also provide specific, appropriate feedback as needed related to their use of word identification strategies. This allows students to have independent practice in the large group under your watchful eye.

INTEGRATION IDEA: Burkins and Yaris (2016) suggest creating a running anchor chart to keep track of strategies that are introduced or discovered during shared readings. It is especially good to capture strategies discovered by students explained in their language. The list helps connect one lesson or experience to the next. This chart can be publicly displayed so it is available to be used as a resource for teaching and learning throughout the day. Students can also maintain a strategy page in their reading and writing notebooks, adding strategies to their charts after something new has been added to the whole class strategy list.

With a short text, it might be valuable to end with a quick rereading of the entire text, so students leave the shared reading with the whole text in their heads. Save a few minutes for self-evaluation techniques and lesson links. These are just as important for early readers and writers as they are for emergent readers and writers. Always make sure learners can see how what was learned during the shared reading can be used during other reading and writing contexts.

Reminders When Reading

- Pace the lesson quickly to stay within the 15- to 20-minute time frame.
- As you read the first part, focus on explanation, demonstration, and modeling (*I do*).
- As you read the second part, focus on use of teacher prompts and strategic questions to allow students to show you what they are learning while you are all together in the large group (*we do*).
- As you read the final part, invite students to "take over" the reading process and show you what they know and are learning. This allows you a chance to observe, monitor, and provide feedback while you are all together in the large group (*you do*).
- When you consider what sound analysis strategies to call attention to, focus on those with which your students need support. (Refer to the guide on pp. 22–23 and Appendix 4 on pp. 176–177.)
- When you consider what high-frequency sight words to call attention to, focus on those with which your students need support, including any that might be identified for students at a specific grade level by your curriculum. (Refer to a standard sight word list.)
- When you consider what structural analysis strategies to call attention to, focus on those with which your students need support. (Refer to the guide on pp. 23–24 and Appendix 5 on pp. 178–179.)
- When you consider what context clue strategies to call attention to, systematically introduce each of the nine common patterns. (Refer to the guide on pp. 25–27 and Appendix 6 on p. 180.)
- Build in time at the end of the lesson for self-evaluation, lesson links, and connections to other reading and writing activities.

Day Two: *Intensifying Instruction toward Outcomes of Teaching Specific Sound Analysis Strategies and Graphophonemic Cues*

To align shared reading with shared writing, the next four days will shift toward cognitive outcomes related to word identification strategies. Each day will focus on one of four specific areas of word identification needed by early readers and writers: sound analysis, sight vocabulary, structural analysis, and context clues. Day two of the shared reading cycle is focused on specific strategies related to sound analysis or phonics to help early readers and writers. For day two, identify your expected outcomes related to sound analysis. Consider what is identified in your curriculum, but also adjust those expectations based on what sound analysis skills and strategies you know your students need. Also, reflect on what connections can be made to any sound analysis skills and strategies explored during the frontloading and initial reading of the text on day one. Remember also to make an effort to align the phonics instruction for your shared reading with the phonics instruction done during the shared writing experience. For example, if you focused on the strategy of using word analogies (i.e., making and breaking words) during the shared writing lesson, focus on using word analogies during this phase of the shared reading cycle. It doesn't have to be the same knowledge (i.e., a word family based on the common phonogram -ing) but should be the same strategy (using common phonograms in words we know to figure out other words we don't know). As you plan your lesson to focus on critical outcomes in this area, remember that the guide in Chapter One (pp. 22–23) and the reminders in Chapter Two (p. 57–61) may help you if your curricular supports are silent on sound-analysis concepts, skills, and strategies. Generally speaking, sound analysis skills and strategies for early readers and writers usually focus on one of three areas: specific sound-symbol relationships, common phonograms or rimes, and consistent vowel-consonant generalizations.

Start the lesson on day two with a quick reading of the text. As the rereading is being done, highlight words and strategies that will be the focus of sound-symbol instruction following the reading. You might model or highlight how you use sound analysis strategies to figure out a few of the words in the class book. For example, you can even intentionally insert a miscue and show how you use a sound-based strategy to cross-check and correct the miscue. Since students are familiar with the text, look for ways to invite them in on this rereading.

Once the text has been reread, move quickly into the focus for the day—systematic and explicit instruction on sound analysis. The lesson should be connected to the text of the shared reading but does not have to be limited only to that text. Other texts with samples and examples can be brought in to reinforce the instruction of sound analysis strategies in a variety of contexts. Many of the activities described for use with the shared writing experience can be modified and used during day two of the shared reading cycle. Let's look at three ways you can get more mileage out of techniques and tools used to address sound analysis concepts, skills, and strategies during the shared writing cycle to provide additional practice during the shared reading cycle.

Specific sound-symbol relationships: As you plan the lesson you will teach, consider specific sound-symbol relationships with which your early readers and writers struggle the most. Use the Sound-Symbol Strategies Record-keeping Sheet (Appendix 4, pp. 176–177) and reminders in Chapter Two (pp. 57–61) to guide your instructional decisions in this area. Many different instructional activities can be modified and used during day two of the shared reading cycle to focus on sound-symbol relationships. For example, you can modify the Sound Scavenger Hunt used to examine the shared writing classroom message (Appendix 8, p. 182) to also examine the text in shared reading. By adding an extra column, repeating the scavenger hunt with the shared reading text, and looking for additional examples of specific sound-symbol relations, patterns, or rules, you can further help students grow in their ability to use sound analysis.

Common phonograms or common rimes: Learning common phonograms or rimes with the ability to use an analogy strategy will help early readers and writers unlock more than 500 of the most common words they will encounter as they read and write. (See Figure 9 on p. 59.) These phonograms are best learned when they are taught as a part of learning an anchor word. Instead of intentionally embedding an anchor word as was done during the shared writing, in shared reading, you need to identify an anchor word already in the text that contains a common phonogram. Remember, this anchor word does not have to be the same one used during shared writing. It doesn't even have to use the same common phonogram because you are not teaching the specific phonogram or anchor word. You are teaching the strategy of using a known part of one familiar word to help you read or spell another similar word. Once an anchor word has been identified in the shared reading text, you can use the same technique used during the shared writing. In fact, replicating the technique during the shared reading instruction will help students see the connections across the two classroom experiences. Remember these steps used in making and breaking words in teaching the anchor word:

1. Isolate the anchor word from the text.
2. Create the word with magnetic letters, with letter cards, or by writing it on a whiteboard.
3. Separate the onset and rime of the anchor word.
4. Show students how to use the known part of the word to figure out new words by replacing the initial consonant sound with others.
5. Have the student copy the new words on their Making Words Grid.
6. Repeat the process with more examples with the students copying each word on their grid.
7. During independent time, students reread the words and add illustrations for each word.

Consistent vowel-consonant generalizations: The shared reading provides an opportunity to teach phonics generalizations and their exceptions. Remember, experts have pointed out that even when a rule doesn't work all the time, it will often get a student close enough to the correct word so the student can use backup strategies to figure out the right word (Stahl, 1992).

With shared writing, words needed could be intentionally embedded in the class message. With shared reading, some of the words that allow for the teaching of high-utility patterns need to be found in the text. You can certainly supplement the words in the texts with other sample and example words to set up the instruction around rules that can be used to figure out new words.

The same analytical approach used during shared writing can be used during shared reading. In fact, one of the best ways to connect the two is to keep the focus on the same generalization, pattern, or rule while adding more samples and examples from the shared reading to a list started with words generated during the shared writing. You can follow the same sequence outlined on day two of the shared writing (pp. 57–61).

Once you have completed the sound analysis instruction, end the lesson by engaging your students in a brief evaluation of their understanding of the content taught. Remind them where and how they can use the skills and strategies taught in other reading and writing contexts away from the shared reading experience. Leave the gathering space with some excitement about what the focus of instruction on day three will be: high-frequency sight words.

Reminders When Teaching Sound Analysis

- Plan the lesson with a clear focus and short length to fit within a 15-minute time frame.
- Plan the lesson with links to sound analysis skills and strategies previously introduced during the frontloading and initial reading on day one.
- Consider the expectations of your curriculum and the needs of students. Plan the lesson to allow you to explain, demonstrate, model, prompt, monitor, and/or give feedback related to sound analysis your students are still in need of instruction on, support with, or practice in. If your curriculum is silent on these strategies, consult the expectations identified by the CCSS. (Use the guide on pp. 28–29.)
- To make sure you actually address teachable moments about sound analysis, try writing reminders on small sticky notes and place these appropriately in the shared reading text so you can make sure you address those items as you read.
- Start with a rereading of the classroom message. Highlight words or strategies during this quick read to connect to the sound analysis instruction that will follow. Remember, you can invite students in using a choral or assisted reading.
- Following the reading, address the identified sound analysis instruction for this lesson. Explain, demonstrate, and model the strategies first (*I do*). Invite students in with strategic questions and prompting as you guide practice of the strategies with students (*we do*). Leave time for students to show an independent understanding of the strategy (*you do*). Be prepared to probe responses and be responsive to unexpected needs that surface.
- Involve students in the self-evaluation of their engagement and performance levels before transitioning from the shared reading experience. End with an intentional link to the next lesson in the shared reading cycle, which will focus on high-frequency sight vocabulary.
- Plan for independent work with sound analysis strategies that will allow students to practice and apply what was learned during the shared reading.

Day Three: *Intensifying Instruction toward Outcomes of Teaching Specific High-frequency Sight Vocabulary*

Like with shared writing, day three of shared reading shifts attention to sight vocabulary. The mastery of high-frequency sight vocabulary words will help students in reading and writing. On the other hand, struggling with these words in reading and writing will cause many students to quickly shut down their efforts. Day three of the shared reading cycle provides another opportunity to help early readers and writers practice specific high-frequency sight words. Review can be linked to any instruction that was introduced during the frontloading and initial reading of the text on day one or connected to the sound analysis instruction conducted on day two. Further consideration needs to be given to alignment with the instruction during shared writing. In the best case scenario, the shared reading lesson should attempt to connect to the text of the classroom message created during shared writing. Keep in mind, it may be difficult to find a shared reading text that offers practice opportunities with the same high-frequency sight words focused on during the shared writing. For example, in the lesson plans provided, even though the class poem featured in the shared reading had eight of the 25 most common sights words in its text, only two were shared by the classroom message: *and* and *the*. In fact, if you want to practice the same sight words during shared writing and shared reading, it may be easier to plan which words to embed in the shared writing message by first looking at what high-frequency sight words will be in the corresponding shared reading text. You don't have to focus on the same high-frequency sight words in the two routines, however, because the end goal is to expand the number of words in the students' sight word vocabularies. Over time, students will need to acquire as many of these words as possible.

Start with a quick reading of the text. Highlight high-frequency words that will be the focus of instruction following the reading. You might model how you use visual strategies to figure out some of the sight words in your message. You can even intentionally insert a miscue on a sight word and show how you use a visually based strategy to cross-check and correct the miscue. Teaching visual strategies is as important as teaching specific words since those strategies can be used to acquire, monitor, and repair sight vocabulary while reading and writing. Following the rereading, move quickly into the focus for the day—systematic and explicit instruction of high-frequency words. Remember, it's not just about focusing on high-frequency words. It's about working on the high-frequency words with which your students need help.

Many different instructional activities can be modified and used during day three of the shared writing cycle. Since these are words you want students to recognize on sight, focus on activities that strengthen visual recognition. For example, the numbered list suggested during shared writing will also work with shared reading. In fact, new sight words in the shared reading can actually be added to the list of sight words reviewed and practiced during shared writing. The Look-Say-Cover-Write-Check technique (Ellery, 2014) introduced with shared writing can be reviewed and used to teach new words during shared reading. Finally, you can bring together the strategies focused on day two and day three using a Sight Word and Sound Grid (Figure 10, p. 63), which can work for shared reading words like it did for shared writing words.

As early readers continue to add to their sight word vocabulary, you may want to involve them in making their own set of cards they can use for word study. Students can be handed a grid and as sight words are introduced, students can copy those words on their word grids. They can cut the words apart and place them in a small, closable plastic bag. They will have those words to use during shared reading experiences, at the guided reading table, or for independent word study activities that are done individually or with a buddy. Buddies can use their cards to play traditional games like Memory. In that game, two students put the words print-side down on the desk. Students then turn over the cards and try to find matches by revealing the words on the other side. If the words don't match, the cards get turned over and students will have to remember what they are to match with another pick. Buddies can also time each other on their words, help each other with word sorts, or come up with their own ways to review the words. Games like these help students in their ability to recognize an increasing number of words automatically on sight. To help with the management of these cards, have students place their initials on the backside of each word card, so they can quickly separate cards during word study activities. It's also easier to help a lost card find the right home if it wanders away from a student during the day.

Richardson (2009) suggests some additional activities to introduce and model during shared reading, to review during guided reading, and to provide some ways for practice when students work more independently. In Guess the Word, the teacher selects a word from the list, then starts to give clues to see if the students can guess the word. For example, the teacher says "I am thinking of a word that has four letters" and continues to give clues until students have guessed the word and confirmed that their guess is correct. The teacher can then help an individual student select a word and be a clue giver to his or her peers, so all know how to play the game away from the teacher. Another game is High Five. In this game, the teacher selects a word from the list. The students then have five chances to guess the word by asking questions (e.g., Does it have four letters?). A hand with five fingers can be used to keep track of how many chances are left. Again, after ample modeling, the teacher can help a student select a word and solicit questions from classmates. The student can learn how to respond to the questions of friends, so all can play the game away from the teacher. Look for activities to introduce and reinforce sight vocabulary in shared, guided, and individual reading situations. It is also best to model a technique that can be used by students as they work individually and with partners to grow their sight word vocabularies.

ENGAGEMENT IDEA: When playing word games during shared reading that require early readers to use word clues and make repeated guesses like High Five and Guess the Word, remember the value of using whiteboards so each child can record a guess. Instead of one or two students making a guess in the large group, all students can write down a guess. Since the words are available on an exposed list, students can copy the word from the list if they need additional support. The students can share their guesses with each other before they flash their whiteboards, which allows you to quickly survey the group for level of understanding.

EVALUATION IDEA: Create a paper trail that can be collected and reviewed when playing word games during shared reading that require early readers to use word clues and make repeated guesses, such as High Five and Guess the Word, create a Guess List. (See Appendix 14, p. 188.) By asking students to record a guess after each question is asked or a clue is given, you can see the flow of students' thinking as they try to determine the secret words. You can record the questions or clues given and then compare them to a student's list of guesses to see if they align with the help given.

Once you have completed the sight word instruction, be consistent by ending the lesson with self-evaluation of students' recognition and memory of the new words. Remind students how they can use these new words and review techniques in other contexts away from the shared reading experience, especially for individual and partner word study. Finally, build some excitement for the focus on day four of the shared reading: the use of structural analysis.

Reminders When Teaching High-frequency Sight Vocabulary

- Plan the lesson with a clear focus and short length to fit within a 15-minute time frame.
- Consider the high-frequency sight vocabulary words that have been identified by the expectations stated in your curriculum. Plan the lesson to allow you to provide maximum practice with the sight words needed by your students. If your curriculum is silent on these words, consult one of the high-frequency lists publicly available to guide you.
- Plan the lesson with intentional links to the high-frequency sight vocabulary words highlighted during the shared writing routine as well as those that surfaced more incidentally.
- Create markers with sticky notes and place them in the shared reading text, so you are reminded to call attention to the specific high-frequency words as they are used in the text. This will help you stay focused on those words.
- Start with a quick rereading of part or all of the shared reading text. Remember to invite students in with a choral reading or an assisted reading. Highlight those sight words that will be the focus of the instruction that will follow.

- Following the reading, address the identified sight words for this lesson through explicit instruction, review, and/or practice.
- Involve students in self-evaluation of their engagement and performance levels before transitioning from the shared reading experience. End with an intentional link to the next lesson in the shared reading cycle, which will focus on structural analysis strategies.
- Plan for independent work with high-frequency sight words that will allow students to practice and apply what was learned during the shared reading.

Day Four: *Intensifying Instruction toward Outcomes of Teaching Specific Structural Analysis Strategies and Syntactic Cues*

Day four of the shared reading will align with day four of the shared writing. The focus of instruction will be strategies for structural or morphemic analysis. The shared reading is another opportunity to support early readers and writers who have grown in their competency to decode shorter one- or two-syllable words and have expanded their sight word vocabularies. Focusing on structural analysis during shared reading is increasingly important for these students. They need to understand structural elements of our language to successfully negotiate demands they will encounter in reading and writing. The starting point for structural analysis instruction during shared reading should be the use of inflected endings. Early readers and writers need to handle components of English syntax related to number, tense, and comparisons. Remembering that 70 percent of all words with endings will have one of these five endings: -s, -es, -ed, -ing, or -ly. This is a "power piece" in English. If shared reading can help early readers and writers master this, they can successfully use it in negotiating syntactical demands in their reading and writing. Day four is designed to help students work on structural analysis strategies.

Shared writing does have one advantage over shared reading. Since the teacher creates the shared writing message, it is easier to embed the language needed to create a springboard for specific skill instruction. With shared reading, you will be somewhat limited to the words already in the text. Almost any shared reading text will have structural elements you can use for instruction. For example, in the class poem featured in the specific sample lessons starting on page 125, a number of structural elements are present in the words in the text. Two words use -ed to represent past tense (*curled* and *dreamed*), one uses -ing for continuous tense (*sleeping*), another uses -er as a comparative (*later*), and another adds -y to change a noun to an adjective (*fuzzy*). The poem includes a word with a prefix (*asleep*), a compound word (*butterfly*), and multisyllabic words (*caterpillar* and *chrysalis*). The poem also includes a number of words that are exceptions to rules related to tense (e.g., *spin* to *spun*, *fall* to *fell*, *can* to *could*, *wake* to *woke*, *is* to *was*). Since it would be nearly impossible to cover all of these structural elements in a single lesson, the key is focusing on one or two critical elements. Consider what the curriculum expects and what the students need in narrowing your focus.

While every text has structural elements, every text may not have the specific structural elements with which your students need the most help. Make sure that is considered in selecting the shared reading text.

You also need the shared reading text to provide instructional opportunities that will align with your shared writing instruction. Keep in mind, if you teach a specific structural analysis skill in shared writing (e.g., working on plurals), you do not need the same words in the shared reading text. You can find other words to work on plurals within the shared reading lesson. In fact, the shared reading text may not have any plural words, but as long as it has some basic root words that can be transformed into plural forms, you can still work on that skill. It helps to stay focused on instruction to teach strategies and rules that transcend specific words and can be generalized across many words. It may also help to look at the shared reading text first—especially if it is selected for you—to see what possible structural analysis skills and strategies are embedded in that text before deciding what skills and strategies to focus on with the shared writing. It's easier to embed a teachable moment in the shared writing message than to find a specific strategy in a required shared reading text. If it is too much of a stretch to align the shared reading with the shared writing, other samples can be brought in to teach the strategies. For example, in the shared reading poem featured in the specific lesson plans (p. 125), there are four common nouns: *caterpillar*, *chrysalis*, *leaf*, and *butterfly*. A lesson on turning single nouns into plural forms is somewhat limited by these choices because only one (*caterpillar*) is transformed by adding an -*s* to the end of the word. *Chrysalis* needs an -*es*, *leaf* changes the *f* to *v* and adds -*es*, and *butterfly* changes the *y* to *i* and adds -*es*. *Caterpillar* might be a good word to use in building on the lesson from the shared writing, but clearly other samples may have to come from outside the class poem.

Since the text has been read at least three times on previous days of the shared reading, you may decide to forgo an additional quick reading of the text. Perhaps all you need to do is reread a part of the text that will be important in addressing your structural analysis instruction. You may want to select part of the reading that allows you to model or highlight how you use structural analysis strategies to figure out words in the shared reading. Select a section where you might be able to intentionally insert a miscue and show the use of syntactic or structural strategies to cross-check and correct the miscue. Use words that won't sound right grammatically and need a structural change to an ending to sound grammatically correct in the sentence.

The heart of the plan for day four is the focus on systematic and explicit instruction on structural elements of words, so move toward that as quickly as possible. You can use a number of activities to support your instruction during the shared reading. For example, the techniques used during shared writing to examine strategies related to the formation of plurals (pp. 64–65) can also be used during shared reading. In fact, using the same instructional activities may help students see the connections between reading and writing. Plural Sheets (Appendix 11, p. 185) given to each student during shared writing can be used during shared reading. The enlarged version of the sheet created during shared writing can be used again during shared reading as you add words to those identified during the shared writing. You can select nouns from the shared reading text to analyze for structural elements. Use the same strategic questioning process from the shared writing to help learners classify the selected word as representing singular (1) or plural (2). Once students have reached consensus on which column it should be assigned to, they can discuss how the word can be transformed to fit the other column. Students can be invited again to find other samples and examples from their reading and writing experiences away from the shared reading experiences.

Activities like making and breaking words using structural analysis can also be used with words from the shared reading. Find a good base word that can be transformed by adding endings—especially critical inflected endings. For example, in the poem featured in the lessons starting on page 125, the word *curled* would be a good choice. The -ed can be removed to change the word into *curl*, -*s* can be added to change it into *curls*, -ing can be added to change it into *curling*, or un- can be added to change it into *uncurl*. These words can be copied by students on individual word grids. Students can add illustrations to show they understand how these changes cause subtle shifts in meaning. If this was modeled during shared writing, it should be easy to build on this during shared reading.

Once you have completed the structural analysis instruction, engage your students in a brief check of their understanding of the content taught. Be sure they can articulate how they can use structural analysis skills and strategies learned in other reading and writing contexts away from the shared reading experience. End by creating some excitement about the focus of instruction on day five: using context clues.

Reminders When Teaching Structural Analysis

- Plan the lesson with a clear focus and short length to fit within a 15-minute time frame.
- Consider structural analysis skills, techniques, and concepts that have been identified by the expectations stated in your curriculum. Plan the lesson to allow you to provide maximum practice with structural analysis strategies your students are in need of instruction on, support with, or practice in. If your curriculum is silent on these strategies, consult the expectations identified by the CCSS. (See the guide on pp. 23–25 or Figure 5 on pp. 28–29.)
- Plan the lesson with intentional links to structural analysis strategies that were highlighted during the shared writing routine.
- Plan the lesson with links to structural analysis strategies that were highlighted on previous days, including those that emerged more incidentally.
- Create instructional reminders on small sticky notes and place these in the shared reading text to keep your focus on identified structural analysis strategies.

- Start with a quick rereading of the shared reading text or an excerpt from it. Remember, you can invite students in with a choral reading or assisted reading. Highlight those words that connect to the structural analysis instruction to follow.
- Following the reading, address the identified structural analysis strategies for this lesson.
- Involve students in the self-evaluation level of their engagement and performance levels before transitioning from the shared reading experience. End with an intentional link to the next lesson in the shared reading cycle, which will focus on the use of context clues.
- Plan for independent work with structural analysis strategies that will allow students to practice and apply what was learned during the shared reading.

Day Five: *Intensifying Instruction toward Outcomes of Teaching Specific Context Clue Patterns and Strategies and Semantic and Syntactic Cues*

The final day of the shared reading cycle will focus on the use of context clues, aligning it to the final day of instruction used during the shared writing experience. The focus of instruction will be contextual analysis strategies—using the words and clues the reader knows in the text to figure out words the reader doesn't know in the text. The shared reading experience provides another opportunity to support early readers and writers as they acquire strategies to use context clues. As early readers get increasingly competent at other word-analysis strategies related to sound, sight, and structure, the ability to use contextual analysis will become more important to handle the demands of higher-level texts. Contextual analysis instruction during shared reading can begin with monitoring what is read for meaning and self-correcting as needed to make sense. The focus is on the use of semantic clues as the text is read in conjunction with other clues (visual, sound, structural, syntax). Eventually, monitoring and self-correcting strategies can evolve into the recognition and use of specific identifiable patterns to figure out the meaning of unknown words. As stated, Artley (1943) identified nine common context clue patterns in English (see pp. 25–26). This is another "power piece" in English. If shared reading can help early readers and writers add this power piece to their word-analysis repertoire, they will have one more tool to meet the semantic demands in their reading and writing. Day five of the shared reading cycle is designed to help students work on specific contextual analysis strategies.

While any shared reading text can provide a platform for teaching the use of context clues, a text that contains some difficult words presented with contextual support may provide an even better platform for teaching contextual strategies. Unlike shared writing, where these words can be embedded in a classroom message surrounded by supporting words or clues, a shared reading text must be selected to support this type of instruction. Remember, with shared reading, your instruction is usually limited to the words in the text. Some strategies, like monitoring and self-correcting, can be taught with virtually any shared reading text. You can intentionally insert a miscue and show how you use a semantic-based strategy to cross-check and correct the miscue. Try this with words that won't make sense and will require changing to a word that would make sense in the sentence. Sometimes an error like this might happen more naturally as you or the students are reading, providing a very good teachable moment. It may be trickier to model or highlight how you use context clue strategies to figure out difficult words in the shared reading text if it doesn't really contain any difficult words. It becomes even harder to model how to identify and use one of the nine common context clue patterns to figure out an unknown word unless one of those patterns exists in the text. As you try to align the lessons for shared writing and shared reading, it may be easier to look first at what can be taught and is needed by the students by using the shared reading text. Then craft the shared writing classroom message to be able to teach that same pattern. You can always bring in samples from other texts to reinforce strategies that can be used to help use context clues in other contexts.

The shared reading should be very familiar to the students by day five. Start with a quick reading of the text. Highlight any words that will be the focus of context clue instruction. Move quickly into the focus for the day—systematic and explicit instruction on context clues. Instructional activities used during the shared writing can be modified and used during day five of the shared reading cycle. Introducing cover-ups during the shared writing will make students familiar when you use them again with your shared reading. Find a section of the shared reading text that contains critical content words. Use sticky notes or masking tape to cover up selected words in that part of the shared reading. Then ask students to think of other words that would make sense and sound right in that part of the text. This technique helps early readers and writers use context clues during shared reading. Covering up words in the text and inviting students to generate other words that would make sense and sound right will enable students to practice the use of semantic and syntactic clues. Asking strategic questions as students generate new words for the sentence frame (e.g., Does that word make sense? Does that word sound right?) will remind students how to monitor their meaning making as they read and write. When you intentionally replace the blanks in the sentence frame with miscues (wrong examples) and ask the same questions, students will also learn how monitoring helps them know when meaning is not being made.

As early readers get good at monitoring and self-correcting words in context to make sense of what they are reading, the focus should include more attention toward being able to figure out unfamiliar words and their meanings. Students will need explicit instruction to help them learn the nine typical context clue patterns. As the thoughtful selection of texts allows, each of these can be taught on a systematic basis during the shared reading experience. Using a gradual release model, start by telling and/or showing how to recognize the pattern within the shared reading text. Using think-alouds, show how to use the pattern to figure out the unfamiliar word. Have additional examples ready within the text or use other texts, so students can practice with guidance how to identify and use the pattern to figure out another unfamiliar word. Prepare additional examples students can use for independent practice in the large group setting during the shared reading experience. Help students use this growing awareness of these patterns with the reading and writing they are doing away from the shared reading experience.

Since this is the end of the shared reading cycle, students should be involved in self-evaluation of the past five days. Have students discuss how they will be using any of the strategies learned during the past five days as they engage in other reading and writing activities away from the shared reading experience. End this final day of the cycle by capturing some excitement about the text shared and strategies learned. Give a preview of what the shared reading experience is going to be like during the next cycle. Do what you can do to keep the momentum gained during this cycle moving forward into the next week.

Reminders When Teaching Context Clues

- Plan the lesson with a clear focus and short length to fit within a 15-minute time frame.
- Consider contextual analysis skills, strategies, and concepts that have been identified by the expectations stated in your curriculum. Plan the lesson to allow you to provide maximum practice with contextual analysis strategies your students are in need of instruction on, support with, or practice in. If your curriculum is silent on these strategies, consult the expectations identified in the guide on pages 25–27.
- Plan the lesson with intentional links to contextual analysis strategies highlighted during the shared writing routine and with links to strategies highlighted on previous days, including those that emerged more incidentally.
- Create instructional reminders on small sticky notes and place these in the shared reading text to keep focus on identified strategies.
- Start with a quick rereading of the shared reading text or an excerpt from it. You can invite students in with a choral or assisted reading. Highlight words that will connect to the contextual analysis instruction.
- Following the reading, address the identified context clue strategies for this lesson. Decide whether you are going to focus on semantic cues, which are doable with almost any message (using a technique like cover-ups), or whether you are going to focus on one of the specific context clue patterns. The latter requires having the pattern embedded in the text of the shared reading and the preparation of additional examples for use in guided and independent practice phases within the lesson.
- Involve students in the self-evaluation level of their engagement and performance levels throughout the week. Since this is day five, self-evaluation may include looking back at the entire five-day cycle. End with an intentional link to the new shared reading with which students will be involved during the next week.
- Plan for independent work with context analysis strategies that will allow students to practice and apply what was learned during the shared reading.

Sample Week of Lessons for Shared Reading (Early Readers and Writers)

To link to the focus of spring seasonal content in the class and a similar focus in the classroom message from the shared writing experience, the text selected for this shared reading is a Capstone Engage Literacy Digital Poster featuring the poem "The Fuzzy Caterpillar" from the Engage Literacy program (EIL3, GRLC). The words of the poem are modified from the song "The Itsy Bitsy Spider." The words of the poem are as follows:

The fuzzy caterpillar
Curled up on a leaf,
Spun her little chrysalis
And then she fell asleep.
While she was sleeping,
She dreamed that she could fly,
And later when she woke up
She was a butterfly!

While students may be familiar with "The Itsy Bitsy Spider," this variation will be a new text for the class. Without a commercial Big Book version available for classroom use, a decision was made to use the digital poster and project the text so that it could be seen by all students during the shared reading experience.

Lesson Plan: *Day One*
Shared Reading (Early Readers and Writers)

1. Move students to the gathering space using name cards. "I am going to move to the gathering space. When you see me flash your last name, move quietly to the gathering space."
2. State purpose: "We are studying the season of spring and all the changes that are taking place. This week, I am going to introduce you to a new poem that is also about changes in spring. It's about a very common change that happens to one very specific animal. Help me with our Rivet. (Prepare a Rivet puzzle that can be seen by the entire group. Create lines for four puzzles for the words *caterpillar*, *chrysalis*, *leaf*, and *butterfly*. See Figure 14, p. 109.) Let's see if we can figure out what animal the poem will be about. It has 11 letters. It starts with the word *cat* (fill in *c-a-t* on puzzle one). The next part of the word is *-er*. Let's add that to *cat* (fill in *e-r* on puzzle one). Can you figure out what the word is? Keep supporting until the students guess *caterpillar*. Invite students to help you spell the rest of the word, *p-i-l-l-a-r*. The title of the poem is 'The Fuzzy Caterpillar.' Let's see if we can figure out the other three words. (Work through Rivet puzzles two through four

for *chrysalis*, *leaf*, and *butterfly*.) As we read our new poem, it will be important to remember these words. We will also learn more strategies we can use when we are trying to figure out words, both when we read and when we write. This will help us get better at both our reading and writing!"

3. Modeling and demonstrating: "Let me read the poem to you." Take the lead in reading the poem. Use a pointer as you read the poem. Seize any potential teachable moments to call attention to features of specific words, especially if you make any intended or unintended miscues as you read. Point out the words *caterpillar*, *chrysalis*, *leaf*, and *butterfly*, which surfaced in the Rivet activity, as you read them in the poem.
4. Guided practice: "Let's read it again and, this time, I want you to join me in the reading." Take the lead in guiding the rereading of the poem. Back away on lines of the poem that may be easier for the students to read and let them take the lead. Intentionally leave blanks in the rereading of the poem, especially around rhyming words and the words highlighted by the Rivet activity. Let the students orally fill in those blanks. Seize any potential teachable moments, especially if any miscues are made by students as they read.
5. Independent practice: "Let's read it one more time and, this time, I want you to do the reading." Select a student to lead the class through the reading using a pointer to pace the reading. Switch leaders for the second half of the poem. Monitor the reading of the poem. Provide support as needed. Seize any potential teachable moments, especially if any miscues are made by students during the third reading of the text.
6. Self-evaluation: Provide individual copies of the poem to students. Encourage students to practice reading the poem with partners or on their own. "Let's rate how well you worked to read the new poem today. Put your hands in your lap. If you worked your hardest, put three fingers in your lap. If you worked pretty hard today, put two fingers in your lap, and if you are going to try to work better tomorrow, put one finger in your lap. On the count of three, show me your fingers. One, two, three." Use name cards to call on students and probe why some students rated themselves that way.
7. Lesson link: "Tomorrow, we are going to use our new class poem to learn more secrets about learning words. Give a thumbs up if you will be ready for that!"

Lesson Plan: *Day Two*

Shared Reading (Early Readers and Writers)

Focus on Sound Strategies (Graphophonemic Cues)

1. Move students to the gathering space using name cards. "Let's move to the gathering space. When you hear me spell your name, move quietly to the gathering space."
2. Warm-up: "Something special about our poem that I didn't tell you yesterday is that it can actually be sung to the tune of 'The Itsy Bitsy Spider.' Let's sing the poem we read yesterday." Lead the students in the singing of the poem.
3. State the purpose: "Yesterday, I told you how we are going to use our new poem to help us learn more strategies about how to figure out words when we read and spell. What we are learning about our words in reading can help us in our writing, and what we know about words in our writing can help us with our reading. Raise your hand if you are working to get better at reading and writing. Wow!"
4. Sound work (phonogram -ell using *fell* as the anchor word): "Remember when we worked on our classroom message, we learned that knowing one word can help you figure out other words. In our classroom message, we started with the word *spring* (show the word card with *spring* on it) and learned how to make *ring*, *king*, and *sing*. (Show the words and have the students say the words with you.) Today I have another special sheet for you to use in making some more new words. Put your name at the top. (Model using a sheet that you have displayed for everyone to see in the shared reading area.) Let's practice our strategy. If you know one word, you can use the sounds and letters of part of that word to help you learn new words. We just learned this word that was in our class poem: *fell*. Let's write that in the first box of our grid. (Model.) Now watch this, boys and girls. I am going to use this part of *fell—ell—*to help me make *bell*. I have *ell*, so all I need to do is add *b* at the beginning. Now don't say it out loud, but whisper to your neighbor what letter makes that sound. Put your hand on your head if you know it. Let's use the name card to call on someone. (Spell out a name and let that student respond.) Let's add *b* to the beginning of the *ell*. Now we have *bell*. Let's write *bell* in our second box. (Model. Repeat the process to make *sell* and *shell*.) Let's check to see if we really know these words." (Display *fell*, *bell*, *sell*, and *shell*. Hold up the picture of a bell. Have students point to it on their sheet. Use a name card to select a student to clothespin it to the display word. Repeat, selecting other students and using other pictures.)
5. Self-evaluation: (Remove the picture cards.) "I am going to point to our four words, and I want you to say them in your head. Now put your hands in your lap and think about how many words you were able to

say—four, three, two, or one. On the count of three, show me your fingers. One, two, three. (Use name cards to probe why some students rated themselves that way.) When you go back to your seats, show me that you really know these words and how to use our strategy by adding an illustration to each of your four boxes."

6. Lesson link: "Remember, you can use what we learned today about using a word we know to figure out how to sound out or spell new words in your reading and writing. We learned *fell*, and we used it to help us with *bell*, *sell*, and *shell*. Tomorrow, let's use our poem to learn some more secrets about learning words, especially words we see and use over and over again. Raise a high five in the air if you will be ready for that!"

Lesson Plan: *Day Three*

Shared Reading (Early Readers and Writers)

Focus on Sight Vocabulary (Visual Cues)

1. Move students to the gathering space using last name cards. "Let's move to the gathering space. When you see your last name, move quietly to the gathering space."
2. Warm-up: "Yesterday we learned how we can sing the words of our new poem. Let's warm up our voices as we sing the poem together. Let's use the name cards to pick one student to lead us through the first part of the poem." (Switch and let another student lead the class in the second part of the poem.)
3. Review: "Yesterday, we learned how if you know one word like *fell*, you can use it to help you sound out or write other words like *bell*, *sell*, and *shell*. Or if you know another word like *spring*, you can use it to help you sound out or write other words like *king*, *ring*, and *sing*. Today when I show your name, I am going to show you one of our new words and see if you can remember it from yesterday. (Use flashcards for *spring, ring, king, sing, fell, bell, sell*, and *shell*.) Everyone can silently say the word I am showing."
4. Restate purpose: "Yesterday, you showed me what you are learning about our words in reading can help us in our writing, and how what we know about words in our writing can help us with our reading. We also learned you can use sounds from a word you know to help you figure out how to read or write a word you are still learning. Today, we will learn another secret about words that will also help us get better at reading and writing."
5. Sight word work (focus on key sight words *and, the, she, was, that*, and *on*): (Pass out individual copies of the poem in plastic pages to the students.) "Today, I want to remind you about another secret we learned about words. There are some words we see over and over again in our reading and we spell them over and over again in our writing. These words are so important that we should remember what

they look like, so we can read and spell them as fast as we can. We have some of these words in 'The Fuzzy Caterpillar.' Let's look for them in your copy, and then I will have someone use our magnifying glass to see if she can spot them in the poem projected on the screen."

[*and*] "This was one of the words we learned working on our class message. Let's see if we can find the word *and* in our class poem. *And* is used a lot in reading and writing. Can you find *and* in your poem and put your finger on *and*? Can you find another *and* in the class poem? Put your finger on that one. Let's pick someone to come up and use the magnifying glass to show us where the *and*s are in our class poem. (Use name cards.) Let's all see if she can find all the *and*s. (Probe student after finding the word.) How did you know that was *and*? Let's say the letters as we remember the word: *a-n-d, and*!"

[*the*] "This was another one of the words we learned while working on our class message. Let's see if we can find the word *the*. *The* is used a lot in reading and writing. Can you find *the* in your poem and put your finger on *the*? Let's pick someone to come up and use the magnifying glass to show us where *the* is in our class poem. (Use name cards.) Let's all see if she can find *the*. (Probe student after finding the word.) How did you know that was *the*? Let's say the letters as we remember the word: t-h-e, the!"

(Repeat process for *she, was, that,* and *on*.)

6. Self-evaluation: "Before we go today, let's see how well we have learned our sight words from our shared writing and shared reading." (Collect the individual messages and sit with students in a circle. Place flashcards with the sight words on them from both the shared writing and shared reading in the middle of the circle. Use duplicate cards as needed so flashcards match the number of students. Use name cards to call on students to find the word you say. After all have had a turn, have each student say one of the words and collect the card until all cards are used up.) "Put your hands in your lap. If you know these sight words very well, put three fingers in your lap. If you know these sight words pretty well, put two fingers in your lap, and if you know you need to work more on your sight words, put one finger in your lap. On the count of three, show me your fingers. One, two, three." (Probe why some students rated themselves that way.) "If you want to practice sight words, I will leave these cards in the gathering area, and you can play the circle game with your buddies during independent work time."
7. Lesson link: "Remember, you can use what we learned today about remembering what a word looks like to read or spell important words in your reading and writing. We learned that *and, is, it, see, the, we, she, was, that,* and *on* (show the words as you say them) are very important because we use them over and over again. Maybe when you are reading your books today, you will find some of these words. Tomorrow, we are going to use our message to learn another secret about learning words that will help us with some of our longer words. Give me a one-hand clap if you will be ready for that!"

Lesson Plan: *Day Four*

Shared Reading (Early Readers and Writers)

Focus on Structural Analysis (Inflected Endings/ Syntactical Cues)

1. Move students to the gathering space. "Let's move to the gathering space. Think about how many parts your first name has when you clap it out. If your first name has one part when you clap it out, like *Mack*, come to the gathering space. If your first name has two parts when you clap it out, like *Ellie*, come to the gathering space. If your name has three or more parts when you clap it out, like *Elizabeth*, come to the gathering space." (Check students' accuracy as they come to the gathering space.)
2. Review: "Over the past few days, boys and girls, we have been learning secrets about how to figure out words. We learned if you know one word like *spring*, you can use it to help you sound out or write other words like *ring*, *king*, and *sing*. (Show flashcards for *spring*, *ring*, *king*, and *sing*.) Or if you know one word like *fell*, you can use it to help you sound out or write other words like *bell*, *sell*, and *shell*. (Show flashcards for *fell*, *bell*, *sell*, and *shell*.) Then we learned some words are used over and over again, so if we remember what they look like, we can use those words in our reading and writing. These words include *and, is, it, see, the, we, she, was, that*, and *on*. (Show flashcards for *and, is, it, see, the, we, she, was, that*, and *on*.) Now, I have put these words on a list. (Show the list of sight words.) Let's say the sight words on the list. (Practice the words on the list in a couple different ways.) Today, when I show your name, I am going to call out a number and see if you can read the words we practiced yesterday. Everyone can silently say the word next to the number, but let your friend have the first chance to say it."
3. Restate purpose: "We keep learning how to figure out how to read or write words. Today, we will learn another secret that will also help us get better at reading and writing. Remember, we want to be the best readers and writers we can be!"
4. Reread: "Every day, it's always good to reread our class poem. It helps us get better at our words. But remember how I said our poem is based on another song, 'The Itsy Bitsy Spider.' (Show a projected version of that poem.) I am going to use my name cards to pick a helper who can use our special microphone to help us reread that old favorite poem we know. (Select a student and lead the rereading. Point out two key words from the poem, *spider* and *spout*. Capture them on notecards.) Now let's review our poem 'The Fuzzy Caterpillar.' (Show

a projected version of the poem.) I am going to use my name cards to pick another helper who can use our special microphone to help us reread our new poem." (Select another reader and lead the rereading. Point out the word *caterpillar* from the current poem. Capture it on a notecard.)

5. Structural word work (focus on singular words that can be made plural like *spider*, *spout*, and *caterpillar*): "With our shared writing, we learned that sometimes you can start with a word you know and add an ending, so the new word makes more sense and sounds better. Sometimes you can start with a word you know and take away an ending to also make a new word that makes more sense and sounds better. Let's use our special word sheet to help practice how to do that." (Pass out copies of Appendix 11 on p. 185, whiteboards, and pencils. Secure two copies of pictures of a bell, shell, caterpillar, spider, and rain spout.)

   [bell] Model how *bell* means one *bell*. Write the word under the "1" column. Have students write along with you.

   [bells] Show a picture with two or more bells. Talk about how we have to change *bell* to *bells,* so it makes more sense and sounds better. Model how to write *bell,* and add *s* to make it plural.

   (Repeat the process, turning *shell* into *shells*, *caterpillar* into *caterpillars*, *spider* into *spiders*, and *spout* into *spouts*.)

6. Self-evaluation: "Let's see if we really know these words. I will call out a word, and you put your finger on the word on your sheet. (Call out five words: *caterpillar*, *spiders*, *bell*, *shells*, and *spouts*. Monitor the students as they respond to the words called out.) Let's rate how well you worked today. Put your hands in your lap. If you figured out all five words, put five fingers in your lap. If you figured out four, put four fingers in your lap; three, if you figured out three; two, if you figured out two; and one, if you figured out one. On the count of three, show me your fingers. One, two, three!" (Probe why some students rated themselves that way.)

7. Lesson link: "Remember, you can use what we learned today about remembering how to make a word mean *one* or *two or more* when you read or spell important words in your reading and writing. When you are reading your books today, you will find some words that mean *one* and some that mean *two or more*. Tomorrow, we are going to use our message to learn how to figure out the meaning of a hard word we come across in our reading. Give me a fingernail clap if you will be ready for that!"

Lesson Plan: *Day Five*

Shared Reading (Early Readers and Writers)

Focus on Context Clues (Semantic and Syntactic Cues)

1. Move students to the gathering space: "Let's move to the gathering space. Think about how many parts your last name has when you clap it out. If your last name has three or more parts when you clap it out, like *Romano*, come to the gathering space. If your last name has two parts when you clap it out, like *Johnson*, come to the gathering space. If your last name has one part when you clap it out, like *Ford*, come to the gathering space." (Check students' accuracy as they come to the gathering space.)

2. Review (start in a circle): "This week, boys and girls, we have been learning secrets about how to figure out words. Let's see if we can use those secrets to figure out our words. First, we learned if you know one word, you can use the sounds and letters of it to figure out other words. (Move around the circle and have the first student say the word *spring*. Then move around the circle to try *ring*, *king*, and *sing*. Show flashcards for *spring*, *ring*, *king*, and *sing*. Then move around the circle to try *fell*, *bell*, *sell*, and *shell*. Show flashcards for *fell*, *bell*, *sell*, and *shell*.) Then we learned that some words are used over and over again, so if we remember what they look like, we can use those words in our reading and writing. (Continue to move around the circle, showing flashcards for *and*, *is*, *it*, *see*, *the*, *we*, *she*, *was*, *that*, and *on*.) Yesterday we learned if you know one word, you can sometimes add an ending to make it sound better and make more sense." (Move around the circle and show cards for *king*, *kings*, *ring*, *rings*, *bird*, *birds*, *flower*, *flowers*, *day*, *days*, *bell*, *bells*, *shell*, *shells*, *caterpillar*, *caterpillars*, *spider*, *spiders*, *spout*, and *spouts*.)

3. Restate purpose: "We keep learning secrets about words. These secrets help you figure out how to read or write words. Today, we will learn another secret about words that will also help us get better at reading and writing. But first, let's play our word card game to see if you really are learning your words. I will show a name card, and that person can find a word he knows. Hang on to your word." (Probe how he knew.)

4. Reread: "Let's sit in our special spots so we can reread our class poem. Every day, it's always good to reread our poem. Rereading helps us get better at our words. I am going to use my name cards to pick a helper who can use our special microphone to help us reread what we wrote." (Spell out a name to select a reader. Have him stand by the message. Lead him in rereading, and invite other students to read along.)

5. Context clue word work (focus on modeling the use of two context clue strategies—making inferences and using graphic clues): "Today, we are going to learn a new secret about words. Sometimes you can use the words around a hard word in a sentence to figure out what it

means. That is called using context clues. Let's look at this line. Read this line with me: *Spun her little chrysalis*. *Chrysalis* is a hard word. Let's use the words around *chrysalis* and see if we can figure out what it means. We know the poem is about caterpillars and it is something that a caterpillar spins. Now read this line: *And then she fell asleep*. So it must be something related to sleeping. What I am doing is using inferencing and using the words around *chrysalis* to figure out what it means."

"Now what is another way we can figure out what *chrysalis* means? (Prompt students to look for the picture clue on the digital poster.) Yes, you can use graphic or picture clues on a page to help you figure out what a hard word on the page means. So we can use two strategies to help us figure out what a hard word means. We can use the words we know around the hard word to help us think about what it might mean, and we can use picture clues on the page to also help us think about what the hard word means. Those are two context clue strategies you can use when you are trying to figure out hard words when you are reading."

(Keep in mind, since this lesson focused on modeling and demonstrating the two strategies, other lessons should focus on guided and independent practice with these two strategies.)

6. Self-evaluation: "Let's see what we have learned about words all week using our class poem. I am going to give you our poem, but it has some things missing. (See Figure 16.) Take it back to your seat, and see if you can use what you have learned about words this week to fill in the missing parts. When you have finished filling in the parts, raise your hand, and I will come and listen to you read your poem with the missing parts filled in."

Figure 16: Swiss Cheese Class Poem

________ fuzzy ________________
Curled up ________ a __eaf,
Spun her little chrysalis
________ then ________ f________ asleep.
While ________ was sleeping,
________ dreamed that ________ could fly,
________ later when ________ woke up
________ was a b________________!

7. Lesson link: "Next week, we will get to share a new class book. Until then, use the secrets we learned about words this week to help with your reading and your writing."

Final Thoughts about Intensifying Your Shared Reading Routine

In this chapter, you have looked at how to intensify your shared reading routine. Along with shared writing, this common routine has an important role to play in literacy and language arts programs for young readers and writers. I hope this chapter has provided you with ways to intensify your use of the shared reading experience to increase its power in reaching more students with what they need to help them grow as independent, strategic readers and writers. If your students are primarily emergent readers and writers, the shared reading experience can be adapted to meet their needs related to concepts of print, alphabetic knowledge, and phonemic awareness. As students grow in their competence and confidence, the same routine can be intensified to address skills and strategies related to sound-symbol relationships, high-frequency sight words, structural and morphological elements, and context clue patterns. For the early phase of reading development, a set of sequenced lessons for a five-day cycle was provided to give you insights and ideas on how to develop similar plans for your students. These ideas will help you to continue to move forward as you use an intensified shared reading routine to more effectively reach your students.

CHAPTER FOUR:
Intensifying Your Word Wall

> Many teachers have Word Walls of one kind or another but don't use them to their full advantage. It is important to distinguish between having a Word Wall and really using a Word Wall.
>
> *Janiel Wagstaff*

What Is a Word Wall?

In wondering how certain practices find their ways into elementary classrooms, Nell Duke (2014) once described what she called the "green tennis ball effect." She recalled how, virtually overnight, it seemed every elementary classroom she entered now had split green tennis balls on the bottoms of the legs of the metal chairs students used at their desks. She wondered how something you once never saw in classrooms suddenly showed up in every classroom you entered. In this case, it was someone's simple idea for reducing noisy chair movements and floor scratching. Soon, school supply catalogs were selling split tennis balls in mass quantities, ready to use and in multiple colors. That probably helped spread the idea across many schools and districts. Duke wondered whether effective teaching techniques could be disseminated in a similar fashion, impacting practice in virtually every classroom.

For educators with more than a few years of experience like me, word walls were a bit like those green tennis balls. Since the idea of word walls has been around for a while, that may surprise many current educators who have always been in classrooms with word walls. But like those green tennis balls, it seemed that, virtually overnight, every elementary classroom (and many beyond the elementary grades) had a word wall where none had previously existed. Putting words up on classroom walls for students to see and use has been advocated by many. The idea seemed to gain popular appeal when promoted more formally by Patricia Cunningham (Lynch, 2005). Cunningham (1991) talked about creating a permanent bulletin board space for a word wall and positioning this resource as a critical part of word work. After her suggestion that classroom environments should include word walls, they started showing up in most classrooms (Lynch, 2005; Ganske, 2006). They were usually organized around the alphabet with a handful of words placed under each appropriate letter on the wall. Cunningham and her colleagues (1991) popularized the use of word walls as a part of her non-ability-grouped, multilevel instruction, known to many teachers as the Four-Blocks Literacy Model. One of the four 30-minute blocks was called Working with Words. It was recommended that, in the beginning of the year, the first 10 minutes of the block be spent working with words on the word wall; as the year progressed and competencies grew, word walls would get less time (Cunningham, Hall, and Cunningham, 2000; Cunningham, 2005).

Combs (2002) described a word wall as a group word bank. Many teachers had students keep individual word banks. These were often small containers in which the student placed word cards they were working on or had learned. A word wall would serve as a similar resource. It would be a place to keep track of all the words the class was working on or had learned. One intent of the word wall is to provide a place to make important words introduced to learners accessible and visible to all, creating a resource learners can use to support their reading and writing (Blamey and Beauchat, 2016; Wagstaff, 1999). It is one of the first references young children learn to use (Pinnell & Fountas, 1998). Another, often overlooked intent of word walls is to help teachers provide a visual record of systematic word study that has taken place in their classrooms (Brabham and Villaume, 2001). Word walls are not only a resource but also a record of what words and strategies have been taught in the class.

Why Is a Word Wall a Critical Resource?

The value of the word wall as a resource is best seen within the broader context of a print-rich classroom environment. Many experts have suggested that children need a print-rich classroom (Zarrillo, 2007; Copple and Bredekamp, 2009). Hill and Ekey (2010) observed that "an authentic print-rich environment supports students in growing independence and literacy (3)." A print-rich environment can be a useful tool for helping stimulate children's literacy development as they work on understandings about letters, sounds, words, and bigger chunks of print (Morrow, 2005). Word walls need to be seen as part of an overall intentional plan for creating an authentic print-rich environment. Thinking about the word wall as one part of a print-rich classroom environment is important because the teaching and learning of words does not need to be limited to placing the word on a word wall. If the expectation is that students will be able to find and use a word in the classroom when they need it, a word wall might not be the only or even the best place to display that word.

Blamey and Beauchat (2016) told of one teacher who was trying to highlight the teaching of the specific word *alone*. After it was initially taught, it was placed near the classroom bathroom door. Not only was it seen more often, but it reminded young students that this was a space involving solo use! Similarly, others recommend the use of labels and captions throughout the room that will match common words to concrete objects (e.g., *clock* near the clock, *door* near the door). In placing these words in strategic locations beyond the word wall, they also might be seen more often and in a more meaningful context, better connecting the abstract word to a concrete object. Some, however, have cautioned that labeling everything may not be the best way to create a print-rich environment (Gerde, Goetsch, and Bingham, 2016). The print needs to be meaningful to the learners. Saunders-Smith (2009) reminds teachers of the importance in engaging students in the labeling of the classroom. She also argues that it may be more effective to use labels that are short sentences or phrases that serve as reminders instead of just words in isolation that serve as labels. The reminder *Wash your hands at the sink*! may be a more meaningful label than just the word *sink*.

Within a print-rich environment, word walls serve two important functions. First as Wagstaff (1999) said: "Word walls serve as permanent records of students' language learning (5)." She recommended four parts to the word wall. Part one is the ABC Wall, where letter-sound correspondences that have been explicitly taught are documented publicly for all to see and continue to use in analyzing new words. Part two is the Chunking Wall, where chunks and spelling patterns, especially related to common rimes and phonograms that were taught, are available to learners to use during their reading and writing. Part three, the Words We Know Wall, is focused on high-frequency sight words that have been learned. The final part is called the Help Wall, where rules about language conventions that were taught are documented. Each of these parts grows as students learn more about words. The word walls capture what they have been taught and, more importantly, what has been learned, so students could be held accountable for those concepts, skills, and strategies in their reading and writing. Often, seeing the value of the word wall as a permanent record of what has been learned is overlooked. Instead, most see the value of the word wall as a resource for teachers and learners to use—which it is—but when the word wall is built and filled with words before students even step into the classroom, one has to wonder if this is the best way to position it as a critical resource. Usually, a predetermined word wall is not the only problem in these environments. Often children walked into classrooms where teacher-created or purchased decorations cover most of the walls. Clayton and Forton (2001) observed that, sometimes, students feel like they have walked into a party store instead of a classroom. As Rose-Duckworth and Ramer (2009) ask: "[H]ow can [students] establish a sense of ownership in this environment? (95)."

What if the students encountered blank spaces when they entered a classroom and were invited by the teacher to help create an alphabetical structure for the word wall as letters are learned or reviewed? Students could even be involved in creating the letter models and visual images to match those letters. Why buy prepared alphabet charts when the students could draw the pictures of words that start with the sounds usually made by those letters (Hayes and Creange, 2001; Hill and Ekey, 2010)? As words are taught and learned, they can be added to the word wall under the appropriate letters. The word wall would grow throughout the year in front of the students and with their help. Wagstaff (1999) argued this shared ownership actually increases the effectiveness of the word wall. Brand (2004) said he learned through the years the benefit of starting with bare walls. As students inquire about the bare walls, he asks them "What do you think should go on the walls?" He shares the ownership of the classroom design with his students. One advantage of shared ownership is it should foster a greater awareness of the resource, the contents on it, and how it could be used by students to help with their reading and writing. As an added bonus, Wagstaff (1999) also observed that any outsider wondering what was taught and learned in a teacher's classroom—especially related to word concepts, skills, and strategies—would see evidence of what was taught. Over time, they would also see the word wall grow from a blank space to a space loaded with learned words and strategies.

This is how I used the word wall in my first-grade classroom. I built the alphabetical structure for the word wall and a word was only placed on the word wall when all my students had demonstrated an ability to read and spell the word accurately. Our word wall became a record of what words were known by all my students. Knowing that allowed me to hold them accountable for reading and spelling those words accurately. Cunningham (2005) also recommended holding students accountable for word wall words, especially high-frequency, irregular words, because spelling those words accurately over and over again made those words more automatic when they were encountered in reading and writing, By also including anchor words—or what Pinnell and Fountas (1998) called "exemplars"—taught to include specific letter-sound correspondences and/or spelling patterns, I also knew what words my students should have been able to spell using strategies they had been taught with those anchor words. Knowing what your students should know makes it a lot easier to find a starting point when conferring with students about editing the spelling in their writing. When trying to decide where to start, you can always begin with the words you know they should know because they are documented on the word wall (Brand, 2004). To emphasize the importance of spelling accuracy and using strategies that had been previously learned, I constructed a "word wall doghouse" that was displayed near the word wall. If one of the word wall words was spelled incorrectly in a piece of student writing, I would put a colored dot on that word. If any word received three dots, it would be moved from the word wall to the doghouse. It would stay in the doghouse until we had enough time to practice and relearn the word. Then it would move back onto the word wall chart.

Wagstaff's second rationale for word walls is they "provide ongoing support for varied language learners (1999, p. 6)." That is probably how most teachers define the value of word walls. They are a handy reference for students who are trying to decode or spell words (Gunning, 2001). Rycik (2002) suggested that word walls actually serve as visual scaffolds that provide students with a reference for words they will need for literacy activities as they transition to more independent reading and writing. These visual scaffolds would include supporting learning of high-frequency words, helping to spell unfamiliar words, developing vocabulary, making connections between words through categorization, and raising savviness about important words (Brand, 2004). The needs for visual scaffolds change, depending on the developmental level of the learners, so a teacher's purpose for word walls may change as the students change.

What Concerns Do Current Theory, Expert Opinion, and Research Raise about Word Wall Practices?

Wagstaff (1999) said, "[T]here is a difference between having a word wall and really using a word wall." Word walls need to avoid two common concerns shared by other forms of classroom print: The print is usually not meaningful to children, and the print is often not used by teachers or children (Gerde, Goetsch, and Bingham, 2016). Anyone who has visited many different classrooms can usually tell two common stories about word walls. Many times, when I visited a classroom at the beginning of the school year, I would notice the word wall was displayed and words were placed on the word wall. When I would return to that classroom, often weeks later, the word wall was still up and the same words were displayed. There was little evidence the word wall had served any purpose other than classroom decoration. On the other hand, I have visited some classrooms where the word wall structure has been built with an expectation that words would be added throughout the year. Returning to that classroom later in the year, I often saw the word wall still waiting for key words to be put on it. Wagstaff reminds us that word walls should be seen as works in progress. I am not sure a word wall structure without words is that much different from one that has a collection of words that never changes. Neither achieves the instructional intents of the word wall. It's a little like the current events bulletin board that has the same article on it in December that was placed there in September. As I have stated before, one of the most difficult things to avoid when using a class routine is for that routine to become routinized. With the word wall, it becomes routinized by being ignored and left in the background. For it to become a more critical resource, it needs to move front and center to be a dynamic, growing resource for interactive teaching and learning.

The lack of intentional interaction with the word wall as a resource is one of the major concerns voiced by many experts. Cambourne (2000) reminds teachers that you can load a classroom with literacy artifacts, but surrounding the learner with artifacts is only part of the equation. The artifacts brought into literacy programs are only valuable if students are engaged in meaningful tasks with them. In one recent study of 68 classrooms, 95 percent of those classrooms had print-rich environments, but less than five percent of the teachers used the print provided to support children's writing (Gerde, Bingham, and Pendergast, 2015). Clearly, teachers need to make more effective use of the print in their classroom environments. They need to draw students' attention to the print in the classroom to help them develop language and literacy skills (Neumann, et al., 2012). That includes word walls. Teachers need to make their word walls more interactive to intensify the engaged use of this resource (Blamey and Beauchat, 2016; Pinnell and Fountas, 1998).

Research has emerged with older learners that suggests the presence of a word wall in and of itself does not result in vocabulary gains. It is the interactive activities using the word wall that lead to growth (Harmon, et al., 2009). In this chapter, I argue that it doesn't require a lot of time to achieve that engagement. At a minimum, words posted on the word wall need to be reviewed periodically (Gunning, 2001). Allington and Cunningham (2007) recommended the use of short activities to make the word wall more interactive. They talked about teachers who used daily, five-minute activities that involved students in clapping, chanting, or writing to call attention to the words on the word wall. They also argued it is important for the teacher to intentionally model how to use the word wall to support reading and writing, referring to it to support spelling and decoding efforts during shared reading and writing activities. Wagstaff (1999) agreed and suggested teachers share quick, daily demonstrations of how to use the word wall to learn about word concepts, skills, and strategies. Like others, she also recommended the use of short word-play activities, interacting with the word wall words to call attention to the words and the resource as a whole. As Hendricks and Rinsky (2007) concluded, "Using the word wall regularly and daily with children keeps the word wall alive (77)."

INTEGRATION IDEA: Many of the best word wall activities can be thought of as "sponges." Sponges are little filler activities teachers can use repeatedly with very little preparation to actively engage students in using literacy and/or language skills to fill a few minutes of downtime (transitions back to class, waiting for a guest speaker, standing in line while another class goes by, etc.). Sponges help teachers "soak up" in a productive way those limited moments of time that often surface in classrooms. Sponges are designed to maximize the value of those moments instead of letting those minutes pass unused. A repertoire of interactive word wall activities can be used as sponges throughout the day when these moments arise. The best sponges require minimal preparation, so they can be done at the drop of a hat. They engage all learners in thinking more deeply about literacy concepts and strategies. Sponges can be reused in a variety of ways. Remember, underutilizing five minutes during the day may not seem like a lot on that day, but it adds up to 900 minutes for the year if that happens every day. Slipping in a sponge curbs that erosion.

Wagstaff (1999) cautions that word walls should not be created in isolation of other reading and writing activities. This seems to be one concern it has in common with shared writing and shared reading—the limited amount of integration of each routine with other aspects of the classroom program. In this chapter, one of the arguments I make is for the need to align the word wall with shared writing and reading instruction. Shared reading and writing should be sources for words added to the word wall. The word wall should be referred to during the shared reading and writing experiences. Instruction during shared reading and writing should be reviewed with systematic visits to the word wall. All of these activities should also be integrated with other aspects of the classroom program. The word wall can be a resource used to connect words and strategies taught in guided reading sessions. Even more importantly, the word wall should be a reference students seek out to support their independent reading and writing. Wagstaff (1999) observed that "[t]he part often missing is constant real application—using the Walls in everyday reading and writing. Daily modeling is the key (p. x)." All of these elements are stronger when they are linked together, showing students the connections between different parts of their literacy and language arts program.

INTEGRATION IDEA: Blamey and Beauchat (2016) recommend an idea from one of the teachers with whom they worked. Words that were taught in a classroom were not only placed on the word wall but were actually made into books that could be used during shared reading, guided reading, and independent reading times. Words can be recorded on sheets, placed in plastic pages, and collected in binders for quick reviews during other contexts with the teacher or left available for students to read more independently. By placing the words in plastic pages, words can be marked up to call attention to specific features and then quickly cleaned up for future use. More words can be easily added as introduced, or retired and removed when mastered.

One way to improve the use of word walls is with targeted classroom visits. Allington and Cunningham (2007) talked about one school where small groups of teachers would visit a classroom in which the teacher had insights and ideas on how to make the word wall a more interactive routine. The groups of teachers would be encouraged to attempt similar ideas in their classrooms to enhance the use of their word walls. Additional teachers would visit those classrooms and grab new insights and ideas until the use of the word wall as an effective interactive routine was more pervasive throughout the school.

How Is a Word Wall Intensified for Emergent Readers and Writers?

What if the word wall for emergent readers and writers became the focus of an additional intensive reading experience (Combs, 2002)? What if it was treated like the texts in the shared writing and reading and revisited over an extended period of time? Like the other classroom routines discussed in this book, this would be one way to intensify the use of the word wall with emergent readers and writers. Revisiting the word wall as a resource will lead young writers and readers to add to their new understandings about print. It can be aligned with shared writing and reading for emergent students. It can involve systematic, explicit instruction in the large group setting, focused on the same three critical outcomes: concepts of print, alphabetic knowledge, and phonological/phonemic awareness. To reinforce the academic language used during the shared writing and reading, it will also be used in word wall activities to further help emergent students make connections between reading and writing. As appropriate, word wall activities will incorporate a gradual release of responsibility to provide direct explanation, demonstrating, modeling, guided practice, and monitored independent practice. Like others who have written about word walls (Cunningham, Hall, and Cunningham, 2000; Rog, 2003), a regular sequence of short lessons will be used, so it can parallel what is done during the shared writing and reading experiences, especially on days three, four, and five of the shared reading and shared writing cycles. Instructional activities will be introduced and modeled that can also be used in small group settings, such as guided reading, or left available for students to use more independently. Keep in mind the sequence that is described in this section is just one way to intensify the use of the word wall for emergent readers and writers. Always feel free to adapt or modify these ideas to better meet the needs of your students as they try to achieve these critical skills and strategies.

What type of word walls may be most appropriate for emergent readers and writers?

Names: The best word walls will contain words or phrases that support instruction related to concepts of print, alphabetic knowledge, and phonological/phonemic awareness strategies. One starting point is a word wall based on names. Many experts recommend starting a word wall with the names of students (Cunningham, 2005). For many students, their name will be one of the words they recognize first. Often the names of friends, which are also visible around the classroom in multiple locations for multiple purposes, are quickly picked up as well (Zarrillo, 2007; Gerde, Goetsch, and Bingham, 2016). Last names can be added as first names are mastered and used for additional instruction about sounds, letters, words, and other aspects of print (Wagstaff, 1999; Rycik and Rycik, 2007). Other important proper nouns, like the names of other significant adults in the school, as well as the name of the school, town, and state, can be added since students may want to use these early on in their writings. Be sure to inventory the names on the word wall, so you know which alphabetic and phonological concepts can be addressed using the posted names. Check the letters in names to see what letters can be easily reinforced using the word wall. Consider what names lend themselves to clear auditory analysis in isolating, identifying, or manipulating sounds.

INTEGRATION IDEA: Gerde and her colleagues (2016) identified 10 different locations for using student names in meaningful ways in a print-rich environment. Some suggestions are usually available in most classrooms, such as labels for cubbies, name tags for center assignments, names on an attendance chart, or assigning names on the classroom job chart. Other ideas might include using name markers to show preferences on classroom graphs, placing names of student authors on contributed pages in class books, passing out personalized student notebooks to allow others to see names repeatedly, and checking off names on class record-keeping charts when completing classroom routines. These experts even recommend creating a class reflection chart for students to post daily reflections labeled with their names. Leaving name cards as resources in a writing center is another idea suggested, but in this book, I talk about the use of name cards as an engagement tool that would also give students repeated exposure to friends' names before they might be placed on a word wall or left in a center.

Environmental print: Another source of words that can be used on word walls with emergent readers and writers is environmental print. Zarrillo (2007) argues for the importance of bringing environmental print into the classroom, especially for emergent readers and writers. Environmental print is words and phrases usually encountered in daily life. These words and phrases are among the first recognized by young children. Think about the quick recognition of *stop* on a stop sign or fast food restaurant names on bags. The consistent graphic presentation of the word is almost always seen in a meaningful context, making it easier to recognize the word. These can be starting points for noticing features about words and letters. Environmental print placed on word walls can also be duplicated in class-made books based on categories like foods or signs (Combs, 2002). The use of environmental print can also go beyond the outcomes for emergent readers and writers. Cunningham (2000) developed a game called Brand Name Phonics, in which a recognizable brand name, such as *Crest*, could be used as an anchor word for using analogies to figure out other words in the word family like *best*, *rest* and *test*. To make sure the environmental print used is culturally relevant across children, solicit samples and examples from all families (Gerde, Goetsch, and Bingham, 2016). As with the names, inventory the environmental print posted to also stay aware of which alphabetic and phonological concepts can be addressed using those words. Knowing what specific concepts, skills, or strategies you need to teach, you may need to find and add environmental print that is more useful when teaching needed letters or working on phonemic awareness strategies.

Words with pictures: Another way to build a word wall for emergent readers and writers is to combine words with pictures. Wasik and Bond (2001) recommend pairing graphic illustrations that match the content of new words introduced to young learners. When a word is placed on a word wall, the picture provides a visual reminder of the word away from the initial introduction to the word. While that may seem like an activity for younger learners, Harmon and her colleagues (2009) found it to be one interactive technique that enhanced vocabulary learning in middle school learners as well. Hiebert (2014) observed connecting written words to concrete objects through illustrations was especially useful for English language learners and students of poverty. Again, be very intentional in selecting the words you will introduce. Add words so you have what you need for subsequent alphabetic and phonological awareness instruction. In using words with pictures on your word wall, create them so they can be separated. Eventually, you want to remove the picture clues so emergent readers and writers focus more on the print features of those words. That allows you to set up matching games in which students can show their understanding of the words in isolation by matching them to their corresponding pictures. For building a word wall with pictures, Hiebert's TextProject Word Pictures may be a very valuable resource since it makes available "a vault of carefully chosen pictures to assist educators in making such connections (2014, p. 18)."

What other considerations should be given to word walls for emergent readers and writers?

If students are going learn from the word wall, the words must be visible and accessible to all. This can be difficult because the space required for a well-developed word wall may not be available in all classrooms. In some schools, teachers are even limited by how many things can be hung on the walls or where things can be placed in creating a print-rich environment. Hanging from ceilings or covering windows may not always be an option in some facilities. In one school, teachers reminded me that their building policy, in accordance with local fire codes, limited paper coverage of walls to 20 percent of their classrooms. On the other hand, even when space is available, it might not be the best. Many word walls occupy a space between the top of the whiteboard and the ceiling—a space almost never in the field of vision for a young child. Word walls work best when those that need them the most can walk right up to them and use them as a resource. It helps to locate the word wall, so a child is able to bring his or her notebook right up to the word wall and copy a needed word instead of having to constantly look up toward the ceiling to transfer a word to the paper below. Teachers may need to get creative in finding a space for a word wall that is visible to all. Cunningham (1995) suggested creating word walls on trifold display boards, like those used to present projects. The trifold can be placed so it is seen by all, but it is also portable, so it can be easily moved to provide greater access to a group of students when needed. It can also be easily stored when the teacher needs to reclaim space for other activities. Others encourage the use of individual word wall resources. Cunningham (1995) also suggested word walls can be replicated on manila file folders and used by students more independently. Similarly, Routman (2000) recommended individual word wall sheets be pasted to the back of reading and writing notebooks students are using. These word walls can contain words introduced in class but can also be personalized (Gunning, 2001).

Another consideration related to visibility and access is the practicality of using the resource. Word walls with permanently affixed words limit the potential use of that resource. Word walls can offer more instructional opportunities if the words are affixed in less permanent ways. Some teachers have found success by creating letter/sound labels with a Velcro tail. Individual words on cards would be made with a Velcro patch on the back. This allows the words to be appropriately placed on the word wall but also provides flexibility to move the words as needed. With an accessible, changeable word wall, students can even borrow a word they need and return it later. If the word wall is on a metal surface, the words can be created with magnetic tags and offer the same advantages in terms of practical use. If modifications like these are difficult to create, some teachers who use a more permanent placement of words on the word wall also attach manila envelopes or plastic pockets under each letter that contain duplicates of the words on the wall for students to take and use (Wagstaff, 1999).

Reminders When Using Word Walls with Emergent Readers and Writers

- Find a space for the word wall that is within the field of vision and reach of young learners. Create it so it facilitates interaction with the posted words.
- Involve your students in the creating of the word wall, especially the alphabetic structure.
- Introduce words to your students before placing them on the wall. Consider your word wall a record of what words your students know or can figure out.
- Start with words that are easily recognizable like student names and environmental print. When other new words are introduced, place them on the word wall with a visual graphic next to them to help students remember them.
- Use your word wall on a daily basis for short periods. Look for sponge activities that can be done with the word wall words, so you can productively fill small moments that surface throughout the day.
- When you are using your word wall for systematic, explicit instruction; plan your lessons with a clear focus and short length not to exceed 10 minutes.
- When introducing and reviewing word wall activities, start with teacher explanation, demonstration, and modeling (*I do*). Then move to guided practice with you taking the lead initially but allowing students to gradually take over with your support. Use teacher prompts and strategic questions to allow students to show you what they have learned (*we do*). End by looking for opportunities to invite students to take over the activities and show you what they know and are learning. This allows you a chance to observe, monitor, and provide feedback while you are all together in the large group (*you do*).
- When selecting a focus for word wall activities, consider connections you can make to cognitive outcomes and expectations (concepts of print, alphabetic knowledge, and phonological/phonemic awareness) to review concepts and strategies aligned with shared writing and shared reading instruction. Plan the word wall lessons to allow you to provide additional practice with concepts, skills, and strategies your students are in need of instruction on, support with, or practice in. If your curriculum is silent on these strategies, consult the expectations identified in the guide on pages 18–22.
- When reinforcing concepts of print with your word wall, remember to use activities that include the academic language introduced during shared writing and reading. Word walls are a good place to review strategies used during shared writing and reading, like counting words, counting letters, comparing lengths of words, tallying frequency of letters, looking for differences and similarities in print features in words, and classifying and categorizing words according to print features. One easy sponge for use with a word wall is Word Wall Yahtzee. Roll a die or dice and find a word on the word wall that has that many letters (Rog, 2003).

- When reinforcing alphabetic knowledge with your word wall, remember to use activities that include looking for differences and similarities in words according to their letter features and classifying and categorizing words according to letter features. One easy sponge for use with a word wall is a scavenger hunt for specific letters: "I'm thinking of a word that starts with an *f* and ends with an *e*. It has four letters and an *i* in the middle. It also has an *r*."
- When reinforcing phonological—including phonemic—awareness strategies with your word wall, remember you can use activities that were used during shared writing and reading, including Secret Word Boxes, Turtle Talk, Blenders, and Transformers games. (See p. 49–50.)
- During word wall activities, be responsive and follow appropriate leads from students that may surface additional instructional opportunities for concepts of print, alphabetic knowledge, and phonological/phonemic awareness strategies, which haven't been planned. Record those moments to help reflection for future lessons.
- Model word wall activities that can be done by students independently during their independent work time.
- Always point out intentional links from the word wall to the reading and writing with which students will be involved. Show how the word wall can be used as a resource during shared writing and reading. Assist in the use of the word wall when guiding and conferring with students in small groups or individually.

How Is a Word Wall Intensified for Early Readers and Writers?

The word wall for early readers and writers should also be seen as an intensive reading experience (Combs, 2002). The word wall routine will be structured with a five-day cycle. It will be revisited each day with a slightly different lens so it can support the connected study of word identification strategies focused on during the shared writing and reading lessons. Like repeated visits to the classroom message and the class book, repeated visits to the word wall will help early readers and writers discover new things about words posted there. Word wall instruction will also be planned as systematic, explicit instruction for the large group. Whenever possible, the instructional activities used with the word wall should be planned using a gradual release model with demonstrations, modeling, guided practice, and monitored independent practice. The activities should be relatively short, requiring less than 10 minutes. Activities will be planned to support instruction for each day of the cycle so they can parallel what is done during the shared writing and reading experiences. They will focus on critical outcomes related to word-analysis strategies: sound analysis (phonics), high-frequency sight words, structural or morphemic analysis, and the use of context clues. Academic language used during shared writing and reading will also be used with the word wall activities to continue to help early readers and writers make important connections between reading and writing. As appropriate, word wall activities should adapt the instructional techniques modeled and used during the shared writing and reading experiences. Instructional activities should also give consideration to activities that can be left for students to do independently, following the large group lessons. The sequence described in the next section is one vision of how to intensify the use of the word wall and align it with the shared writing and reading experiences for early readers and writers. The presented sequence can be adapted or modified to better help students achieve these critical word-analysis outcomes.

What type of word walls may be most appropriate for emergent readers and writers?

Words selected for the word wall should be developmentally appropriate and based on student needs (Wagstaff, 1999). The previous sources of words for word walls for emergent readers and writers (names, environmental print, and words with pictures) may still be appropriate for use with early readers and writers. As those words are mastered by learners, however, they might be retired from the word wall to make room for new words used in instruction. Experts recommend keeping the word wall simple and uncluttered (Wagstaff, 1999; Ganske, 2006). Retired words can be left near the word wall in portable containers, like library pockets, so they can still be accessed if needed (Wagstaff, 1999; McCarrier, Pinnell, and Fountas, 2000). Wagstaff (1999) reminds teachers to be intentional about the words selected to put on the word wall. The word wall needs to become a resource for sound analysis, high-frequency sight words, structural analysis, and context clues. These word-analysis strategies are critical outcomes for early readers and writers. Therefore, the word wall needs to be built to provide opportunities for instruction in those areas.

Sound-symbol relationships: A word wall that supports sound analysis or phonics instruction needs three key components. The first component is matching alphabet letters to their typical sound-symbol relationships. A word wall organized by the alphabet with visual images matching the typical initial sound made by that letter may help early readers and writers with these critical sound-symbol relationships. If words with pictures are being used, effort should be made to introduce each critical sound with an anchor word. It is helpful if the word represents a fairly concrete concept by which the pronunciation of the word has a clean, clear representation of the sound in the initial position. Eventually, anchor words with those sounds in middle and final positions can be taught and added to the word wall. While there are only 26 letters and 44 phonemes, there are more than 200 letter-sound combinations in English (Dow and Baer, 2012). Narrow your word wall words to focus on the most common sound-symbol relationships early readers and writers will encounter in their reading and writing.

Phonograms: The second key component for sound analysis is phonograms. As previously discussed, the 37 common phonograms will help early readers and writers unlock 500 of the most common words they will need for early reading and writing. A word wall for early readers and writers would incorporate common rimes and phonograms. Anchor words for each of the common phonograms would be introduced and added to a traditionally organized word wall. These anchor words should represent concrete meanings and contain the most regular spellings of those phonograms. Some have called this building a "chunking wall" (Wagstaff, 1999; Rycik and Rycik, 2007; Rog, 2003), in addition to or as an alternative to the traditional word wall. McKenna (2002) suggests word walls could actually be organized around the rime families. It may be difficult to have both a traditional word wall and a chunking wall. If the anchor words are on the word wall, word families built on phonograms might be developed on separate sheets of chart paper. In my first-grade classroom, we made these charts and attached them to hangers. We had a small, self-standing hanging rod, where the charts could be stored, pulled out, and displayed for instruction and selected when needed by students to support their reading and writing. Anchor words and word families should help support instruction about how to use word analogies to analyze and spell words more independently.

Generalizations: The third key component is generalizations. To teach the basic common consonant-vowel patterns, anchor words or exemplars that represent common vowel patterns should be introduced and added to the word wall. As previously identified, these anchor words would identify short vowel patterns like VC and CVC. Anchors words would also be taught to teach long vowel patterns like CV, VCe, and VV. Generalizations about other sound-symbol relations might also be addressed through exemplars, like distinguishing patterns for hard and soft /c/ and /g/ or different sounds for /y/. Since many of these patterns or generalizations have exceptions, words that follow the rules might be color coded one way and those that don't another way (Cunningham, 2005).

High-frequency sight words: In addition to sound analysis, the word wall for early readers and writers needs to address high-frequency sight vocabulary. Initial suggestions for word walls argued for the use of word walls to display high-frequency sight vocabulary words that students will use repeatedly in their reading and writing (Allington and Cunningham, 2007; Brand, 2004; Rycik, 2002). Hiebert (2011) reminds teachers, "relatively few words in English account for a majority of the total words that are read in text. In English, approximately 100 words account for almost 50 percent of the total words in text, and approximately 5,500 words account for 80 percent of the total words (p. x)." Many of these are also irregularly spelled words and frequently misspelled by young learners. These include words like *they*, *were*, *friend*, *from*, and *said*. Making words like these visible and accessible on the word wall will help students grow increasingly competent with these words. This is especially true if the teacher calls attention to the words on the wall with interactive practice activities. Rog (2004) described one interactive activity to call attention to these words. She suggested students should choose one or two of the high-frequency words from the word wall, grab a section of a newspaper, and circle every time they see the word. This will also help students see the words within the context of sentences and phrases.

As Saunders-Smith (2009) reminded teachers, the "true power of sight words is realized in a greater context (p. 29)." She would agree with Cunningham (2005), who suggests building meaning for high-frequency words by including them in phrases. *Of* makes more sense when it is presented in phrases like *a piece of cake*, *a box of cookies*, and *a bowl of soup*. In his book, *The Fluent Reader*, Rasinski (2003) actually provides lists of useful phrases based on 300 of the most common words in English. These phrases could be recorded and added to word walls.

Structural analysis: If the word wall is to become a useful resource for early readers and writers who are becoming increasingly competent with easy-to-decode words and high-frequency sight vocabulary words, it needs to also include anchor words and exemplars to teach about structural or morphemic analysis. This starts by addressing the inflected endings (-s, -es, -ed, -ing, -ly, -er, -est) early readers and writers will encounter and need in their reading and writing. In looking at the inflected endings in particular, the easiest way to include these on the word wall is to look for base words already on the word wall. Once the base word is on the word wall, inflected endings can be added to the base word and also placed on the word wall. When these words are linked, students can see how to build a structural word family (*bug, bugs, bugged, bugging*), much like how phonograms were used to build sound-based word families (*bug, mug, tug, rug, hug*). It is important to remember that adding inflected endings can result in variations, impacting the spelling and pronunciation of base words. For example, with tense, sometimes you just add the inflected ending, sometimes you have to double the final consonant before adding the inflected ending, and sometimes you have to drop the final -e before adding the inflected ending. It would be helpful to have exemplars that show all three of the spelling rules so students can start to see patterns across the words as they theorize what they need to do and when they need to do it. These exemplars can even be color coded to call attention to the patterns. Remember, there are also many exceptions to these rules, so noting or adding exceptions on the word wall will support structural analysis instruction. Creating these exceptions in a different color might be helpful for students. Other exemplar words with structural elements that early readers and writers will need, like contractions and compounds, can also be added to word walls to support instruction. A final area of need to address related to structural analysis is the use of syllabication strategies to help early readers and writers pronounce and determine the meanings of longer words. Exemplar words that show basic patterns of syllabication division can be introduced and added to the word wall. These might be based on the teaching of the CLOVER strategies discussed on the next page. Once basic structural elements like these are mastered by students, increasingly sophisticated structural elements can be addressed through the word wall, like words with prefixes and derivational suffixes or families based on Greek and Latin roots.

ENGAGEMENT IDEA: Jill Hoda (2016) from the Mississippi Office of Elementary Education and Reading shared a way to generate a little more interest in learning about syllable types. Since this topic may not be inherently interesting to young learners, anything we can do to raise their level of interest may lead to more engagement in learning these important concepts. Using the CLOVER acronym to teach syllable types, Hoda suggested each of the syllable types could be linked to a kind of candy with which most children would be familiar. You could adapt this to honor healthier alternatives, like fruits or vegetables. The following might be appropriate connections:

C =	closed syllable	= plum
L =	CLe syllable	= apple
O =	open syllable	= coconut
V =	vowel team	= green beans
E =	silent E	= grape
R =	R-controlled vowel	= corn

The word wall would be a good location to place environmental print from grocery ads and food labels representing each of the syllable types.

Contextual analysis: Since the use of context clues often involves the use of surrounding words and clues, isolated words on a word wall may not be the best place to review and reinforce these strategies. The exception might be three types of words that need context in order to determine their meanings, spellings, and/or pronunciations. Placing some of these words on the word wall may give you instructional opportunities to show the importance of contextual analysis. First are multiple-meaning words. These are words that are spelled and pronounced the same but have potentially different meanings. Think of words like *run*, *duck*, or *park*. Very few words have a solitary definition, so context will be needed to determine which meaning is appropriate in a given phrase, sentence, or longer piece of text. These words are often called homographs. Within the group of homographs, there are many that are spelled the same but pronounced differently. The 10 most common in English are *use*, *number*, *live*, *does*, *read*, *house*, *close*, *wind*, *lead*, and *row*. Second are words that are pronounced the same but have different spellings and meanings. Context is needed to determine which meaning is needed before knowing which spelling is appropriate. These words are called homophones. Some of the most easily confused homophones in English include *hear/here*, *buy/by/bye*, *there/they're/their*, *to/too/two*, *your/you're*, *bear/bare*, *one/won*, and *break/brake*. The third category is unfamiliar words. The word wall should occasionally include a couple of unfamiliar words. These can be used as starting points. Once students have figured out their meanings, they can place them in sentences and phrases to provide a meaningful context.

Let's remember the word walls previously described have often focused on a single feature of a word. Any word can be explored in multiple dimensions at one time. In *Exceptional Expressions for Everyday Events*, Folkins and Hiebert (2011) select everyday "events" (e.g., *listen*, *talk*, *look*) and explore multiple aspects of those words, creating a comprehensive word web for each of those. The base everyday event is explored in terms of its multiple meanings with connected synonyms, idioms that use the word, common phrases including the word, inflected endings attached to the word, derivational suffixes attached to the word, compounds involving the word, and even cognate connections to other languages, especially Spanish.

INTEGRATION IDEA: Readers may have noticed references to the work of Elfrieda Hiebert in these discussions of vocabulary. Hiebert's TextProject website is promoted as "strategies, tools, and texts to bring beginning readers and struggling readers up to high levels of literacy." Much of the thinking about vocabulary in this section of the book has been informed by the recent work of Hiebert's. Educators can access all of that professional information without cost to inform curricular decisions about vocabulary instruction at the local level. The website also includes instructional materials (like the word picture cards previously discussed) and lesson plans for teaching things like the Everyday Expressions described above. Teachers may appreciate freely accessible texts that can be used in instructional contexts, including short informational texts written more like magazine articles in her "FYI for Kids" section. It's the kind of website that offers many insights, ideas, and resources for integrating reading instruction across content areas.

What other considerations should be given to word walls for early readers and writers?

Many of the considerations for word walls discussed for emergent readers and writers are still important for early readers and writers. The word walls must be visible and accessible to all.

Word walls work best when students can walk right up to them when they need to use them. They will offer more instructional opportunities if the words are affixed in less permanent ways. The use of portable, trifold word walls and individual word wall resources (Cunningham, 1995) may work even better with early readers and writers who are growing in their understandings about words. Additional resources, like commercially available word books, may be another way to give early readers and writers easy access to words they need for their reading and writing. These resources often include alphabetical lists of commonly used high-frequency sight words but also have spaces to record additional words that have been collectively learned by the class or the student needs for individual, personal use.

One additional concern for word walls with early reading and writing is the potential for clutter that actually may interfere with the effective use of the resource. If the word wall takes on too many words too quickly, it may be overwhelming for some students to use. As the growth of early readers and writers takes off, it may not be possible to keep track on the word wall of every word taught. The focus of the word wall may shift more to capturing anchor words and exemplars so students can use them to figure out every word. In other words, the word wall may not need to contain every word that can be made using the phonogram -ight as long as a few anchor words are available to help spell another word with -ight in it. The word wall might not contain every base word transformed into past tense as long as a few anchor words show how adding -ed to a word changes the spelling and/or pronunciation of words. Some additional spaces may need to be created to store words previously introduced to students. As was described before, word families may be placed on chart paper and stored on hangers until needed. Similarly, the individual commercial word books described above provide students access to many common words that can eventually be retired from the word wall.

Reminders When Using Word Walls with Early Readers and Writers

- Find a space for the word wall that is within the field of vision and reach of young learners. Create it so it facilitates interaction with the posted words.
- Involve your students in the creation of the word wall, especially the alphabetic structure.
- Introduce words to your students before placing them on the wall. Initially, use your word wall as a record of what words your students know or can figure out. As words or strategies become more automatic across students, some words can be retired to make room for others. This avoids making the word wall too cluttered for effective use.
- Introduce words that serve as key anchor words or exemplars for sound-symbol relationships, phonograms, and phonics generalizations. To guide decisions in these areas, consider the expectations of your local curriculum. If your curriculum is silent on these outcomes, consult the guide on pages 22–23. Activities related to graphophonemic strategies can include those also used during the shared writing and reading, like secret word boxes, classifying and categorizing words according to sound-symbol patterns, analytical phonics lessons, and building sound-based word families using an anchor word from the wall. Adapt sponges used for other skills, like the scavenger hunt, but this time for specific sounds ("I'm thinking of a word that starts with the blend /tr/, ends with the sound /k/, and has a short /u/ in the middle. What's the word wall word? *Truck*!")
- Add words that are high-frequency sight words for early readers and writers. To guide decisions about these words, consider expectations from your local curriculum. If your curriculum is silent on these expectations, consult any readily available, high-frequency sight word list. Activities related to sight words can include those used during the shared reading and writing, including classifying and categorizing

according to visual features and changing words by changing their letters. The scavenger hunt sponge for sight words should focus on visual patterns ("I'm thinking of a word that looks like *the* in the beginning and *where* at the end. What's the word wall word? *There*!").

- Transform base words already on your word wall as anchor words or exemplars for structural analysis. Start with inflected endings. Create words that show the variations in how adding the endings affects spellings or pronunciations. Later, consider how words with common suffixes and prefixes can be added to your word wall. Use exemplars to also address contractions, compounds, and syllable types. To guide decisions in these areas, consider the expectations of your local curriculum. If your curriculum is silent on these outcomes, consult the guide on pages 23–24. Activities for structural analysis could include changing words by changing structural elements, classifying and categorizing words according to structural elements, using analytical structural lessons, and building structural word families by adding structural elements to a base word. Think about how to adapt word activities through a structural lens like the scavenger hunt sponge ("I'm thinking of a word that has an -ing ending. I had to double the final /m/ to add the end. What's my word wall word? *Swimming*!").
- Add words that will lend themselves to instruction about the importance of using contextual analysis. Adding common homophones and homographs to the word wall allows for activities using context to figure out the meaning, pronunciation, and/or spelling of these words. Include a few unfamiliar new words to the word wall that, once learned, students can create meaningful contexts around those words. Activities can include cloze or Swiss cheese sentences, where students have to select words from the word wall that would make sense. These are especially useful for sorting out homophones. Creating sentences to contextualize words on the word wall can be used to sort out homographs and surround a new, less familiar word with a sentence that reveals its meaning. A scavenger hunt could focus on specific semantic connections ("I'm thinking of a word that means the same as ..." or "I'm thinking of a word that is the opposite of ..."). Word wall words can be classified and categorized according to semantic features ("Let's find all the word wall words that are living things.")
- Use your word wall on a daily basis for short periods. Look for sponge activities with the word wall words so you can productively fill small moments that surface throughout the day.
- When you are using your word wall for systematic, explicit instruction, plan your lessons with a clear focus and short length, not to exceed 10 minutes.
- When introducing and reviewing word wall activities, start with teacher explanation, demonstration, and modeling (*I do*). Then move to guided practice with you taking the lead initially but allowing students to gradually take over with your support. Use teacher prompts and strategic questions to allow students to show you what they have learned (*we do*). End by looking for opportunities to invite students to take over the activities and show you what they know and are learning. This allows you a chance to observe, monitor, and provide feedback while you are all together in the large group (*you do*).

- When selecting a focus of word wall activities, consider connections you can make to cognitive outcomes and expectations (sound analysis, sight words, structural analysis, and contextual analysis) to review concepts and strategies aligned with shared writing and shared reading instruction. Plan the word wall lessons to allow you to provide additional practice with concepts, skills, and strategies your students are in need of instruction on, support with, or practice in. If your curriculum is silent on these strategies, consult the expectations identified in the guide on pages 22–29.
- During word wall activities, be responsive and follow appropriate leads from students that may surface additional instructional opportunities for sound analysis, sight words, structural analysis, and contextual analysis strategies that haven't been planned. Record those moments to help reflection for future lessons.
- Model word wall activities that can be done by students during their independent work time.
- Always point out intentional links from the word wall to the reading and writing with which students will be involved. Show how the word wall can be used as a resource during shared writing and reading. Assist in the use of the word wall when guiding and conferring with students in small groups or individually.

Sample Week of Lessons for the Word Wall (Early Readers and Writers)

Lesson Plan: *Day One*

Word Wall (Early Readers and Writers)

As we saw with the first lesson in the emergent readers and writers, the first day of the five-day cycles for shared writing and shared reading with early readers and writers is focused on preparing, writing, and reading texts. These lessons are usually focused beyond the word level, making alignment with the word wall more difficult. So day one of the word wall lessons would again be used for one of two activities. Day one could be used to review any aspect of word strategies previously introduced and related to sound analysis, sight words, structural analysis, and/or context clues. This might be a perfect day to do activities that involve the use of a combination of these strategies related to sound, sight, structure, and context. These review activities can be short sponge activities done when time allows during the day. It could also be a time for a more structured, explicit lesson to reteach something previously taught but still in need of review by the students. Day one can also be used to show how a challenging moment during the shared reading and writing was solved with the use of strategies related to sound, sight, structure, and context. That provides a natural opportunity to link to the word wall and show how it can be used as a resource to help address challenges in words when reading and writing.

Lesson Plan: *Day Two*

Word Wall (Early Readers and Writers)

Focus on Sound Strategies (Graphophonemic Cues)

1. Restate the purpose: "Today, with our classroom message and class poem, we learned that what we know about our words in reading can help us in our writing, and what we know about words in our writing can help us with our reading. Today, let's use our word wall words to see what we learn. Let's focus today on what we know about sound-symbol relationships in the words we have learned!"
2. Sound work (review word analogy strategy with phonograms): "Remember when we worked on our classroom message and class poem today, we learned that knowing one word can help you to figure out other words. In our classroom message, we started with the word *spring* (point to the word on the word wall) and learned how to make *ring*, *king*, and *sing*. (If not added to the word wall, show the words previously printed on flashcards and have the students say the words with you.) In our class poem, we started with the word *fell* (point to the word on the word wall) and learned how to make *bell*, *sell*, and *shell*." (If not added to the word wall, show the words previously printed on flashcards and have students say the words with you.)
3. Model and demonstrate: (Select another word on the word wall that contains one of the common phonograms. Model how to start with the word and, using consonant substitution, change the word wall word into other words. Use a small whiteboard to show how the word is spelled, not just pronounced.) "Let's start with this word on the word wall from our class poem." (Point to the word *woke* on the word wall.) "Raise your hand if you remember what this word from our class poem is. Don't tell me. Tell your partner. On the count of three, let's all say the word. One, two, three. *Woke*! Now I am going to think about a word that rhymes with *woke*. How about *joke*? If I didn't know how to spell *joke*, I could look at *woke* and use this part of *woke* (run your finger under the *oke*) to help me spell that part of *joke*. (Write the *oke* on your whiteboard.) Then I would have to think about what letter I would have to change the *w* to in order to start *joke*. I am hearing /j/, and I know that *j* usually makes that sound. So I am going to write that at the beginning. (Add the *j* to *oke* on the whiteboard. Run your finger on the whole word *joke*, stopping between the onset and rime.) Now what if I didn't know this word *choke* when I was reading? (Write the word *choke* on the whiteboard.) I see that it shares this part with *woke*. (Run your finger under the *oke* in *choke*.) Now I can use that to help me read the same part in this word: /ōk/. Then I can look at these letters and think about what sound they make to finish the word. (Run your fingers under the *ch*.) *Ch* together usually makes /ch/. /Ch/ plus /ōk/ equals *choke*. (Run your fingers under each part and then under the whole word as you say it.) I can use a word I know on the word wall to help me spell or say a new word that I need for my reading and writing." (Repeat with other words as time allows using think-alouds.)

4. Guided practice: "Friends, let's work together to see if we can practice our sound strategy with another word wall word. (Guide your students to select another word on the word wall that contains one of the common phonograms. You might narrow the choice and have students vote on two or three possibilities.) Now let's start with the word *day* from our class message that we put on our word wall. (Write it on the whiteboard.) What if I need to spell the word *stay*? How would I change this word to make that word? Help me spell it. (Write the spelling with help from students on the whiteboard. Call on students.) What part stayed the same? Why did we keep it the same? What part did we change? How did we know how to change it? What if I was trying to read this word? (Write *spray* on the whiteboard.) How could I figure it out? What part would sound the same as *day*? How did you know? What part did you need to change? How did you know?" (Repeat with other words using strategic questioning and probing so students are invoking their metacognitive language.)

5. Monitored independent practice: "Friends, let's use our name cards to see if you can use our strategy independently. (Select a student to pick a word from the word wall that contains one of the common phonograms. Assist in the choice as need.) Now start with that word from our word wall. (Have the student write it on the whiteboard.) Now what if I need to spell the word _______? How would you change this word to make that word? (Invite the student to spell the word with classmates' help as needed. Write the new word on the whiteboard. Probe the student's effort.) What part stayed the same? Why did you keep it the same? What part did you change? How did you know how to change it? (Select additional students to work with the same word from the word wall.) What if I was trying to read this word? (Write a new word from the word family on the whiteboard.) What is the word? How did you figure it out? What part would sound the same as _______? How did you know? What part did you need to change? How did you know?" (Repeat with other students as you monitor their abilities to identify appropriate words, use analogies to spell a new word, use analogies to decode a new word, and use metacognitive language to explain actions. Provide scaffolded support as needed.)

6. Lesson link: "Remember, you can use the word wall as a resource anytime during the day! You can use what we learned today about using a word wall word you know to figure out how to sound out or spell new words in your reading and writing. Tomorrow, we are going to use our word wall to review some more secrets about learning words, especially words we see and use over and over again."

Lesson Plan: *Day Three*

Word Wall (Early Readers and Writers)

Focus on Sight Vocabulary (Visual Cues)

1. Restate purpose: "Yesterday, you showed me what you are learning about our words in reading can help us in our writing and how what we know about words in our writing can help us with our reading. We also learned how our word wall can help us do that. You can use parts of a word wall word you know to help you figure out how to read or write a word you are still learning. Raise your hand if you are working to get better at reading and writing. Today, we will use our word wall to practice another strategy about words that will help us get better at reading and writing. Let's try to work hard and be the best readers and writers we can be!"

2. Sight word work (focus on key sight words *and, is, it see, the, we, she, was, that,* and *on*): "Today I am going to add some words to our word wall that we see over and over again in our reading and spell over and over again in our writing. These words are so important that we should remember what they look like so we can read and spell them as fast as we can. These are the words we worked on in our class message and in our class poem. (Prepare the words to be added to the word wall. Show each word.) Let's say the words together: *and, is, it, see, the, we, she, was, that,* and *on.*"

3. Model and demonstrate: "Let's add *and* to the word wall. I want to remember *and* because it is used over and over again. Let's use our Look-Say-Cover-Spell-Check strategy to help us really remember the word before we put it on our word wall. First I am going to look closely at the word *and* to try to remember what it looks like. Now I am going to say the word: *and.* Now I am going to cover up the word and try to spell it. (Cover the word and write the word on a whiteboard.) Now I'll look at the word again and check to see if I spelled it right: *a-n-d.* It is spelled right, so I will add it to the word wall. I will remember that if I ever need to check how to spell it, I can use the word wall as a resource to help me. Since the word *and* is on the word wall, I expect myself to spell it correctly whenever I am ready to share my writing with others." (Repeat the demonstration with a new word as needed if time allows.)

4. Guided practice: "Together, let's add this word to the word wall. Raise your hand if you know this word. (Show the word *see* to the class.) Don't tell me. Tell your partner. Let's all say it on the count of three. One, two, three. *See*! Let's use our Look-Say-Cover-Spell-Check strategy together to help us really remember the word before we put it on our word wall. We want to remember the word because it is used over and over again. Grab a sheet of scratch paper. Let's use our strategy. First, let's look closely at the word *see* and try to remember what it looks like. Now let's say the word: *see.* Now I'll cover up the word, and you try to spell it on your scratch paper. Think about everything you remember about the word. (Cover the word and give students a chance to write it on their papers.) Now I'll show you the

word again and let you check to see if you spelled it right: *s-e-e*. Raise your hand if you spelled it correctly. If you need to correct it, go ahead and spell it again. I will add it to the word wall. If you ever need to check how to spell it, the word wall is a resource that can help you. Now that the word *see* is on the word wall, let's all make sure we hold ourselves to the expectation to spell it accurately in our writing and remember it when we are reading." (Repeat the guided practice with more words as needed if time allows.)

5. Monitored independent practice: "Now let's see if you can use the Look-Say-Cover-Spell-Check strategy on your own to do a final review of the remaining sight words before we put the word on the word wall. (Display the remaining high-frequency sight words from the shared reading and writing: *is*, *it*, *the*, *we*, *she*, *was*, *that*, and *on*.) Pick any of the remaining words and use the Look-Say strategy on your own to do a final review of one of our high-frequency words. (Give students time to select a word and use the strategy on their scratch paper.) Let's use our name cards to call on individuals to come up, pick one of our remaining words, and tell us what they noticed when they use the strategy. (Monitor performances of individuals and provide support as needed. Repeat until all words have been reviewed, if time permits.) So, if you ever need to check how to spell one of these words, what can you use as a resource to help you? Yes, the word wall can help you. And if a word is on the word wall, what should we expect? Yes, let's expect ourselves to spell the word accurately in our writing and remember it when we see it in our reading."
6. Lesson link: "We keep learning how our word wall can be a helpful resource when we are reading and writing. Tomorrow, we are going to use our word wall to review some more strategies we've learned about words. We will look at the structure of words we know to help us learn new words."

Lesson Plan: *Day Four*

Word Wall (Early Readers and Writers)

Focus on Structural Analysis (Inflected Endings/ Syntactical Cues)

1. Restate purpose: "We keep learning strategies about words. These help you figure out how to read or write words. Today during our shared reading and writing, we learned another secret about words that will also help us get better at reading and writing. We learned that thinking about word parts can help us figure out words we see when we read and words we need when we write. This is just one more way we are getting better at reading and writing because we are learning to be the best readers and writers we can be!"
2. Structural analysis word work: "With our class message, we learned that sometimes you can start with a word you know and add an ending, so the new word makes more sense and sounds better when you are reading or writing. With our class poem, we also learned that

sometimes you can start with a word you know and take away an ending to also make a new word that makes more sense and sounds better. Let's play a game called One or Two with some of our words on our word wall."

3. Model and demonstrate: "I am going to select a word from the word wall. I want you to tell me if it is one of that thing by putting up one finger or two or more of that thing by putting up two fingers. I will show you how it works. If I say the word *bell*, I would ask myself if that is one or two or more. If I think it is one thing, I would put one finger in my lap. If I think it is two or more things, I would put two fingers in my lap. When I hear *bell*, I know that it is one *bell*, so I would put one finger in my lap and then flash one finger when it's time to answer."

4. Guided practice: "Now I would like you to play the game with me. I am going to select another word from the word wall. I want you to tell me if it is one of that thing by putting one finger in your lap or two or more of that thing by putting two fingers in your lap. Here's the word: *ring*. Is that one or two or more? Put your fingers in your lap. On the count of three, let's flash our answers. One, two, three, flash. (Survey student answers and probe responses.) How did you know it was one? Does it sound right to say *one ring*? Would it sound right to say *two ring*? How would you have to change *ring* to make that sound right? When you are spelling, how would you change *ring* to *rings*? Yes, you would add an -s to the word *ring*." (Repeat the guided practice with more words as needed if time allows.)

5. Monitored independent practice: "One or Two is a game you can play with your partners during your independent work time. Let's use our name cards to have a student play the game with you. (Select a student to lead the game with the other students.) You can pick a word from the word wall, or you can use your own word. Remember, the best words are usually things. Whisper your word to me first. (Check to see if the word is appropriate.) Go ahead and say your word. (Let the student say the word. Give students time to decide one or two or more.) OK, go ahead and count for flashing answers. (Let the student do the count and survey the group.) What did you friends decide—one or two or more? Is that right? How do you know?" (Probe whether the answer sounds right grammatically with the student's word, whether the other answer would sound right grammatically, and how the student's word would need to be changed so it would sound right. Repeat with other students as you monitor their abilities to identify appropriate words, evaluate the accuracy of other students' answers, judge syntactical appropriateness, and repair syntactical miscues. Provide scaffolded support as needed.)

6. Lesson link: "Remember, you can use what we learned today during our word wall work to help you make a word mean *one* or *two or more* when you are reading or writing. This is just one more way our word wall can be a good resource to use when we are reading and writing. We will use our word wall again tomorrow to help us with one more important strategy that helps us figure out the meaning of tough words we come across in our reading."

Lesson Plan: *Day Five*

Word Wall (Early Readers and Writers)

Focus on Context Clues (Semantic and Syntactic Cues)

1. Review: "All week, we have learned so many strategies we can use to help us learn about words. Let's use our word wall to play a game to see if you are really learning your words. I will show a name card and that person can find one word he or she has learned this week and point to it on our word wall." (Quickly call on students to go to the word wall and point to a word they have learned. Probe responses with strategic questions like, "How do you remember that word?" or "How do you know that word isn't ______?" Monitor students as they select and say words. Provide scaffolded support as needed.)
2. Context clue word work: "Today during our shared reading, we learned that sometimes you can use the words around a hard word in a sentence to figure out what it means. That is called using context clues. Remember how we used clues in our poem to figure out what the tough word *chrysalis* meant? We used inferencing and picture clues to help us figure out that word."
3. Modeling and demonstrating: "To show how the words around a hard word can help you figure out what the word is, I am going to use some Swiss cheese sentences. Swiss cheese is the cheese with holes in it, so these Swiss cheese sentences also have some holes in them. You have to find a word on the word wall that would fill the hole in the Swiss cheese sentence. You have to think about what would make sense and what would sound right. Let me show you how that might work. *When the* [*blank*] *rings at noon, it is time for lunch.* Hmm, I am looking for a word on the word wall that would make sense and sound right. I think the word *bell* would work. I am going to fill the hole with that word. *When the bell rings at noon, it is time for lunch.* That does sound right. It sounds like the way we talk. Now I want to check if it makes sense. A *bell* is something that rings and it does signal it is time for lunch. Yes, it makes sense. Just by knowing the familiar words around a word, I was able to figure out the word I didn't know."
4. Guided practice: "Raise your hand if you are ready to try a Swiss cheese sentence using our word wall words. Let's see if you can use the familiar words around an unknown word to fill the hole in my next Swiss cheese sentence. Let's use our scratch paper. Here is my sentence: *We saw the __________ at the fire department.* Search the word wall or any other print you can see in the room, and fill the hole. You can use one word or more than one word, but let's remember two things that need to be true. What's one thing that has to be true? Yes, it has to sound right. What's the other thing? Yes, it has to make sense. OK, start searching the room for words to fill the hole. (Give students

time to write a word or phrase on their scratch paper.) Let's share with our partners. Have your partner check two things: Does it sound right and does it make sense? (Give students time to work as partners.) OK, who has some good ways to fill the hole? (Call on students, probe syntactic and semantic appropriateness, and provide scaffolded support as needed.) Yes, that fills the hole. See how you were able to think about the words around a word you didn't know to figure it out?"

5. Monitored independent practice: "You can use a Swiss cheese sentence with your partners. Let's use our name cards to have a student come up with a Swiss cheese sentence for you to fill the hole. (Select a student to lead the game with the other students. Have him whisper his Swiss cheese sentence to you. Help the student adjust the sentence as needed.) Go ahead and say your Swiss cheese sentence. (Let the student say the sentence. Give other students time to decide words to fill the hole and write those on their papers.) Share your answer with a partner first before our Swiss cheese maker calls on some of you. Let's share with our partners. Have your partner check two things: Does it sound right and does it make sense? (Give students time to work as partners.) Let's have our Swiss cheese maker call on some of you. (Let the student call on a student for a response.) Does that one work? How do you know? (Monitor the student to see if he can check the response for syntactic and semantic appropriateness. Let him call on others to fill the hole and check as well. Repeat, with other students creating different Swiss cheese sentences as time allows. Monitor students' abilities to create an appropriate sentence, evaluate the accuracy of other students' answers, judge syntactical and semantic appropriateness, and repair syntactical and semantic miscues, if required. Provide scaffolded support as needed.) Look at how you were able to think about the words around a word you didn't know to figure it out."

6. Self-evaluation: "Before we go today, let's check ourselves to see what we have learned about using our word walls. Let's put a hand in our lap. Put one finger in your lap if you know at least one way to use the word wall to help you with your reading and writing. If you know two ways to use the word wall as a resource, put two fingers in your lap. If you know three ways to use the word wall during reading and writing, put three fingers in your lap. Now on the count of three, flash your fingers. One, two, three, flash! (Probe students' responses to review some of the key strategies learned this week with shared reading, shared writing, and the word wall.) You have worked hard this week to learn about words."

7. Lesson link: "Remember, you can use the word wall as a resource any time you need help with your reading or writing. Next week, we will see how to use the word wall in your reading and your writing."

Final Thoughts about Intensifying Your Word Wall

Those green tennis balls appear to be headed for a long life in elementary classrooms. They may have shown up overnight, but they seem to be here to stay. Such was the case with word walls. They might have shown up overnight, but now almost 20 years later, they are still found in most classrooms. This chapter acknowledged that and provided insights, issues, and ideas to consider as you work to intensify the use of this resource to maximize its value for the readers and writers in your classroom. If your students are emergent readers and writers, I hope you have learned how to position your word wall as a class routine to support your shared writing and reading and address concepts of print, alphabetic knowledge, and phonological—including phonemic—awareness. If your students are early readers and writers, I hope you can see how the word wall can evolve as a routine to be a strong resource that supports teaching and learning word strategies, including sound analysis, high-frequency sight words, structural analysis, and context clues. To provide you a practical vision of how that can happen in your classroom, a five-day sequence of lessons has been developed for the early phase of literacy development. Blamey and Beauchat (2016) observed in their research: "Teachers often discover that an effective word wall does more than merely display words; it engages students in conversations surrounding the words (p. x)." That seems to be the best outcome to strive toward when intensifying the use of your word wall. Get your students to become interested in words. Interest raises awareness and awareness increases attentiveness. The more your students find words interesting and attend to them, the more they will learn about their patterns, spellings, structures, and meanings.

CHAPTER FIVE:

Putting It All Together

> When the time is right for you, take the first step.
> And another. And another.
>
> It gets easier, huh?
>
> *Marla Frazee*

In her book, *Walk On! A Guide for Babies of All Ages*, Marla Frazee reminds us it is all about taking that first step (and then another and another...). In this chapter, let's look at how to take that first step, how to get started, and how to bring it all together.

The good news is that, for most teachers, these are three routines—shared writing, shared reading, and word walls—with which you are already familiar. For most teachers, these are already a part of the school day and the literacy and language arts programs. So the first step is really making a decision to tighten up your current practices and pick a doable change that would help you move in that direction. Once you have decided that, the following steps might be helpful in guiding you to move forward.

Step one: Start by thinking generally about the learners sitting in front of you. While you may use the first part of the year to get to know your readers and writers on a more individual basis, you can start by thinking about the common patterns of development that they often share. If you have taught that grade before, you can draw upon your experience of former students and where they were at to find a starting place for your instructional decisions. When you look across your learners, you will be able to see whether the common pattern they share is primarily one of emergent readers and writers or early readers and writers. Figure 17 [adapted from Ford (2016)] on the next page will give you additional guidance in looking for common patterns in your learners.

Figure 17: Phases of Readers

	Emergent Phase	Early Phase
Key questions the learners are trying to answer	What is print? What is reading and writing all about?	How do I unlock print when I read and write?
Major instructional focus (but not exclusively!)	Print	Tools
Major areas of cognitive attention	• Expand oral language. • Expand world knowledge. • Understand concepts of print. • Develop phonological and phonemic awareness. • Gain alphabetic knowledge. • Make meaning through shared reading and writing.	• Use sound analysis. • Increase sight vocabulary. • Analyze word parts through structural analysis. • Analyze word meanings through text analysis. • Use searching, monitoring, and cross-checking strategies. • Identify main idea, theme, and text elements. • Make predictions and draw conclusions based on text evidence.
Major areas of affective attention	discovering the joy developing a positive identity	developing self-efficacy knowing you can read, wanting to read, and knowing how to read

Step two: Once you have determined the common pattern of development shared by your students, select ONE of the routines you would feel the most comfortable with intensifying using the insights and ideas from this book. Try to avoid overwhelming your efforts by taking on all of the routines at the same time. Give yourself permission to get comfortable and confident intensifying one of your routines first, before taking on another. Remember, what you learn from intensifying one routine may help you as you try to intensify another. It might be most helpful to start with a routine that you are already using, especially one for which you have already set aside time in your schedule. This will lessen both concerns about how to do the routine and where to find the time to schedule it. Be sure to consider expectations of required programs and frameworks. Many of those incorporate at least one of the routines, providing another good starting point.

Step three: Now that you have determined where your students are at and what routine you want to intensify, use the insights and ideas in this book to help you plan your first sequence. If you start with your shared writing experience, use Chapter Two to guide you in your planning and implementation of a manageable next step forward. If you start with your shared reading experience, use Chapter Three. If you start with your word wall, use Chapter Four.

Step four: For your first attempts at intensification, use the planning sheets in the Appendices to help you structure a five-day sequence of instructional activities for the routine you have chosen. If you are planning a text for the shared writing experience, use the planning sheets on pages 189–190 and 195–196. If you are using a text for the shared reading experience, use the planning sheets on pages 191–192 and 197–198. For your word wall activities, use the planning sheets on pages 193–194 and 199–200. Select the planning sheet that is designed for the developmental phase of the students with whom you will be working. Use the planning reminders in previous chapters to double check the thoroughness of your plan.

Step five: Implement day one of your plan. Once completed, find time to reflect on your instruction. You'll notice the planning sheets contain space for you to note observations of your students from your teaching on each day. Look at what you intended to teach on day two. Adjust your initial plan as needed, in light of how your instruction went on day one. Give yourself permission to make changes. Don't feel compelled to move forward with your initial plans if you know how to adjust them to facilitate better teaching and learning on day two. Also, remember these sessions are intended to be fairly short. If you can get everything done on one day, remind yourself that you can pick up from where you left off on the next day. That is probably much better than squeezing something else into one lesson just for the sake of making sure it was covered on the day it was planned. Your goal is not just covering content but uncovering opportunities to learn.

Step six: Continue the subsequent days of your plan, repeating your cycle of reflection and adjustment. The end of your first five-day cycle provides another good opportunity to reflect on how the week went overall. Begin to plan for the next week of your cycle for the same routine. Think deeply about what you observed throughout the week. Think about whether the focus for your plans should repeat the previously taught skills and strategies to provide needed practice and/or review. Also consider whether your plans should move to address different skills and strategies based on the learning you observed, especially if most students seem ready to move in a new direction. Remember, students may be at different points. Some may need more practice, and some may need a new direction. Look across your group for what seems to be the prevailing pattern. Use your additional small group and individualized instructional opportunities to address those variations. If most students seem ready to move on, it might be the better instructional decision to do so. Those with a need for additional practice will be in a socially supportive, large group structure with you there to adjust levels of support. They may also benefit from the modeling and insights of their peers as they explore the new strategies and skills. Also keep in mind that any cycle of plans can include some review integrated with the introduction of new content.

Step seven: Once you are more comfortable and confident implementing the five-day cycle for your first routine, select a second routine. Use what you have learned from your intensification efforts with the first routine to inform your thinking as you plan to add a second routine. If you want to focus on just the new routine, temporarily set aside the first routine to raise your competence and confidence levels with the new routine. When you are ready, start to bring the two routines together. Eventually, you want to find as many connections across the two routines to incorporate into your daily lessons. Remember, the key is to align the focus for each routine every day. Once aligned, the routines will reinforce common language and consistent skills and strategies instruction across the parallel processes of reading and writing.

Step eight: Continue your planning, implementation, reflection, and adjusting of your plans within the five-day cycles. As you reflect, be sure to not only look at each lesson for each routine, but also look at how the two routines are working together. Once your comfort and confidence have grown working with two routines, add the final routine. As soon as you feel comfortable, start to plan all three together. Now you can look for potential connections across all three routines. Be very cognizant of how you schedule the three routines to give each the time necessary for systematic, explicit instruction. A pacing and alignment guide for the three routines in these developmental levels is provided on page 167.

Step nine: Remember, when all three of the routines are operationalized, there will be one daily lesson with the shared writing (15–20 minutes), one lesson with the shared reading (15–20 minutes), and one transitional activity lesson, as needed, interacting with the word wall (5–10 minutes). Always look at these time allotments with consideration of what is being addressed in other aspects of the language arts program. The lessons for the routines should supplement the language arts program. They are not the entirety of the program. It is also important to keep that in mind when you feel some frustration with trying to teach everything you need to through the routines. You can teach skills and strategies at other times during your literacy and language arts program.

Step ten: Even Marla Frazee points out in her book *Walk On* that it is very common to fall down as you are trying to learn how to walk. Give yourself permission to fall down. Don't work on being perfect. Work on getting better. If things are not going in the direction you desired, be ready to stand back and reflect on what you have been doing. As Frazee advises, "Fix whatever you can before you start over." If it is too hard to juggle three intensified routines with other expectations, narrow your focus. If getting each routine in every day on the five-day cycles is too overwhelming, stretch out the cycles and maybe try to implement the routines on alternating days or alternating weeks. My intent in this book was not to show the one right way to do classroom routines. My intent was to help expand our vision of how we see classroom routines by providing new insights and ideas. As was said throughout the book, you always have the right to modify ideas for what will work best for you and your students.

Final Thoughts

Regie Routman once observed about herself, "I wonder about literacy all the time." Her passionate, lifetime commitment to exploring issues, insights, and ideas for administrators, teachers, families, and students definitely supports that. For me, this book began in a similar manner. After visiting and working in many primary literacy and language programs—including my own—I began to wonder about how to improve the use of three of the most popular routines used in those classrooms. Believing in their value, but wondering whether all their potential was being achieved, I began to explore and experiment with ways to intensify their power. I hope this resource will help other educators do the same. Physicist Lisa Randall once said, "Speculation and the exploration of ideas beyond what we know with certainty are what lead to progress." I invite you to speculate, explore, and ask "I wonder what would happen if…."

Figure 18: Pacing and Alignment Guide

Emergent and Early Literacy	Monday: Day One	Tuesday: Day Two	Wednesday: Day Three	Thursday: Day Four	Friday: Day Five
Shared Reading	15–20 minutes	15–20 minutes	15–20 minutes	15–20 minutes	15–20 minutes
Weekly Message	15–20 minutes	15–20 minutes	15–20 minutes	15–20 minutes	15–20 minutes
Word Wall Transitional Activity	5–10 minutes	5–10 minutes	5–10 minutes	5–10 minutes	5–10 minutes
Total Time Allocation	35–50 minutes	35–50 minutes	35–50 minutes	35–50 minutes	35–50 minutes
Balance of Language Arts Program (based on a two-hour block)	70–85 minutes	70–85 minutes	70–85 minutes	70–85 minutes	70–85 minutes

Appendices

Appendix 1: Concepts of Print Record-keeping Sheet . . . 170

Appendix 2: Alphabetic Knowledge Record-keeping Sheet . . . 172

Appendix 3: Phonological/Phonemic Awareness Record-keeping Sheet . . . 174

Appendix 4: Sound-Symbol Strategies Record-keeping Sheet . . . 176

Appendix 5: Structural Analysis Strategies Record-keeping Sheet . . . 178

Appendix 6: Context Clues and Semantic Analysis Strategies Record-keeping Sheet . . . 180

Appendix 7: Concepts of Print Scavenger Hunt . . . 181

Appendix 8: Sound Scavenger Hunt . . . 182

Appendix 9: Phonogram Grid . . . 183

Appendix 10: Sight Word Practice Sheet . . . 184

Appendix 11: Plural Sheet . . . 185

Appendix 12: Patterned Sentence Page . . . 186

Appendix 13: Sample Interactive Guide . . . 187

Appendix 14: Guess List . . . 188

Appendix 15: Planning Sheet for Emergent Readers and Writers Routines: Shared Writing . . . 189

Appendix 16: Planning Sheet for Emergent Readers and Writers Routines: Shared Reading . . 191

Appendix 17: Planning Sheet for Emergent Readers and Writers Routines: Word Wall Activities . . . 193

Appendix 18: Planning Sheet for Early Readers and Writers Routines: Shared Writing . . . 195

Appendix 19: Planning Sheet for Early Readers and Writers Routines: Shared Reading . . . 197

Appendix 20: Planning Sheet for Early Readers and Writers Routines: Word Wall Activities . . 199

Appendix 1: Concepts of Print Record-keeping Sheet

Note date(s) task was completed.					
	Introduced	**Guided Practice**	**Independent Practice**	**Mastered**	**Reviewed**
Starts writing at the top on the left					
Moves writing from left to right					
Moves writing from top to bottom					
Return sweeps at the end of the line					
Starts sentences with a capital letter					
Ends sentences with a punctuation mark					
Uses spaces between words					
Writes words from left to right					
Has voice-print match					
Understands term *letter*					
Understands term *word*					
Understands term *page*					
Understands terms *capital/uppercase*					
Understands terms *small/lowercase*					
Understands terms *start, beginning,* and *first*					
Understands terms *end, back,* and *last*					

Appendix 1: Concepts of Print Record-keeping Sheet *continued*

Note date(s) task was completed.					
	Introduced	**Guided Practice**	**Independent Practice**	**Mastered**	**Reviewed**
Understands terms *print* and *picture*					
Understands terms *line* and *sentence*					
Understands a period					
Understands a comma					
Understands a question mark					
Understands an exclamation point					
Understands quotation marks					
Other:					

Appendix 2: Alphabetic Knowledge Record-keeping Sheet

Note date(s) task was completed.					
	Introduced	**Guided Practice**	**Independent Practice**	**Mastered**	**Reviewed**
Understands what a letter is					
Can sort letters by specific features					
Matches and distinguishes between letters					
Understands that letters form words					
Understands that letters stand for sounds					
Recognizes uppercase letters (note letters addressed)					
Check off key uppercase letters introduced, practiced, and mastered	A B C D E F G H I J K L M N O P Q R S T U V W X Y Z				
Recognizes lowercase letters (note letters addressed)					
Check off key lowercase letters introduced, practiced, and mastered	a b c d e f g h i j k l m n o p q r s t u v w x y z				
Identifies uppercase letters (note letters addressed)					
Check off key uppercase letters introduced, practiced, and mastered	A B C D E F G H I J K L M N O P Q R S T U V W X Y Z				

Note date(s) task was completed.					
	Introduced	**Guided Practice**	**Independent Practice**	**Mastered**	**Reviewed**
Identifies lowercase letters (note letters addressed)					
Check off key lowercase letters introduced, practiced, and mastered	a b c d e f g h i j k l m n o p q r s t u v w x y z				
Prints uppercase letters (note letters addressed)					
Check off key uppercase letters introduced, practiced, and mastered	A B C D E F G H I J K L M N O P Q R S T U V W X Y Z				
Prints lowercase letters (note letters addressed)					
Check off key lowercase letters introduced, practiced, and mastered	a b c d e f g h i j k l m n o p q r s t u v w x y z				
Knows when to use uppercase (capital) and lowercase (small) letters					
Knows letters can appear in slightly different forms (fonts) but are the same					
Other:					

Appendix 3: Phonological/Phonemic Awareness Record-keeping Sheet

Note date(s) task was completed.					
	Introduced	**Guided Practice**	**Independent Practice**	**Mastered**	**Reviewed**
Hears and identifies individual words in sentences (word awareness)					
Hears and identifies parts or chunks in words (syllable awareness)					
Hears and identifies ending clusters of sounds in words (awareness of rimes)					
Hears and identifies the same ending cluster of sounds in different words (rhyming)					
Hears and identifies individual sounds in words (sounds in initial, medial, and final positions)					
Hears and isolates individual sounds in words (sounds in initial, medial, and final positions)					
Adds individual sounds to words (sounds in initial, medial, and final positions)					
Blends individual sounds into words					

Appendix 3: Phonological/Phonemic Awareness Record-keeping Sheet *continued*

Note date(s) task was completed.					
	Introduced	**Guided Practice**	**Independent Practice**	**Mastered**	**Reviewed**
Segments all the individual sounds in a word					
Substitutes one individual sound for another in a word (sounds in initial, medial, and final positions)					
Other:					

Appendix 4: Sound-Symbol Strategies Record-keeping Sheet

Note date(s) task was completed.					
	Introduced	**Guided Practice**	**Independent Practice**	**Mastered**	**Reviewed**
Can use analogies (onsets and rimes) to identify new words					
Check off key phonograms as introduced, practiced, and mastered	-ack, -ail, -ain, -ake, -ale, -ame, -an, -ank, -ap, -ash, -at, -ate, -aw, -ay, -eat, -ell, -est, -ice, -ick, -ide, -ight, -ill, -in, -ine, -ing, -ink, -ip, -it, -ock, -oke, -op, -ore, -ot, -uck, -ug, -ump, -unk				
Can use single-consonant sound-symbol relationships to decode words					
Check off key single-consonant sound-symbol relationships introduced, practiced, and mastered	b, d, f, h, j, k, l, m, n, p, r, s, t, v, w, y, z				
Can use variable-consonant sound-symbol relationships to decode words					
Check off key variable-consonant sound-symbol relationships as introduced, practiced, and mastered	hard and soft sounds of c hard and soft sounds of g multiple sounds of x distinguishing vowel and consonant sounds of y distinguishing vowel and consonant sounds of w				
Can use consonant blends to decode words					
Check off key consonant blends as introduced, practiced, and mastered	Initial blends: br, cr, dr, fr, gr, pr, tr, bl, cl, fl, gl, pl, sl, sc, scr, sk, sm, sn, sp, spl, spr, st, str, sw, and tw Additional ending blends: ld, mp, nt, nd, lt, ft				

Note date(s) task was completed.					
	Introduced	**Guided Practice**	**Independent Practice**	**Mastered**	**Reviewed**
Can use consonant digraphs to decode words					
Check off key consonant digraphs introduced, practiced, and mastered	Initial digraphs: ch, th, wh, sh Ending digraphs: ng				
Can use short vowel patterns to decode words					
Check off key short vowel patterns as introduced, practiced, and mastered	VC CVC				
Can use long vowel patterns to decode words					
Check off key long vowel patterns as introduced, practiced, and mastered	CV VVC VCe				
Can use irregular vowels to decode words					
Check off key irregular vowels as introduced, practiced, and mastered	schwa consonant-controlled diphthongs unique vowel digraphs				
Other:					

Appendix 5: Structural Analysis Strategies Record-keeping Sheet

Note date(s) task was completed.					
	Introduced	**Guided Practice**	**Independent Practice**	**Mastered**	**Reviewed**
Ability to use chunks (syllables) within words to help analyze and use words					
Ability to analyze and use words with inflected endings					
Check off key inflected ending as introduced, practiced, and mastered	-s, -es, -ed, -ing, -ly, -er, -est				
Ability to analyze and use words with common suffixes					
Check off key common suffixes as introduced, practiced, and mastered*	-able, -ible, -al, -ial, -en, -er, -or, -ful, -ic , -ion, -tion, -ation, -ition, -ity, -ty, -ive, -ative, -itive, -less, -ment, -ness, -ous, -eous, -ious, -y				
Ability to analyze and use words with common prefixes					
Check off key common prefixes and inflected endings as introduced, practiced, and mastered	ab-, ad-, be-, com-, con-, co-, col-, de-, dis-, di-, en-, ex-, in-, il-, ir-, pre-, pro-, re-, sub-, un-				
Ability to analyze the structure of compound words					
Ability to analyze the structure of contractions					
Ability to analyze the structure of possessives					

Appendix 5: Structural Analysis Strategies Record-keeping Sheet *continued*

Note date(s) task was completed.					
	Introduced	**Guided Practice**	**Independent Practice**	**Mastered**	**Reviewed**
Ability to use syllabication generalizations to identify unfamiliar longer words					
Check off key syllabication generalizations as introduced, practiced, and mastered	**C** = **C**losed Syllables (VC/CV, VC/V) **L** = Consonant-**L**e Syllable (/CLe) **O** = **O**pen Syllables (V/CV, V/DIGRAPH V, V/BLEND V) **V** = Double **V**owel Syllable **E** = Vowel-Consonant-**E** Syllable **R** = **R**-controlled Syllable				
Other:					

*Honig, B., Diamond, L. & Gutlohn, L. (2000). *Teaching reading sourcebook: For kindergarten through eighth grade*. Core Literacy Training Series. Novato, CA: Arena Press.

Appendix 6: Context Clues and Semantic Analysis Strategies Record-keeping Sheet

Note date(s) task was completed.					
	Introduced	**Guided Practice**	**Independent Practice**	**Mastered**	**Reviewed**
Can monitor and self-correct for meaning when working with print					
Able to use typographical clues to identify unfamiliar words					
Able to use structural clues to identify unfamiliar words					
Able to use direct definition to identify unfamiliar words					
Able to use antonyms and synonyms to identify unfamiliar words					
Able to use similes and metaphors to identify unfamiliar words					
Able to use graphic clues to identify unfamiliar words					
Able to use inferences to identify unfamiliar words					
Able to use background knowledge to identify unfamiliar words					
Other:					

Appendix 7: Concepts of Print Scavenger Hunt

My name is: ______________________________

What to Look for	My Guess	Class Answer
How many sentences are in our message?		
How many words are in our message?		
How many letters are in our message?		
How long is the longest sentence?		
How short is the shortest sentence?		
How long is the longest word?		
How short is the shortest word?		
What word do we see the most times?		
What letter do we see the most times?		
Bonus question:		

Appendix 8: Sound Scavenger Hunt

My name is: ____________________

	In the Class Message	**From My Reading and Writing**
Find a word that starts with a /d/ sound.		
Find a word that starts with a /w/ sound.		
Find a word that has an /ē/ sound in it.		
Find a word that has an /ā/ sound in it.		
Find a word that starts with a /b/ sound.		
Find a word that starts with the blend /fl/.		
Find a word that ends with the rime /ing/.		
Bonus question:		

Appendix 9: Phonogram Grid

My name is: ______________________________

Appendix 10: Sight Word Practice Sheet

My name is: ______________________________

Write and check the words	**Look at and say the words**	Cover the words (fold over to cover up the words you are studying)
	and	
	is	
	it	
	see	
	the	
	we	

Appendix 11: Plural Sheet

My name is: ______________________________

1	2

Appendix 12: Patterned Sentence Page

My name is: ______________________________

We see __________________ and __________________.	

Appendix 13: Sample Interactive Guide

My name is: ______________________________

What do you think we are going to read about today?	*Tell me what you already know about that topic.*
Write down one thing you learned about the topic from the picture walk.	*How well did you think you worked during the shared reading today?*

Guess List

My name is: ____________________

	First Secret Word	**Second Secret Word**	**Third Secret Word**
First Guess			
Second Guess			
Third Guess			
Fourth Guess			
Final Guess			

Appendix 15: Planning Sheet for Emergent Readers and Writers Routines: Shared Writing

<table>
<tr><td colspan="2">Message:</td></tr>
<tr><td>Day One: Focus on Interactive Writing</td><td>Notes from observation of students during lesson:</td></tr>
<tr><td>Day Two: Focus on Rereading</td><td>Notes from observation of students during lesson:</td></tr>
</table>

Day Three: Focus on Concepts of Print	*Notes from observation of students during lesson:*
Day Four: Focus on Alphabetic Knowledge	*Notes from observation of students during lesson:*
Day Five: Focus on Phonological/Phonemic Awareness	*Notes from observation of students during lesson:*
Reflection on the week (insights and ideas for the next cycle of lessons):	

Appendix 16: Planning Sheet for Emergent Readers and Writers Routines: Shared Reading

Shared reading text:	
Day One: Focus on Preparing to Read	*Notes from observation of students during lesson:*
Day Two: Focus on Rereading	*Notes from observation of students during lesson:*

Day Three: Focus on Concepts of Print	*Notes from observation of students during lesson:*
Day Four: Focus on Alphabetic Knowledge	*Notes from observation of students during lesson:*
Day Five: Focus on Phonological/Phonemic Awareness	*Notes from observation of students during lesson:*
Reflection on the week (insights and ideas for the next cycle of lessons):	

Appendix 17: Planning Sheet for Emergent Readers and Writers Routines: Word Wall Activities

Key words for focus:	
Day One: Review	*Notes from observation of students during lesson:*
Day Two: Review	*Notes from observation of students during lesson:*

Day Three: Focus on Concepts of Print	*Notes from observation of students during lesson:*
Day Four: Focus on Alphabetic Knowledge	*Notes from observation of students during lesson:*
Day Five: Focus on Phonological/Phonemic Awareness	*Notes from observation of students during lesson:*
Reflection on the week (insights and ideas for the next cycle of lessons):	

Appendix 18: Planning Sheet for Early Readers and Writers Routines: Shared Writing

Message:	
Day One: Focus on Interactive Writing and Rereading	*Notes from observation of students during lesson:*
Day Two: Focus on Sound Analysis	*Notes from observation of students during lesson:*

Day Three: Focus on High-frequency Sight Vocabulary	*Notes from observation of students during lesson:*
Day Four: Focus on Structural and Morphological Elements	*Notes from observation of students during lesson:*
Day Five: Focus on Context Clues	*Notes from observation of students during lesson:*
Reflection on the week (insights and ideas for the next cycle of lessons):	

Appendix 19: Planning Sheet for Early Readers and Writers Routines: Shared Reading

Shared reading text:	
Day One: Focus on Preparing to Read	*Notes from observation of students during lesson:*
Day Two: Focus on Sound-symbol Relationships (Sound Analysis)	*Notes from observation of students during lesson:*

Day Three: Focus on High-frequency Sight Vocabulary	*Notes from observation of students during lesson:*
Day Four: Focus on Structural and Morphological Elements	*Notes from observation of students during lesson:*
Day Five: Focus on Context Clues	*Notes from observation of students during lesson:*
Reflection on the week (insights and ideas for the next cycle of lessons):	

Appendix 20: Planning Sheet for Early Readers and Writers Routines: Word Wall Activities

Key words for focus:	
Day One: Review	*Notes from observation of students during lesson:*
Day Two: Focus on Sound-symbol Relationship (Sound Analysis)	*Notes from observation of students during lesson:*

Day Three: Focus on High-frequency Sight Vocabulary	*Notes from observation of students during lesson:*
Day Four: Focus on Structural and Morphological Elements	*Notes from observation of students during lesson:*
Day Five: Focus on Context Clues	*Notes from observation of students during lesson:*
Reflection on the week (insights and ideas for the next cycle of lessons):	

References

Adams, A., Farnham, D., McQuillen, C. & Peabody, D. (2003). *Morning message: Dozens and dozens of instant and engaging ideas for morning messages that build skills in reading, writing, math and more.* New York, NY: Scholastic.

Akhavan, N. (2008). *The Title I teacher's guide to teaching reading.* Portsmouth, NH: Heinemann.

Allington, R. L. (2012). *What really matters for struggling readers: Designing research-based programs.* New York, NY: Pearson.

Allington, R. L. & Cunningham, P. M. (2007). *Schools that work: Where all children read and write.* Boston, MA: Allyn & Bacon.

Artley, A. S. (1943). Teaching word meaning through context. *Elementary English Review,* 20(2). 68–74.

Bear, D. R., Invernizzi, M., Templeton, S. & Johnston, F. (2015). *Words their way: Word study for phonics, vocabulary and spelling instruction, 6th edition.* Upper Saddle River, NJ: Merrill Prentice Hall.

Beck, I. L., McKeown, M. G. & Kucan, L. (2002). *Bringing words to life.* New York, NY: Guilford Press.

Blamey, K. L. & Beauchat, K. A. (2016). *Starting strong: Evidence-based early literacy practices.* Portland, ME: Stenhouse Publishers.

Bomer, R. (1998). Transactional heat and light: More explicit literacy learning. *Language Arts, 76*(1), 11–18.

Boushey, G. & Moser, J. (2014). *The Daily 5: Fostering literacy independence in the elementary grades, 2nd ed.* Portland, ME: Stenhouse Publishers.

Boyles, N. N. (2009). *Launching RTI comprehension instruction with shared reading: 40 Model lessons for intermediate readers.* Gainesville, FL: Maupin House.

Brabham, E. & Villaume, S. (2001). Questions and answers—building walls of words. *The Reading Teacher, 54,* 700–703.

Brand, M. (2004). *Word savvy: Integrated vocabulary, spelling & word study, grades 3–6.* Portland, ME: Stenhouse Publishers.

Bromley, K. (2007). Nine things every teacher should know about words and vocabulary instruction. *Journal of Adolescent & Adult Literacy, 50*(7), 528–537.

Buehl, D. (2013). *Classroom strategies for interactive learning.* Newark, DE: International Reading Association.

Burkins, J. M. & Croft, M. M. (2010). *Preventing misguided reading: New strategies for guided reading teachers.* Newark, DE: International Reading Association.

Burkins, J. M. & Yaris, K. (2016). *Who's doing the work? How to say less so your readers can do more.* Portland, ME: Stenhouse Publishers.

Calkins, L. & Ehrenworth, M. (2016). Growing extraordinary writers: leadership decisions to raise the level of writing across a school and a district. *The Reading Teacher, 70*(1), 7–18.

Cambourne, B. (2000). Observing literacy learning in elementary classrooms: Nine years of classroom anthropology. *The Reading Teacher, 53*(6), 512–515.

Cambourne, B. (2001). Conditions for literacy learning: Why do some students fail to learn to read? Ockham's razor and the conditions of learning. *The Reading Teacher, 54*(8), 784–786.

Clay, M. (1993). *An observation survey of early literacy achievement*. Portsmouth, NH: Heinemann.

Clay, M. (2013). *An observation survey of early literacy achievement, 3rd edition*. Portsmouth, NH: Heinemann.

Clayton, M. K. & Forton, M. B. (2001). *Classroom spaces that work*. Greenfield, MA: Northeast Foundation for Children.

Combs, M. (2002). *Readers and writers in primary grades: A balanced and integrated approach*. Upper Saddle River, NJ: Prentice Hall.

Copple, C. & Bredekamp, S. (2009). *Developmentally appropriate practice in early childhood programs serving children from birth through age 8*. Washington, DC: National Association for the Education of Young Children.

Cunningham, P. M. (1991). *Phonics they use*. New York, NY: HarperCollins.

Cunningham, P. M. (1995). *Phonics they use: Words for Reading and Writing, Second Edition*. HarperCollins.

Cunningham, P. M. (2005). *Phonics they use: Words for Reading and Writing, Fourth Edition*. Upper Saddle River, NJ: Pearson/Allyn & Bacon.

Cunningham, P. M. & Allington, R. L. (2016). *Classrooms that work: They can all read and write, 6th ed*. Upper Saddle River, NJ: Pearson.

Cunningham, P. M., Hall, D. P. & Cunningham, J. W. (2000). *Guided reading the Four-Blocks way, grades 1–3: The Four-Blocks literacy model book series*. Greensboro, NC: Carson-Dellosa Publishing.

Cunningham, P. M., Hall, D. P. & Defee, M. (1991). Non-ability-grouped, multilevel instruction: A year in a first-grade classroom. *The Reading Teacher, 44*(8), 566–571.

Cutting, B. (1989). *Getting started in whole language*. Bothell, WA: Wright Group/McGraw-Hill.

DeMeo, W. (2013). *When nothing else works: What early childhood professionals can do to reduce challenging behaviors*. Gryphon House, Inc.

Dorn, L. J. & Jones, T. P. (2012). *Apprenticeship in literacy: Transitions across reading and writing, K–4, 2nd ed*. Portland, ME: Stenhouse Publishers.

Dow, R. S. & Baer, G. T. (2012). *Self-paced phonics: A text for educators*. Upper Saddle River, NJ: Pearson Higher Ed.

Duke, N. K. (2014, June 20). *Teaching students to comprehend and compose informative/explanatory and persuasive text using a project-based approach*. Paper presented at the 33rd Annual UW Reading Research Symposium. (Milwaukee, WI).

Eldredge, J. L., Reutzel, D. R. & Hollingsworth, P. M. (1996). Comparing the effectiveness of two oral reading practices: Round-robin reading and the shared book experience. *Journal of Literacy Research, 28*(2), 201–225.

Elkonin, D. B. (1963). The psychology of mastering the elements of reading. *Educational psychology in the USSR*, 165–179.

Ellery, V. (2014). *Creating strategic readers: Techniques for supporting rigorous literacy instruction*. Huntington Beach, CA: Teacher Created Materials.

Elley, W. B. & Mangubhai, F. (1983). The impact of reading on second language learning. *Reading Research Quarterly, 19*(1), 53–67.

Epstein, A. S. (2007). *The intentional teacher: Choosing the best strategies for young children's learning.* Washington, DC: NAEYC.

Fisher, D. & Frey, N. (2013). *Better learning through structured teaching: A framework for the gradual release of responsibility.* Alexandria, VA: ASCD.

Fitzgerald, J. (1999). What is this thing called "balance"? *The Reading Teacher, 53*(2), 100–107.

Folkins, A. F. & Hiebert, E. H. (2011). *Exceptional expressions for everyday events.* Santa Cruz, CA: TextProject.

Ford, M. P. (2016). *Guiding reading: What's new, and what's next?* North Mankato, MN: Capstone.

Ford, M.P. (1996, Fall). Tightening up: Working toward balanced literacy. *The Whole Idea*, pp. 1, 12–15.

Fountas, I. C. & Pinnell, G. S. (1996). *Guided reading: Good first teaching for all children.* Portsmouth, NH: Heinemann.

Fountas, I. C. & Pinnell, G. S. (2016). *The Fountas & Pinnell literacy continuum: A tool for assessment, planning and teaching.* Portsmouth, NH: Heinemann.

Fox, B. J. (2014). *Phonics and word study for the teacher of reading: Programmed for self-instruction.* Upper Saddle River, NJ: Prentice Hall.

Fox, B. J. (2003). *Word recognition activities: Patterns and strategies for developing fluency.* Upper Saddle River, NJ: Merrill/Prentice Hall.

Fox, M. (2013). What next in the read–aloud battle? Win or lose? *The Reading Teacher, 67*(1), 4–8.

Fry, E. (1980). The new instant word list. *The Reading Teacher, 34*(3), 284–289.

Ganske, K. (2006). *Word sorts and more: Sound, patter, and meaning explorations K–3.* New York, NY: Guilford Publications.

Ganske, K. (2013). *Word journeys: Assessment-guided phonics, spelling, and vocabulary instruction, 2nd ed.* New York, NY: Guilford Publications.

Gaskins, I. W., Ehri, L. C., Cress, C., O'Hara, C. & Donnelly, K. (1996). Procedures for word learning: Making discoveries about words. *The Reading Teacher, 50*(4), 312–327.

Gerde, H. K., Bingham, G. E. & Pendergast, M. L. (2015). Reliability and validity of the Writing Resources and Interactions in Teaching Environments (WRITE) for preschool classrooms. *Early Childhood Research Quarterly, 31*, 34–46.

Gerde, H. K., Goetsch, M. E. & Bingham, G. E. (2016). Using print in the environment to promote early writing. *The Reading Teacher, 70*(3), 283–293.

Goodman, Y. & Marek, A. (1996). *Retrospective miscue analysis.* Katonah, NY: RC Owens.

Gunning, T. G. (2001). *Building words: A resource manual for teaching word analysis and spelling strategies.* Boston, MA: Allyn & Bacon.

Harmon, J. M., Wood, K. D., Hedrick, W. B., Vintinner, J. & Willeford, T. (2009). Interactive word walls: More than just reading the writing on the walls. *Journal of Adolescent & Adult Literacy, 52*(5), 398–408.

Hayes, K. & Creange, R. (2001). *Classroom routines that really work for prek and kindergarten.* New York, NY: Scholastic.

Hearron, P. & Hildebrand, V. (2013). *Guiding young children.* Upper Saddle River, NJ: Pearson.

Hendricks, C. & Rinsky, L. A. (2007). *Teaching word recognition skills.* Upper Saddle River, NJ: Pearson/Merrill Prentice Hall.

Hiebert, E. (2014). *Great free stuff from TextProject: Resources for knowledge, vocabulary, and automaticity.* http://textproject.org/assets/library/powerpoints/Hiebert-2014-07-31-Great-Free-Stuff-from-TextProject.pdf. Retrieved December 2016.

Hiebert, E. H. (2011). *Growing capacity with the vocabulary of English language arts programs: Vocabulary megaclusters.* Santa Cruz, CA: TextProject.

Hill, B. C. & Ekey, C. (2010). *The next step guide to enriching classroom environments.* Portsmouth, NH: Heinemann.

Himmele, P. & Himmele, W. (2011). *Total participation techniques: Making every student an active learner.* Alexandria, VA: ASCD.

Hoda, J. (2016, December 5). *Building literacy foundational skills: The 123s of the ABCs.* Paper presented at the Mississippi Reading Association Conference. (Biloxi, MS).

Hoffman, J. V., McCarthey, S. J., Elliott, B., Bayles, D. L., Price, D. P., Ferree, A. & Abbott, J. A. (1998). The literature–based basals in first–grade classrooms: Savior, Satan, or same-old, same-old? *Reading Research Quarterly, 33*(2), 168–197.

Holdaway, D. (1979). *The foundations of literacy.* Sydney, Australia: Ashton Scholastic.

Honig, B., Diamond, L. & Gutlohn, L. (2000). *Teaching reading sourcebook: For kindergarten through eighth grade. Core Literacy Training Series.* Novato, CA: Arena Press.

Hornsby, D. (2000). *A closer look at guided reading.* Armdale, Victoria, Australia: Eleanor Curtain Publishers.

Jett-Simpson, M. (1984). *Parents and beginning reading.* Atlanta, GA: Humanics Limited.

Johnson, P. & Keier, K. (2010). *Catching readers before they fall: Supporting readers who struggle, K–4.* Portland, ME: Stenhouse Publishers.

Kelly, S. & Turner, J. (2009). Rethinking the effects of classroom activity structure on the engagement of low-achieving students. *The Teachers College Record 111:* 1665–1692.

Kinzer, C. K. & Leu, D. J. (2014). *Phonics, phonemic awareness, and word analysis for teachers: An interactive tutorial, 11/e.* Upper Saddle River, NJ: Pearson.

Layne, S. L. (2009). *Igniting a passion for reading: Successful strategies for building lifetime readers.* Portland, ME: Stenhouse Publishers.

Leu, D. J. & Kinzer, C. K. (2012). *Phonics, phonemic awareness, and word analysis for teachers: An interactive tutorial, 9th ed.* Boston, MA: Pearson.

Lynch, J. (2005). *Making word walls work.* New York, NY: Scholastic.

McCarrier, A., Pinnell, G. S. & Fountas, I. C. (2000). *Interactive writing: How language and literacy come together K–2.* Portsmouth, NH: Heinemann.

McKenna, M. C. (2002). *Help for struggling readers: Strategies for grade 3–8.* New York, NY: Guilford.

McLaughlin, M. (2012). Reading comprehension: What every teacher needs to know. *The Reading Teacher, 65*(7), 432–440.

Mooney, M. E. (1990). *Reading to, with, and by children.* Katonah, NY: RC Owens.

Moore, R. & Gilles, C. (2006). *Reading conversations: Retrospective miscue analysis with struggling readers.* Portsmouth, NH: Heinemann.

Morrow, L. M. (2005). *Literacy development in the early years: Helping children read and write, 5th ed.* Needham Heights, MA: Allyn & Bacon.

National Governors Association (2010). *The Common Core State Standards.*

Neumann, M. M., Hood, M., Ford, R. M. & Neumann, D. L. (2012). The Role of Environmental Print in Emergent Literacy. *Journal of Early Childhood Literacy, 12*(3), 231–258.

Oczkus, L. D. (2007). *Guided writing: Practical lessons, powerful results.* Portsmouth, NH: Heinemann.

Oczkus, L. D. (2010). *Reciprocal teaching at work: Powerful strategies and lessons for improving reading comprehension.* Newark, DE: International Reading Association.

Opitz, M. & Ford, M. (2015). *Classroom catalysts: 15 efficient practices that accelerate readers' learning.* Portsmouth, NH: Heinemann.

Opitz, M. F. & Ford, M. P. (2014). *Engaging minds in the classroom: The surprising power of joy.* Alexandria, VA: ASCD.

Pardo, L. S. (2004). What every teacher needs to know about comprehension. *The Reading Teacher, 58*(3), 272–280.

Pearson, P. D. & Gallagher, M. C. (1983). The instruction of reading comprehension. *Contemporary Educational Psychology, 8*(3), 317–344.

Piasta, S. B. (2014). Moving to assessment–guided differentiated instruction to support young children's alphabet knowledge. *The Reading Teacher, 68*(3), 202–211.

Pinnell, G. S. & Fountas, I. C. (1998). *Word matters: Teaching phonics and spelling in the reading/writing classroom.* Portsmouth, NH: Heinemann.

Pressley, M., Allington, R. L., Wharton-McDonald, R., Block, C. C. & Morrow, L. M. (2001). *Learning to read: Lessons from exemplary first-grade classrooms.* New York, NY: Guilford Press.

Rasinski, T. V. (1990). Effects of repeated reading and listening-while-reading on reading fluency. *The Journal of Educational Research, 83*(3), 147–151.

Rasinski, T. V. (2003). *The fluent reader: Oral reading strategies for building word recognition, fluency, and comprehension.* New York, NY: Scholastic.

Reutzel, D. R., Hollingsworth, P. M. & Eldredge, J. L. (1994). Oral reading instruction: The impact on reading development. *Reading Research Quarterly*, 41–62.

Richardson, J. (2016). *The next step forward in guided reading.* New York, NY: Scholastic.

Richardson, J. (2009). *The next step in guided reading.* New York, NY: Scholastic.

Rodgers, E., D'Agostino, J. V., Harmey, S. J., Kelly, R. H. & Brownfield, K. (2016). Examining the nature of scaffolding in an early literacy intervention. *Reading Research Quarterly, (3)*51, 345–360.

Rog, L. J. (2012). *Making the most of the 18-minute guided reading lesson.* Markham, Ontario, Canada: Pembroke Publishers Limited.

Rog, L. J. (2003). *Guided reading basics: Organizing, managing and implementing a balanced literacy program in K–3.* Markham, Ontario, Canada: Pembroke Publishers Limited.

Rose-Duckworth, R. & Ramer, K. (2009). *Fostering learner independence: An essential guide for K–6 educators.* Thousand Oaks, CA: Corwin Press.

Routman, R. (2000). *Conversations: Strategies for teaching, learning, and evaluating.* Portsmouth, NH: Heinemann.

Routman, R. (2003). *Reading essentials: The specifics you need to teach reading well.* Portsmouth, NH: Heinemann.

Routman, R. (2008). *Teaching essentials: Expecting the most and getting the best from every learner, K–8.* Portsmouth, NH: Heinemann.

Rycik, M. (2002). How primary teachers are using word walls to teach literacy strategies. *Ohio Reading Teacher, 35*(2), 13.

Rycik, M. & Rycik, J. (2007). *Phonics and word identification: Instruction and intervention, K–8.* Upper Saddle River, NJ: Pearson/Merrill Prentice-Hall.

Saunders-Smith, G. (2009). *The ultimate guided reading how-to book, 2nd ed.* Thousand Oaks, CA: Zephyr Press.

Schwartz, R. (2005). Decisions, decisions: Responding to students during guided reading. *The Reading Teacher, 58*(5), 436–443.

Shagoury, R. (2016). "Language in the classroom: Using a recorder as a teaching resource." https://www.choiceliteracy.com/articles-detail-view.php?id=929. Retrieved December 2016.

Shanahan, T. (1988). The reading-writing relationship: Seven instructional principles. *The Reading Teacher, 41*(7), 636–647.

Stahl, S. A. (1992). Saying the "p" word: Nine guidelines for exemplary phonics instruction. *The Reading Teacher, 45*(8), 618–625.

Stead, T. (2009). *Good choice! Supporting independent reading and response in K-6.* Portland, ME: Stenhouse.

Sulzby, E. (1985). Children's emergent reading of favorite storybooks: A developmental study. *Reading Research Quarterly, 20*(4), 458–481.

Swartz, S. L., Shook, R. E. & Klein, A. F. (2002). *Shared reading.* Carlsbad, CA: Dominie Press.

Wagstaff, J. M. (1999). *Teaching reading and writing with word walls.* New York, NY: Scholastic.

Wasik, B. A. & Bond, M. A. (2001). Beyond the pages of a book: Interactive book reading and language development in preschool classrooms. *Journal of Educational Psychology, 93*(2), 243.

White, T. G., Sowell, J. & Yanagihara, A. (1989). Teaching elementary students to use word-part clues. *The Reading Teacher, 42*(4), 302–308.

Wilhelm, J. D. (2001). *Improving comprehension with think-aloud strategies.* New York, NY: Scholastic.

Wood, D., Wood, H., Ainsworth, S. & O'Malley, C. (1995). On becoming a tutor: Toward an ontogenetic model. *Cognition and Instruction, 13*(4), 565–581.

Yopp, H. K. (1992). Developing phonemic awareness in young children. *The Reading Teacher, 45*(9), 696–703.

Zarrillo, J. (2007). *Are you prepared to teach reading? A practical tool for self-assessment.* Upper Saddle River, NJ: Prentice Hall.

Children's Book and Text Resources

Fancy Nancy by Jane O'Connor (HarperCollins, 2005)

Mrs. Wishy-Washy by Joy Cowley (Philomel, 1999)

Brown Bear, Brown Bear, What Do You See? by Bill Martin, Jr. (Henry Holt, 1996)

Double Trouble in Walla Walla by Andrew Clements (21st Century, 1997)

This Book Just Ate My Dog! by Richard Byrne (Henry Holt, 2014)

The Itsy Bitsy Spider by Iza Trapini (Charlesbridge, 1998)

Walk On! A Guide for Babies of All Ages by Marla Frazee (HMH Books, 2006)

Capstone Engage Literacy Digital Poster Resources

"The Fuzzy Caterpillar" from the Engaged Literacy program (Capstone, 2013)

Other titles from the Engaged Literacy program that could be used in shared reading routines include posters based on traditional rhymes and songs such as the following:

"The Grand Old Duke of York"

"Five Little Ducks"

"Teddy Bear, Teddy Bear"

Some digital posters feature new lyrics to traditional songs such as the following:

"Color Song" (based on the tune of "*Itsy Bitsy Spider*")

"We Like to Come to School" (based on the tune of "*The Farmer in the Dell*")

"When the Bugs Come Out in Spring" (based on the tune of "*When the Saints Go Marching In*")

Other digital posters have content to support and extend discussions of the season of spring presented as the focus for shared writing and shared reading for early readers in this book such as the following:

"Snail"

"Wonderful Weather"

"The Little Plant"

Maupin House
capstone

At Maupin House by Capstone Professional, we continue to look for professional development resources that support grades K–8 classroom teachers in areas, such as these:

Literacy	Language Arts
Content-Area Literacy	Research-Based Practices
Assessment	Inquiry
Technology	Differentiation
Standards-Based Instruction	School Safety
Classroom Management	School Community

If you have an idea for a professional development resource, visit our Become an Author website at:

http://www.capstonepub.com/classroom/professional-development/become-an-author/

There are two ways to submit questions and proposals.

1. You may send them electronically to: proposals@capstonepd.com
2. You may send them via postal mail. Please be sure to include a self-addressed stamped envelope for us to return materials.

Acquisitions Editor
Capstone Professional
2 N. LaSalle Street, Floor 14
Chicago, IL 60602